Perspectives in Landscape Archaeology

Papers presented at Oxford 2003-5

Edited by

Helen Lewis
Sarah Semple

BAR International Series 2103
2010

Published in 2016 by
BAR Publishing, Oxford

BAR International Series 2103

Perspectives in Landscape Archaeology

ISBN 978 1 4073 0579 0

BAR Publishing is the trading name of British Archaeological Reports (Oxford) Ltd.
British Archaeological Reports was first incorporated in 1974 to publish the BAR
Series, International and British. In 1992 Hadrian Books Ltd became part of the BAR
group. This volume was originally published by Archaeopress in conjunction with
British Archaeological Reports (Oxford) Ltd / Hadrian Books Ltd, the Series principal
publisher, in 2010. This present volume is published by BAR Publishing, 2016.

Printed in England

BAR
PUBLISHING

BAR titles are available from:

BAR Publishing
122 Banbury Rd, Oxford, OX2 7BP, UK
EMAIL   info@barpublishing.com
PHONE   +44 (0)1865 310431
FAX   +44 (0)1865 316916
www.barpublishing.com

Contributors

Adrian Chadwick
Archaeology Service, Environment Directorate, Gloucestershire County Council, Shire Hall, Gloucester, UK, GL1 2TH

Niall Finneran
Department of Archaeology, University of Winchester, Winchester, UK SO22 6HY

Joe Flatman
Institute of Archaeology, University College London, 31-34 Gordon Sq., London, UK WC1H 0PY

Charles French
Department of Archaeology, University of Cambridge, Downing St., Cambridge, UK, CB2 3DZ

Mark Gillings
School of Archaeology and Ancient History, University of Leicester, University Rd., Leicester, UK, LE1 7RH

Rodney Harrison
Faculty of Arts, The Open University, Walton Hall, Milton Keynes, UK, MK7 6AA

Della Hooke
Cheltenham and Gloucester College of Higher Education, PO Box 220, The Park, Cheltenham, Gloucestershire, UK, GL50 2QF

Helen Lewis
School of Archaeology, University College Dublin, Belfield, Dublin 4, Ireland

Joshua Pollard
Department of Archaeology and Anthropology, University of Bristol, 43 Woodland Rd., Clifton, Bristol, UK, BS8 1UU

Alexandra Sanmark
Centre for Nordic Studies, Department of Cultural Studies, University of the Highlands and Islands Millennium Institute, Kiln Corner, Kirkwall, Orkney, UK, KW15 1B5

Sarah Semple
Department of Archaeology, Durham University, South Rd., Durham, UK, DH1 3LE

Stephen Yeates
Wolfson College, Linton Rd., Oxford, UK, OX2 6UD

Table of Contents

Preface and acknowledgements

Helen Lewis and Sarah Semple

This book derives from a seminar series held at the Oxford University Institute of Archaeology in 2003-2004 and a second brief series in spring 2005. The Landscape Archaeology seminars aimed to provide a meeting place for students in two new master's degrees at the university: the MSc in Applied Landscape Archaeology at the Department for Continuing Education (OUDCE), and the MA in Landscape Archaeology at the Institute itself. The idea was to bring the students together with academic and professional archaeologists engaged in doing interesting work in landscape archaeology, who could present recent thinking about ancient landscapes from a variety of perspectives, using various approaches, and with a number of different aims.

The first, year-long series, funded jointly by the Institute of Archaeology and through Career Development Fellowship funds, and with the added institutional support of the Department for Continuing Education at Oxford, was highly successful, attracting not only our target student audiences, but also undergraduates, PhD students, researchers and lecturers from Oxford, as well as audience members from London, Bristol and Southampton. The quality of the papers was excellent, and reflected the myriad of approaches involved in landscape archaeology, as well as, altogether as a series, catching the scale and extensive nature of this field. While the second series was a much smaller affair, the talks were again fascinating and well-received, and several of the 2005 speakers are contributors to this volume.

The editors are grateful to all of our contributors and our speakers over the two years, and to the students, staff and interested members of the public who attended the series. We would like to especially thank Barry Cunliffe, Gary Lock, Chris Gosden and Helena Hamerow, the Oxford University Institute of Archaeology, Department for Continuing Education, and School of Archaeology for their support, and particularly Lidia Lozano, Liz Strange, Francesco Menotti and Zena Kamesh, and the support staff at the Institute of Archaeology at Oxford for their help with everything that needed doing. We are also extremely grateful to our referee for comments and suggestions.

Although we tried to get all of the speakers to contribute to this volume, many had committed themselves elsewhere and only a selection of the wonderful papers given are presented here, along with two by the editors. The papers are of variable lengths and organisation, reflecting the style of each author. The full list of speakers and their talks is given at the end of the preface.

Anyone looking over the list of speakers will note a strong geographical bias towards the UK, both in the research presented and in the origin of speakers; this can be seen to reflect two things (in addition to our budgetary constraints). First, it reflects the health and breadth of research in landscape archaeology in the UK, both applied to local archaeological problems, and to international issues through overseas research carried out by UK-based scholars. Second, it reflects our own teaching aims in organising the seminar series, in particular regarding the development of a new (at that time) MA in Applied Landscape Archaeology through OUDCE, whose students were strongly interested in British landscape archaeology, especially for their dissertation research. Nevertheless, we also aimed to show our students that there is a bigger world out there, with equally interesting archaeology for them to engage with. Having speakers present projects from other parts of the world was also important in reflecting the scope of landscape archaeology at Oxford in general, and generating interest in the series in other disciplines and departments.

For all speakers, we chose to invite people who we knew were doing interesting research in landscape archaeology, and who could present a case study showing the application of theoretical and practical methodologies to a real-life archaeological situation. This was partly to simply inform our students, colleagues and ourselves of new and interesting research, but also to give an example for landscape archaeology dissertation writing of how research studies using a wide variety of approaches could be conducted and presented.

On a more personal level, we both greatly enjoyed running this series, as all of the papers given fed into our own interests in themes in landscape archaeology. One of the most satisfying and fascinating things was to see how all of these incredibly diverse talks engaged with similar issues (of scale, of theory, of methodology), while approaching completely different archaeological questions, materials and localities, and using a wide variety of analytical techniques and interpretative frameworks. Even the few papers in this volume, which are essentially random, being simply those that were sent to us out of the whole list of twenty-eight talks, reflect this similarity and diversity.

For instance, many of the papers presented here deal with the meaning of landscape change, from perspectives ranging from how one site can reflect major changes in the interpretation of the past, to how proposed regional (pre-)historical cultural changes are seen, or not seen, in archaeological landscapes. Some papers deal with major changes in religious beliefs, and the relationship of this to archaeological landscapes, and others with the inter-relationships between cultural and environmental changes, including how these influence present-day landscapes. Many authors suggest that multi-scalar landscape approaches provide a stronger interpretative basis than site-specific studies or national-scale studies; indeed, sometimes the choice of scale for addressing a landscape was made to encompass and investigate the full range of participatory experience – intra-site, local, regional, national and international. In this way, new landscape approaches are addressing issues not visible at, or for which little additional insight could be gained at 'traditional' scales of approach.

Several of the papers present the results of various types of landscape archaeology field studies, often combined with historic and/or ethnographic research, looking at issues such as the understanding of movement through a landscape, or of land-use change in landscape history, while others are more 'text-based' in their focus on using landscape approaches to re-address old issues in regional archaeology.

Given the location of the venue, Oxford, it is not surprising that several of the papers in this volume focus on the geographical area of southwest England and Wales, discussing a variety of approaches to the fascinating record of this famous archaeological region. Other papers describe studies of a variety of north-western and northern European landscapes, associated with different cultural groups, and from very different perspectives. The papers that stand out geographically, discussing work in southern Europe, Australia, southwest Asia, Africa and North America, are nevertheless linked thematically to others in the book and the lecture series, describing geoarchaeological, historical and/or ethno-historical perspectives to religious and agricultural landscapes.

Over the series it became clear to us that landscape archaeology is difficult to define because it is truly a holistic approach, one which can embrace everything that we do as archaeologists, as long as we are interested in doing archaeology at a certain geographical scale. Although a topic of the moment, the seminar series convinced us, at least, of the potential longevity of landscape archaeology; the utility and flexibility of investigation at a landscape scale is still only just barely conceived of, just beginning to be theorised, its limitations just starting to be explored, and it is a unifying approach in an often divided discipline.

The hiatus between the completion of the seminar series in 2005 and the publication of this collection of papers which derive from events across 2003-5 is the result of the developing careers of both editors who have moved between several institutions and departments since 2005. It is a delight to both of us to see this volume finally emerge and we would like to offer our thanks to all the contributors for their patience and commitment to the volume in the intervening four years.

Helen Lewis and Sarah Semple 2009

Landscape Archaeology Seminars at Oxford, October 2003-April 2005

Graeme Barker *The prehistory of rainforest foraging and farming in Southeast Asian landscapes: reinvestigating Niah Cave*

John Barrett *Do we really understand the nature of landscape transformation? The case of the late Neolithic to early Iron Age in southern Britain*

Richard Bradley *Seeing in the dark: new light on stone circles in the prehistoric landscape of Scotland?*

Stefan Brink *Power and religion in the Viking Scandinavian landscape*

Gabriel Cooney *Interpreting an island landscape: Lambay Island*

Barry Cunliffe *In site of Danebury: studying the first millennium landscape in detail*

Tom Evans and Angela Boyle *Chariots for the dead: issues of landscape and regionality in the two-wheeled vehicle burials of Yorkshire and Champagne*

Niell Finnerann *Syncretism of landscape: the Christianisation of Ethiopian space*

Joe Flatman *Wetting the fringe of your habit: medieval monasticism and landscapes*

Andrew Fleming and Helen Wickstead *Reviewing the Dartmoor reaves*

Charles French *Discovering ancient agricultural landscapes in Yemen and New Mexico: sustainability in semi-arid systems*

Dorian Fuller *Neolithic landscapes of South and North India*

Chris Gosden *Landscapes and colonialism in Papua New Guinea and Britain*

David Griffiths *Birsay and Skaill, Orkney: landscape survey 2003*

Rodney Harrison *'Where the cattle went, they went': towards a phenomenological archaeology of cattle mustering in the Kunderang ravines, New South Wales, Australia*

Della Hooke *The nature and distribution of early medieval woodland and wood-pasture habitats*

Lila Janik *Visualising the landscapes in the rock art of northern Europe*

Matthew Johnson *W.G. Hoskins, William Wordsworth and the development of English landscape archaeology*

Robert Johnston *A social archaeology of garden plots in the Bronze Age of northern and western Britain*

Andrew Jones *A biography of stone: rock art and landscape in Kilmartin, Argyll, Scotland*

Tom Kiely *Tombscapes in Bronze Age Cyprus*

Mike Parker Pearson *The Stonehenge landscape - a new view from Durrington Walls*

Josh Pollard and Mark Gillings *Building histories and memories in the Neolithic of the Avebury landscape*

Niall Price *Landscapes of the mind: sorcery and sorcerers in the Viking world*

Andrew Reynolds *Sight and sound in the late Anglo-Saxon landscape: civil defence in the localities*

Julia Shaw *Locating Buddhism in the landscape: approaches to religious change in ancient India*

Andrew Sherratt *Routes and resources; the eternal dialectic – as illustrated by the cultural landscapes of the Fertile Crescent*

Stephen Yeates *Still living with the Dobunni*

Sarsen stories

Joshua Pollard and Mark Gillings

'I shall conclude with the stones called the Grey Wethers; which lye scattered all over the downes about Marlborough… and in many places they are, as it were, sown so thick, that travellers in the twylight at a distance take them to be flocks of sheep (wethers) from whence they have their name…Of these kind of stones are framed the two stupendous antiquities of Aubury and Stoneheng.' (Aubrey 1847, 44)

Putting people and stones back together

Behind the dualist paradigms of the western scientific tradition lies an essentialist comprehension of the world, a notion that substances, actions and states carry with them fixed and immutable values. We are now aware of the problematic, or at least highly specific, nature of the dualist categories created in such schemes, of nature/culture, subject/object, mind/body and so forth, but how do we counter the legacy of essentialist comprehensions of the world? A lead is provided by Descola and Pálsson when they state that 'going beyond dualism opens up an entirely different intellectual landscape, one in which states and substances are replaced by processes and relations' (1996, 12). So we overcome the problematic recourse to fixed categories by adopting forms of interpretation that seek to define the contingent and shifting networks that bind together people, and people and things. One way of achieving this is through a contextual and biographical approach to particular phenomena, an approach that explores the shifting networks of engagement and relationships between humans and non-humans that are created through the on-going process of landscape inhabitation. Here such an approach is employed in investigating the changing contextualisation of a particular geological *affordance*: sarsen stone.

Sarsen is a resilient form of sandstone, often of a greyish to yellowish colour, or reddish-brown when stained with oxidised iron (Fig. 1). It occurs in several areas of southern England, but the most extensive and impressive spreads of this stone are found in the area of the Marlborough Downs and the Upper Kennet valley in Wiltshire. Erosion has left patches of sarsen within the landscape, the remains of locally hardened beds of sand of Tertiary age, often taking the form of 'trails' or 'trains' of stone along former drainage lines in the base of valleys bisecting the chalk downland (Geddes 2000, 63). The name sarsen is thought to derive 'from either the Anglo Saxon *sar stan* or "troublesome stone", or from *saracen*, meaning "alien" or "stranger"' (*ibid.* 60). Whatever the precise etymology, this stone clearly troubled the Anglo-Saxon mind.

A highly visible component of this distinctive landscape, sarsen was famously employed in the construction of the late Neolithic henge monuments at Avebury and Stonehenge (Fig. 2), as well as in a number of allied constructions dating to the fourth and third millennia BC, including the West Kennet long barrow and other chambered tombs in the Upper Kennet valley (Barker 1985).

There has been a tendency in accounts of the region's archaeology to think of sarsen simply as a convenient building material, or as an obstacle to clearance and cultivation, but this ignores its many symbolic and ontological dimensions. The history of stone and the history of human occupation of the region are intimately woven together, and it is human engagement with stone that created many of the conditions through which this landscape was inhabited.

Figure 1 In situ sarsens in Lockeridge Dene.

Woodland stones

Our biography of stone begins with the periodic visits made to the area by Mesolithic gatherer-hunters. Groups travelled through the region, camping here briefly and making occasional hunting forays. One feature that must have struck those moving through the landscape would have been the encounter with extensive trails of stone 'hidden' in the wooded valley floors. Microliths have been found around former sarsen trails in the dry valley to the south of Avebury, but occupation looks to have been fleeting, and there is a sense that it was not respectful to dwell too long among the stones. Like many other 'stonescapes', these spreads of sizable and distinctive blocks could have accrued considerable mythical and symbolic significance. In other parts of the world, such as in areas of New Caledonia, stones have names and biographies (Kahn 1990). Elsewhere in Melanesia stones act as anchoring points or mnemonic devices for tales, myths and personal histories, while for the Erromangan, stones have even deeper power as non-human agents. They are seen to assist in human affairs or, if improperly treated, to hinder and bring harm (Roe and Taki 1999).

Perhaps seen to embody varied forms of agency and potency, it is not too difficult to imagine how stones were worked into the myths and understandings of Mesolithic communities moving through the Upper Kennet valley. Perhaps it was the encountering of these stonescapes that created the conditions under which the region became the focus for traditions of monument building during the subsequent Neolithic (Pollard and Reynolds 2002). It was stone that made this landscape special.

The labour of transformation

Sustained occupation of the Upper Kennet valley only really began at the start of the Neolithic, here perhaps as late as the end of the first quarter of the fourth millennium BC (Whittle 1993). That process of occupation, living within this stonescape, created new and distinctive relationships between people and sarsen. Not least, from then on stones were always the focus for a variety of laboured practices.

It is tempting to envisage a developing association between stones and sacred realms, culminating in the employment of massive quantities of sarsen to construct the stone circles and avenues of later Neolithic Avebury. The significance of sarsen may have accrued with time as stones became more firmly embedded not only in routine practices, but also in stories and myths about the landscape.

Whether constructing monuments or when engaged in other practices, the dealings Neolithic communities had with sarsen frequently revolved around processes of accumulation and re-working, material connections being drawn out through acts of construction and deposition. Sarsen fragments were placed along the base of ditches at the Windmill Hill enclosure, mixed with other materials such as antler, bone, flint and carved chalk (Whittle *et al.* 1999). These discreetly placed groups imply reverential burial, a care for this stone, while the mixing of sarsen with the debris of occupation served to reinstate the material connections of life and labour. Sarsens were made into querns, but querns were then smashed and fragmented before being deposited at Windmill Hill (e.g. *ibid.* 45, 66). How can such 'violence' be equated to the care they were afforded in deposition? The focus of so much labour, perhaps these were stones that became inalienable, and so closely linked to the lives of their users that they, like human bodies, were broken-up or disarticulated upon the death of these relationships.

In other contexts stones were woven into the fabric of monuments. At the Beckhampton Road long barrow, the edge of the mound was deliberately laid out to take in a small boulder, implying the pre-existing significance attached to this one particular stone. At the analogous site of South Street, a 'cairn' of nine large sarsen blocks, conceivably a pre-barrow shrine, provided the focus for the construction of a long mound, in fact being incorporated into the very fabric of that monument (Ashbee *et al.* 1979). These stones occupied the same position within the mound as mortuary deposits under comparable monuments. Indeed, there are reasons for seeing a close metaphorical connection between stone and the transformed remains of the human dead during the early Neolithic. Sarsen blocks provided the material for constructing chambers at West Kennet and other long mounds in the region associated with large mortuary deposits. The dead were, quite literally, encased in stone.

Figure 2   A recumbent stone at the east entrance, Avebury, c. 1910.

Following this thread, Parker Pearson and Ramilisonina (1998) have argued that during the later Neolithic a much closer metaphorical connection developed between sarsen, as a durable and enduring substance, and the immutable and timeless domain of ancestors. Because of the general absence of later Neolithic mortuary deposits, the connection is not always immediately apparent for this period, but in the early Bronze Age there developed a close contextual association between burials and stones. A number of Beaker burials were interred at the feet of megaliths, while flat burials were repeatedly placed adjacent to or covered by sarsens, as were those under round barrows (Pollard and Reynolds 2002, 129-30). Here links were created between individual social personae and individual stones, in such a way that their identities became mutually subsumed. Perhaps the stones that made up the great monuments of Avebury and Stonehenge always had an identity of their own, whether one that linked them to certain people, or an identity borne of their 'stoniness' and places of origin (Gillings and Pollard 1999; 2004).

But let us not fall into the trap of assuming that stone only took on significance through its reworking into the fabric of monuments. Other sarsens, left in place across the landscape, became the locations for the working and deposition of other stones. Finds of flint-working debris have been reported from around large *in situ* boulders, as at the site of Falkner's Circle to the south of Avebury, just as knapping debris was placed around the feet of standing stones (Pollard and Reynolds 2002, 104).

A number of large and distinctive blocks were utilized during the fourth millennium BC for grinding and polishing stone axes (Fig. 3). Some of these *polissoirs* display deep grooves created through repeated working over decades or generations. Woven into the taskscape of Neolithic communities, these stones became places in their own right. Other stones, particularly the largest blocks and those with distinctive surface features, or stones in clearings or along woodland paths, would also have developed an identity, becoming known, even named, components of the occupied landscape (Gillings and Pollard 1999). They provided fixed and known points in a landscape of semi-mobile settlement (e.g. Whittle *et al.* 2000). It is easy to imagine people gathering at stones, working other stones (flint and axes of distant stone with its own identity), and telling stories about the world around them. Sarsens participated in the construction of real and imagined worlds.

We would now like to jump forward nearly four millennia to a point where the known world gets split in two. In the early modern world the categorisation of sarsen came to be worked according to the relative distance of stone from human practice. This is a separation according to context: with *in situ* spreads being identified as of 'nature', and those employed in building projects as of a 'cultural' domain.

Figure 3   Traces of axe polishing on a Beckhampton Avenue stone.

The labour of scholars
> 'It is the unalterable belief of many, and that not of the uneducated only, that these stones grow!'(Smith 1885, 28)

It is telling that while recognising the earthworks of the henge, the megalithic settings at Avebury initially received little attention from early antiquaries. The stones were largely ignored by Camden (1610, 255), who thought them more 'naturall than artificiall' in their setting. Furthermore, perhaps because of their unmodified form, Camden took the avenues to be natural lines of rocks. It is claimed this was a view shared by many of the locals, but in pre-modern rural England there was little sense of a natural history against which a world of culturally-constructed things was counter-posed. Rather, there were works of God, works of man as an agent of God, and works of unholy supernatural agencies.

Against this was the emerging rationalism of a nascent science, epitomised by bodies such as the Royal Society. It was John Aubrey in 1649 who first recognised the megalithic settings at Avebury for what they were, and William Stukeley who undertook the first systematic survey of the region's archaeology in the 1720s (Stukeley 1743). A colleague of Newton, Stukeley brought an emerging scientific discourse to the study of antiquities and natural phenomena (Haycock 2002). His *Abury* of 1743 provides the first detailed natural history of sarsen, though one worked within an accepted theological context. His description of the formation of this stone is telling of a new science:

> 'As this chalky matter harden'd at creation, it spew'd out the most solid body of the stones, of a greater specific gravity than itself; and assisted by the centrifuge power, owing to the rotation of the globe upon its axis, threw them upon its surface.' (Stukeley 1743, 16)

His work makes a very clear distinction between 'natural' and humanly-made things in the landscape, and he finds it difficult to comprehend how people could not have seen the artifice in a monument like Avebury (Fig. 4). It is science and romanticism that created 'nature'. But Stukeley's reading of the Avebury sarsens was not the only, or dominant, one. Not everyone invested the megalithic settings with a sense of antiquarian value, or appreciated the romance and sublime qualities of their ruinous grandeur, least of all those who lived and laboured around Avebury.

Turning sheep-stones into sugar lumps
> 'Those huge stones may be broken in what part of them you please without any great trouble. The manner is thus: they make a fire on that line of the stone where they would have it to crack; and, after the stone is well heated, draw over a line with cold water, and immediately give a smart knock with a smyth's sledge, and it will break like the collets at the glasse-house.' (Aubrey 1847, 44)

> 'The Sarsen Stones, or Grey Wethers, are slowly disappearing from the Marlborough Downs.

Intractable to all ordinary methods, they have for some years past, been split into blocks for building and paving, by tools of iron of extraordinary hardness, made for the purpose. Holes are bored in them, by sharp picks, at certain distances, and into these iron wedges are inserted, which are driven by hard hammers. In this way the stones are cloven into quadrangular blocks of from six to twelve inches, like immense lumps of sugar.' (Long 1858, 70)

We do not know what agencies the locals thought lay behind the megalithic settings, though by the seventeenth century AD names given to these, such as the 'Devill's Coytes' and the 'Devil's Chair', imply a degree of association with unholy agencies, but it was more complicated than that. By the early post-medieval period, sarsens had variously become relics of paganism, a hindrance and, once modified, a commercial resource (Gillings et al. 2004).

Avebury during the later seventeenth and early eighteenth centuries AD was at the heart of a systematic campaign of stone breaking, the blocks being used for building houses, garden walls and the village chapel. A more marked re-contextualisation of this material had never before taken place. Stones were toppled and broken through fire-setting. These actions of stone-breaking sat at the centre of a complex web of local politics, and ultimately theological dissent. All the active stone-breakers were dissenters and non-conformists who, following the visit of King Charles II to Avebury in 1663, now identified the stones of the henge both with superstition and, worse still, with a Royalist Anglican establishment and antiquarianism (Gillings et al. 2004).

Stukeley's description of the fire-setting of stones as akin to an *Atto de fe* (a reference to Catholic burning of heretics), is a revealing description of the process. The burning of the stones was analogous to contemporary burnings of papal effigies, and the connections in technological practice could not have been lost on the non-conformist stone breakers. Here the stones were at the nexus of conflicting contemporary theological opinion. The local reading of the megaliths as symbols, perhaps even agents, of unholy ways stood in stark contrast with Stukeley's idealistic Druidic interpretation of the Avebury monuments. For Stukeley these were the works of a nature-centred Druid religion that represented an early patriarchal Christianity (Haycock 2002).

The politics of stone must always have been a feature of the medieval and early post-medieval periods in the Upper Kennet valley, whether in the context of clearance, the acquisition of stone for building, or the testimony of stones in boundary disputes.

There had been earlier episodes of 'destruction' of Avebury's standing stones. Many were buried during the fourteenth to seventeenth centuries AD. The motivations behind stone burial are still poorly understood, some

arguing it was driven by the Church wishing to destroy the focus of relict pagan worship (e.g. Burl 1979), but reasons are likely to have been multifarious (Gillings et al. 2004). Whatever the motivations, the details of this practice tell of local understanding of the ontology of sarsen. The care with which stones were buried, in carefully-shaped pits that followed the size and shape of the stones, suggests some respect for these stones. Here was an act of re-planting, putting the stones back into the ground from which they grew.

It was commerce that really spelled the end for many of the sarsen trails on the Downs and in surrounding valleys. A sarsen industry, with its own craft tradition, employing its own techniques and tools, had developed on the Marlborough Downs by the late nineteenth century AD (King 1968). 'Natural' sarsens, now valued in a radically different manner to their cousins making up the megalithic complexes at Avebury and Stonehenge (and protected by law with the first Ancient Monuments Act of 1882), were broken up to make tram setts and curbing. Context was everything: sarsens were either a component of a national prehistoric heritage, or a commercial resource for the taking.

Figure 4 Stukeley's view of the Southern Inner Circle at Avebury (Stukeley 1743, pl. 17).

It was a strange hybrid of romanticism, science and post-war ecological awareness that finally saved the remaining downland sarsens. Once so common, sarsen spreads had become so much diminished that the surviving trails on Overton and Fyfield Downs, and at Lockeridge and Piggledean, were purchased and preserved by English Nature and the National Trust (Geddes 2000, 64).

The 'romance' of sarsen was fuelled in no small part by a mystery of antiquity and the resurrection of many fallen and buried megaliths at Avebury by Alexander Keiller during the 1930s (Smith 1965). His work was a fight against the legacy of gravity and earlier depredations. The stones reacquired an agency, an ability to affect. Their physicality and connection with remote pasts, their contorted and textured surfaces, their sentinel-like presence, became inspiration for artists:

'Last summer I walked in a field near Avebury where two rough monoliths stand up, sixteen feet high, miraculously patterned with black and orange lichen, remains of an avenue of stones which led to the Great Circle. A mile away, a green pyramid casts a gigantic shadow. In the hedge, at hand, the white trumpet of a convolvulus turns from its spiral stem, following the sun. In my art I would solve such an equation.' (Paul Nash, in Read 1934)

What the history of sarsen reveals is not a story of fixed and bounded categories, but a mutual involvement of people and substances within the projects of life. Meanings, categories and encounters are so fluid that the attribution of these things to distinct domains is at the very least misleading. Just as the identity of people is constructed through a network of relationships, and is always shifting, contingent and contextual, so too is the identity of stone.

Bibliography

Ashbee, P., Smith, I. and Evans, J. 1979. Excavation of three long barrows near Avebury, Wiltshire. *Proceedings of the Prehistoric Society* 45, 207-300.

Aubrey, J. 1847. *The Natural History of Wiltshire*. Edited by J. Britton. London: Wiltshire Topographical Society.

Barker, C. 1985. The long mounds of the Avebury region. *Wiltshire Archaeological and Natural History Magazine* 79, 7-38.

Burl, A. 1979. *Prehistoric Avebury*. New Haven and London: Yale University Press.

Camden, W. 1610. *Britannia*. London.

Descola, P. and Pálsson, G. (eds.) 1996. *Nature and Society: Anthropological Perspectives*. London: Routledge.

Geddes, I. 2000. *Hidden Depths: Wiltshire's Geology and Landscapes*. Bradford on Avon: Ex Libris Press.

Gillings, M. and Pollard, J. 1999. Non-portable stone artefacts and contexts of meaning: the tale of Grey Wether. *World Archaeology* 31, 179-93. (www.museum.ncl.ac.uk/Avebury/stone4.htm)

Gillings, M. and Pollard, J. 2004. *Avebury*. London: Duckworth.

Gillings, M., Peterson, R. and Pollard, J. 2004. The destruction of the Avebury monuments. In Cleal, R. and Pollard, J. (eds.) *Monuments and Material Culture. Papers in Honour of an Avebury Archaeologist: Isobel Smith*, 139-63. Salisbury: Hobnob Press.

Haycock, D.B. 2002. *William Stukeley: Science, Religion and Archaeology in Eighteenth-century England*. Woodbridge: Boydell Press.

Kahn, M. 1990. Stone-faced ancestors. The spatial anchoring of myth in Wamira, Papua New Guinea. *Ethnology* 29, 51-66.

King, N.E. 1968. The Kennet Valley sarsen industry. *Wiltshire Archaeological and Natural History Magazine* 63, 83-93.

Long, W. 1858. *Abury Illustrated*. Devizes: H. Bull.

Parker Pearson, M. and Ramilisonina. 1998. Stonehenge for the ancestors: the stones pass on the message. *Antiquity* 72, 308-26.

Pollard, J. and Reynolds, A. 2002. *Avebury: The Biography of a Landscape*. Stroud and Charleston: Tempus.

Read, H. (ed.) 1934. *Unit One: The Modern Movement in English Architecture, Painting and Sculpture*. London: Cassell.

Roe, D. and Taki, J. 1999. Living with stones: people and the landscape in Erromango, Vanuatu. In Ucko, P.J. & Layton, R. (eds.) *The Archaeology and Anthropology of Landscape*, 411-22. London: Routledge.

Smith, A.C. 1885. *A Guide to the British and Roman Antiquities of the North Wiltshire Downs*. Devizes: Wiltshire Archaeological and Natural History Society.

Smith, I.F. 1965. *Windmill Hill and Avebury: Excavations by Alexander Keiller, 1925-1939*. Oxford: Clarendon Press.

Stukeley, W. 1743. *Abury, A Temple of the British Druids, with Some Others Described*. London.

Whittle, A. 1993. The Neolithic of the Avebury area: sequence, environment, settlement and monuments. *Oxford Journal of Archaeology* 12, 29-53.

Whittle, A., Davies, J., Dennis, I., Fairbairn, A. and Hamilton, M. 2000. Neolithic activity and occupation outside Windmill Hill causewayed enclosure, Wiltshire: survey and excavation 1992-93. *Wiltshire Archaeological and Natural History Magazine* 93, 131-80.

Whittle, A., Pollard, J. and Grigson, C. 1999. *Harmony of Symbols: the Windmill Hill Causewayed Enclosure, Wiltshire*. Oxford: Oxbow.

Syncretism of space: the Christianisation of the Ethiopian landscape?

Niall Finneran

Introduction

When we speak of syncretism, mainly in relation to the material culture of ideology *sensu lato,* we arguably use the term to refer to the synthesis of different symbolic ideas within a single ritual framework (Stewart and Shaw 1994 *passim*): 'a process of religious amalgamation, of blending heterogeneous beliefs and practices' (Van der Veer 1994, 208, cited in Insoll 2001, 19). We can draw upon many case studies from a notional archaeology of world religion that show how elements of certain belief systems survive the conversion process, and continue to play an important role in the development of a 'new' cosmological system. Using the case study of Caribbean and Latin American variants of Voodoo (ideologies which mediate a variety of western African traditional cosmologies of the dominated – slaves – with the Roman Catholic religion imposed from above by the slave owners and colonial authorities), I have argued that we can speak of a *syncretism of personalities*, where, for instance the Voodoo goddess Erzulie takes on traits akin to those of the Blessed Virgin Mary; a *syncretism of ritual*, where the Voodoo rite borrows heavily from elements of the Roman Catholic mass, yet re-conceptualises them in a format more appropriate to the desired ends of the Voodoo mass; and finally a *syncretism of time*, where the sacred calendar of the Roman Catholic Church is appropriated to fit the cycle of Voodoo ritual – for example, the Feast of All Souls on November 1st becomes a more sinister necromantic 'day of the dead' (Finneran 2002, 17-18).

In this paper I wish to take the idea of syncretism further, and attempt to understand how ideology impacts upon our spatial environment, how the same sacred loci within the Ethiopian early Christian landscape are re-conceptualised and re-used as zones of Christian ideological importance (Markus 1994). This is something that would not be regarded as being an original approach in the realms of, say, western European late antique/medieval archaeology, where we find many examples of the reuse of 'sacred' sites, examples of a strong social memory of the 'past in the present' (e.g. Blair 1996; Semple 1998; Williams 1998). My argument here is based upon two key and interrelated contentions. First that ideological change is not only visible through change in the fabric of pre-existing social organisation and material culture, but it also impacts upon the organisation and quantification of the spatial environment. My second contention is that any theoretical analysis of this space has to be based upon a fluid and nuanced approach; there are no rigid boundaries and no fixed readings of space as would be recognised in

a purely (and admittedly old-fashioned) structuralist analysis of space.

Phenomenology lends itself particularly well to understanding how an entity, a human, moves through and reacts with space; the generalised analytical framework outlined here is based largely upon the approach articulated by Tilley (1994) in his analysis of later prehistoric ritual landscapes of southern and western Britain. Such an approach demands fluidity of analysis, and recognition of multi-vocal meanings of space; a landscape analysed thus is recognised as being 'invested with powers, capable of being organised and choreographed in relation to sectional interests, and is always sedimented with human significances' (*ibid.* 34). In attempting to bring some order into the analysis of these fluid and changing meanings in space and place, I propose two operational scales of spatial analysis, based upon Tilley's scheme (*ibid.* 15), although they are not mutually exclusive: the 'taskscape', a secular, pragmatic perception of space (cf. Ingold 1993; a combination of Tilley's (*ibid.*) 'somatic', 'perceptual' and 'architectural' space), and psychogeographic space, a combination of Tilley's 'existential' and 'cognitive' space (*ibid.*). These two scales of space would accord with what Lefebvre (1991, 254) has termed 'material' and 'imagined' space.

The former is a quantifiable form of space: secular, social, economic, functional space, concrete localities; the latter is more amorphous, probably naturally rather than culturally constructed, invested with symbolism (see also Bradley 2000, 104; Lefebvre 1991, 30; Tuan 1974, 142 *ff.*), and accessed, I would argue, through a phenomenological approach as articulated by Tilley *inter alia.* The idea of psychogeography is a concept that could be better explored in our examination of symbolic space. A useful operational definition of this concept is found in the philosophical and artistic manifesto that first introduced the idea in post-war Italy:

> 'The study of specific effect of the geographical environments consciously organised or not, on the emotions and behaviour of individuals' (Anon 1958).

Today, the psychogeographical approach is perhaps best known from avant-garde travel writers, such as Iain Sinclair, whose evocation of psychic space in contemporary London in *Lights out for the Territory* (1997) is an example of this literary genre. In a sense this form of spatial analysis is recognisable to archaeologists as a phenomenological approach, and I do feel that we can learn much from the methods by which situationist theory defines spatial perception. We need to be more aware of the possibilities and layers of meanings in space and place, and attempt to access, as suggested in the quote above, the effect of environments upon individuals, especially during periods of immense change in their lives – such a portal of analysis would open itself, metaphorically, during periods of religious conversion, here 'Christianisation', for instance.

The term 'Christianisation' itself can be rightly critiqued as being problematic and having overtly teleological associations (e.g. Kilbride 2000; Milis 1986). A society can never be wholly 'Christianised' (or Islamicised, or Judaicised); there is clearly too much scope for continual ideological evolution and there is never a total acceptance of any new cosmology. An Anglocentric historical trajectory for Christianity over the last 1500 years or so, would, for instance, recognise initial patchy and piecemeal conversion, continuing 'pagan' survivals, religious dissent, emergence of rationalistic atheism and the twentieth century establishment of a multi-faith, yet also secular and arguably syncretic 'new age' ideology. The same situation may be predicted in any notional 'Christianisation' of space; in short, space is never wholly 'Christianised'; Christianity rewrote pre-existing landscape and spatial texts.

It is worth making another observation on a more religion-specific basis, namely that Christianity is not, primarily, a religion of nature (Davies 1994). The 'natural place' does not figure highly in Christian perceptions of landscape; Christianity acculturated natural places as they were dangerous places, redolent of pre-Christian, pagan, superstitious belief (after all the word 'pagan' derives from the Latin *paganus*, denoting country dweller). Such notions were clearly understood by the earliest Christian hermits of Egypt, who sought out places of spiritual danger, deserts, domains of demons, and by constructing a Christian hermitage controlled dangerous natural places (this much is clear from contemporary accounts of the psychogeographical landscape of early eastern ascetics as presented, for instance, in John Moschos' *Pratum Spirituale* (1992). Arguably, in some Christian societies – often far from the centre of the organised, political powerbase of the Church – traditional concepts of sacred natural place did survive, albeit recast in a Christian form (e.g. Barnish 2001). One example may be found in the continuing veneration of sacred wells of pre-Christian sacred significance in the western Celtic fringes of Britain, specifically in Wales; here curative waters took on the identity of a local saint rather than a pagan earth force (e.g. Jones 1954). There are similar meanings in Ethiopian Christianity, where Christianity has sought to organise and control the natural world; for example, the baptistery within the church building represents a symbolic organisation of a water source. Whereas the earliest Christians were democratic and used rivers for baptism, increasing Roman imperial patronage and the acquisition of power saw the increasing delineation of place within the church building, and the closing off and control of the baptismal area. Before examining these themes in relation to the Ethiopian picture, it is worth briefly considering the historical context of Ethiopian Christianity, placing special emphasis on the creation of its own distinctive syncretic identity.

The historical context of Ethiopian Christianity

According to the Christian historian Rufinus, Christianity was introduced to the Aksumite court of King Ezana of northern Ethiopia in the mid-fourth century AD (scholars disagree on the exact date; Munro-Hay 1991, 205-6) by a Syrian from Tyre named Frumentius. Christianity replaced a pre-existing Aksumite cosmology (which itself had its roots in South Arabia), which emphasised the worship of sun and moon deities, as well as other minor gods and goddesses (*ibid.* 196-202). Although physically situated beyond the fringes of the eastern Mediterranean late antique trading sphere (*koine*), the outlook of the Aksumite polity was decidedly internationalist – this much is attested by contemporary textual sources such as the *Periplus of the Erythraean Sea* and the results of recent archaeological work at Aksum, demonstrating the scale of international trade here during the apogee of the Aksumite polity from the second to sixth centuries AD (e.g. Phillipson 2000). In short, both artefacts and ideas flowed up and down the Red Sea, and given the progress of contemporary 'Nestorian' (Church of the East) missions along the Silk Road into China and into northern Arabia, it is obvious that the Christian world was expanding greatly during the fourth century AD. The conversion of Aksum was just one small part of a much larger ideological exchange sphere.

Ostensibly, the archetype for Aksumite conversion should follow a 'top down' model (Finneran 2002, 187). This scenario compares, for example, with the conversion of the Kingdom of Edessa, the medieval Nubian states, Armenia and, in Britain, the Anglo-Saxon kingdoms of Northumbria, Kent and the East Saxons (even if in the case of the latter there was often a relapse into paganism) *inter alia*, and contrasts with the general picture of the Roman world where Christianity grew only slowly, and under the threat of persecution, within a generally lower-class, mercantile, urban Judaic population (*i.e.* a 'bottom up' model). The material culture corollary of these models should be fairly clear: ideological changes enforced from a position of power should see a relatively rapid and far-reaching 'Christianisation' of all aspects of life (and death), and of perception of space and material culture (Finneran 2002, 185). Conversely the 'bottom up' model for conversion – frequently played out against a background of anti-Christian persecution – would result in a less visible Christian material culture, manifesting itself, for example, in the use of a *domus ecclesiae* (house church) and discreet worship, and interment in catacombs.

But, as ever, the picture is not clear cut; it is possible that the Aksumite king Ezana (perhaps like the Roman emperor Constantine after AD 313) was never actually baptised, and although nominally Christian, did not enforce Christianity rigidly from on high (Kaplan 1982). In attempting to understand the wider conceptual re-ordering of space, we need to examine the motivations for Ezana's acceptance of this new cosmological order. The process of conversion is a two-way dynamic, which offers benefits for the convertor and converted, and in many cases subsumes a number of social, political and economic decisions as well as the straightforward ideological message (Urbanczyk 2003); this dynamic is clearly seen in recent archaeological studies of mission activity in southern Africa in the nineteenth century (Lane 1999). One clear socio-economic benefit of Ezana's conversion to Christianity would have been to cement links with the Roman trading sphere of the eastern Mediterranean. The act of conversion could be viewed as being as much an economic as an ideological choice, creating a new institution of power at the centre of the Aksumite polity, and a tool for social *and* economic control that has arguably dominated highland Ethiopian society to this day.

The form of Christianity that developed in Ethiopia took on, from the outset, a very individualistic and syncretic character. Within the wider Christian socio-cultural context, the evangelisation of Ethiopia was a product of the western Syrian Christian world, but the Church was actually controlled from Alexandria, thus giving Ethiopian Christianity a very eastern Christian flavour. The shift away from the Mediterranean Christian world, dominated by Rome and Constantinople, was sealed by the refusal of the eastern Churches of Egypt, Syria, Ethiopia and Armenia to accept the recommendations of the Council of Chalcedon in AD 451 concerning the points of fundamental Christology (these Churches are erroneously referred to as monophysite churches), and this arguably contributed to the unique socio-cultural aspects of these 'oriental' Churches which flourished 'beyond Byzantium'. Both physical and, for want of a better word, theological isolation served to foster a distinctive Ethiopian Christian identity, one enhanced by a number of idiosyncratic and arguably syncretic socio-ideological facets: Ethiopian Christians do not eat shellfish or pork (essentially following *halal* or *kashrut* prohibitions), and celebrate the Sabbath on the Saturday. These are very distinct socio-cultural motifs which have been variously suggested as being survivals of a relic Jewish religion in the area, or perhaps representing a common pan-Semitic cultural trait (Pawlinkowski 1974). It is equally possible that these pre-existing ideological rules were adapted to fit the new Christian perspective, and were maintained as a means of making acceptance of the new faith easier for the masses.

It is thus significant that the Ethiopian Orthodox Church embodies a number of seemingly contradictory dichotomies, a Christian veneer laid over a deep social ideological memory, a faith that served to bring disparate ethnic peoples together within the context of the nation state – a created Ethiopia – and that has survived repeated pressures from Muslim peoples from the south and east. This picture strengthens the critique of the idea of 'Christianisation'. This social memory, this syncretic ideological system, is mirrored in the perception of Ethiopian space and place. Using archaeological case studies drawn from three different areas of highland Ethiopia (Fig. 1) – the Aksumite landscape in the first seven centuries AD, the city of Lalibela which became the capital city of the Zagwe dynasty during the twelfth century AD (Finneran and Tribe 2004), and the landscape of Shire in the northwest of the country, which finally became integrated politically and ideologically into the Ethiopian Empire as late as the fifteenth century AD (Finneran and Phillips 2003) – we will try to understand how Christianity impacted upon the constructed social and ideological space of highland Ethiopia.

Landscapes of conversion
It is clear that the Aksumite Empire was evangelised from the 'top down'; hypothetically this would see the placement of Christianity at the centre of secular power and would result in a highly visible Christian culture in the major towns and cities of the Aksumite polity, with greatest power concentrated close to the king at Aksum itself. The most obvious archaeological indicator of Christianity is the presence of a church building, and Aksumite-period churches have been found at the important urban sites of Adulis (Paribeni 1907), Enda Cherqos (De Conteson 1961), Matara (Anfray 1974), Ouachatei Golo (De Contenson 1961) and Yeha (Doresse 1957, 231) among others (Munro-Hay 1991, 212). At Aksum itself two basilicas were excavated on the summit of Beta Giyorgis hill in the 1970s (Ricci and Fattovich 1987), but there is no evidence for the many churches of the town listed in the *Book of Aksum* (Conti-Rossini 1910), apart from the Cathedral of Maryam Zion, which occupies the site of a much older basilica destroyed in the sixteenth century AD. The presence of churches in urban zones probably reflects a bias in archaeological research, but it is equally probable that Christianity, in its initial phase of expansion, was a religion of the town alone and that the countryside had yet to be brought into the new cosmological sphere.

A secondary Christian evangelisation of the Aksumite polity occurred in the fifth to sixth centuries AD, with the influx of the Syrian 'nine saints' as well as 'Roman' Christians or *sadqan* – probably anti-Chalcedonian refugees (Munro-Hay 1991, 207), and it is at this time, with the establishment of monasteries in the countryside across the state by the nine saints, that we begin to see the integration of the rural ideological system with that of the urban centres. Monasteries, then, effected the Christianisation of the countryside, a motif also reflected

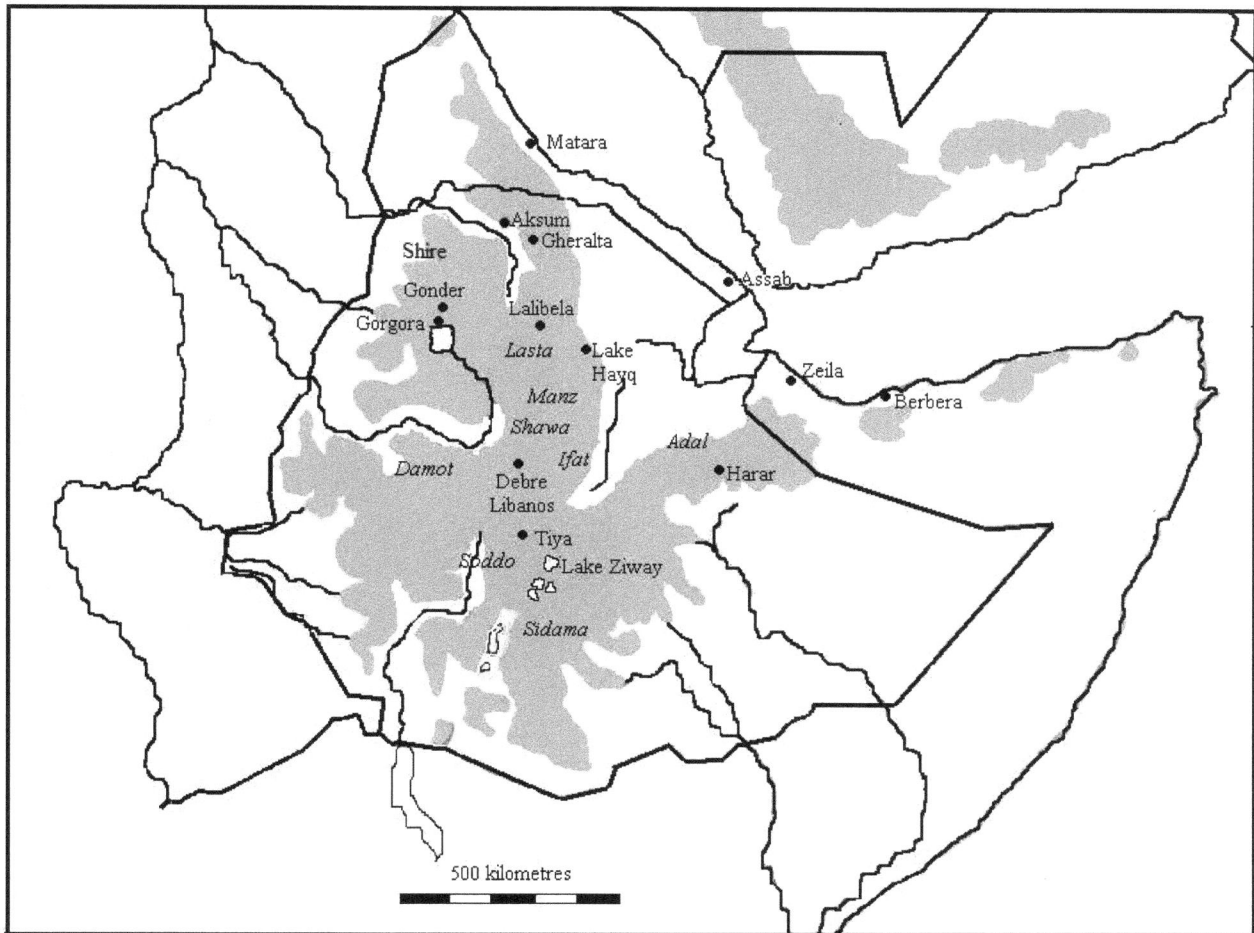

Figure 1 Map of Ethiopia showing sites mentioned in the text.

in the late antique countryside of western Europe (James 1981). This process left its impact upon the way in which the landscape was perceived and 'quantified' or labelled. Rural toponyms occasionally refer to identifiable personages (saints) connected with the missionary process; this is a feature that is also noted in the preponderance of saints' dedications in, for example, the landscape of early medieval Cornwall (Padel 2002).

It is noticeable that in many regions, be they subject to 'top down' or 'bottom up' models of Christian conversion, the countryside was always the last area to be evangelised. Christian influence was focused upon the town or city, the base of secular power (although not always – for instance in early medieval Ireland, Christianity was not mapped onto an urban landscape as towns simply did not exist), whilst the countryside, with its psycho-geographical network of natural places and shrines was inherently dangerous. In Ethiopia it took the establishment of a monastery within this rural space to bring about a gradual reordering of the landscape; the monastery was a mission station in every sense of the word, a conduit for Christianity. In the urban centres the church was kept close to secular power; physically the building would be monumental, it would make an explicit

statement of secular and ideological power through sheer scale (Trigger 1990), and the site of the church would naturally be regulated according to the outlook of the ruler. Ezana, we would assume, was positive about accepting Christianity and as such accorded the Church access to spaces of power. In some instances drawn from the historical literature of the mission process in southern Africa, we see how rulers centralised or isolated the Christian mission building according to their perceptions of the benefits (or otherwise) of accepting Christianity (Lane 1999). Our preliminary model for the landscape of conversion defines a simple two-tier scenario which sees the Christianisation of urban centres in the first phase, and a secondary evangelisation of the countryside through the establishment of a monastic network. But how did this gradual conversion to Christianity affect the symbolic and cultural outlook of the Aksumite people?

Ideological change and material culture in life and death
The clearest evidence for the actual pace and depth of Christian penetration into Aksumite society is seen in changes of burial practice and in decorative motifs in coinage and ceramics from elite and domestic contexts. In

15

the case of the coinage the predominant motif above the head of the ruler changes from the pre-Christian crescent moon to a cross; a fly whisk is substituted by a hand cross, and the epigraphy on the coins possibly reflects a more monotheistic outlook, and occasionally uses recognisably Christian formulae (Munro-Hay 1991, 190). It is scarcely surprising that the coinage should undergo such a rapid change; based upon pre-Diocletian Roman coinage standards, Aksumite coins have been found in Arabia and across north-eastern Africa. The adoption of overt Christian motifs made it clear to an international audience that the king of Aksum was now answerable to a far greater power.

The character of burial traditions also changes in Christian times, although we must be wary about employing burial evidence alone as an indicator of ideological change and status (Parker Pearson 1982). High-status individuals were interred in large subterranean tombs, marked by large, free-standing and often decorated stelae, in a delineated zone in what may have been the centre of the city (the Central Stelae Park at Aksum). The tombs were well appointed, and even though phases of robbing have clouded the archaeological picture, it is clear that many high-status, luxury grave goods were routinely placed alongside the corpse. Evidence for lower-status burial is less equivocal; excavations on the Gudit Stelae Field to the southwest of the town have shown a differential treatment of the dead, with simple pit tombs marked by rough, undecorated stelae (Phillipson 1998, 95-111). The actual practice of marking the burial place of the dead by free-standing monoliths is well attested in prehistoric contexts in the Sudan-Ethiopia borderlands, and is not uniquely associated with Aksum (Fattovich 1987); the Aksumite stelae are notable, however, for their size and intricate decoration, which skeuomorphically may recall the construction of Aksumite domestic buildings. A recent excavator of Aksum, David Phillipson, has suggested that the practice of stela erection did not survive the coming of Christianity; a door on the upper side of the fallen stela 1 was defaced, its handle deliberately chipped away, perhaps by Christians who were uncomfortable with this symbolism of the pre-Christian afterlife (Phillipson 1994).

Certainly there are no Aksumite Christian burials within the elite burial zone, and the stelae were left largely untouched; the pre-Christian elite burial zone, however, continues to play a part in the symbolism and ritual of the Ethiopian Orthodox Church to this day. At the Feast of Maryam Zion, stela 3 is the focus of a key part of this important Christian ritual, the enthronement of the Patriarch and a symbolic drawing together of pre-Christian past and Christian present, a strong social memory (Fig. 2).

Two unequivocally Christian-period tombs at Aksum (the tombs of Kaleb and Gebre Maskel) are sited to the north of the town, on a ridge away from the presumed focus of secular and holy power. It seems that these tombs – still

unquestionably 'elite' in terms of scale and construction – are distanced from the centre of secular power, and do not present the same monumental visual impact in the landscape as the stelae. Built as if to echo an ecclesiastical building, and decorated with crosses, it is probable that these tombs date to the sixth century AD (Phillipson 1998, 109). It is clear that only more archaeological survey will solve the riddle of the missing Christian tombs; what is clear at least is that while burial zones did shift, pre-Christian cemeteries were respected. The contemporary picture sees differential burial space allotted according to religion; it is noticeable that in Axum, the holiest site in Ethiopian Christendom, the cemetery for the town's Muslim population is distanced to the north-west of the town whilst modern Christian burial zones are more centralised.

Figure 2 Syncretism of space and social memory: Christian ritual at stela 3, Aksum, 1996. (Niall Finneran).

The sacred place

> 'The Christianisation of archaeological spaces would amount to much more than negating the previous cultural system....it is instead an example of the construction of a new social and ideological order based on the appropriation of the past' (Oubina *et al.* 1998, 174).

Central to the theoretical thread of this paper is the contention that social memory resides in places in the landscape, and in order to effectively surmount pre-Christian ideological traditions these places have to be seized and reconfigured in a Christian context: this results in syncretism of place (this idea brings us back to the notion of rewriting ritual texts discussed above). There are many case studies that show how new faiths impinge upon the sacred places of older religions, and this may be explained both as an act of basic economic pragmatism, a reuse of an existing social space, or a symbolic act of appropriation and statement of new ownership. The historian of the English Church, Bede, reports that Mellitus, Augustine's cohort in the evangelisation of Kent, was enjoined by Pope Gregory not to destroy pagan temples, but to convert them where possible (Blair 1996); the Council of Arles was also concerned by the

16

predominance of worship at 'natural places' (see Morris 1989, 6ff, 60) and urged their destruction or conversion.

In many newly-Christianised societies, temple building (*sensu lato*) represented a continued threat, a possible focus for pagan recrudescence. Spatially the temple was configured in a different way, something unlike the form of the church, which may have been a relatively democratic space for meeting; the temple was closed-off, secretive, the house of the god, a place of demons for early Christians. These were places in the landscape that demanded eradication or reconceptualisation. Emperor Theodosius understood this and the conversion (if not destruction) of the temple was at once a pragmatic step to take advantage of an existing place of worship, and at the same time a symbolic statement of intent (Brown 1995, 6 ff.). The newly-enfranchised Christians of Egypt enthusiastically wrecked the urban temples of Alexandria, and placed churches within their space. It is commonly suggested that Pharaonic temple complexes were also subject to large-scale spatial revision in the early Christian period, but this is not borne out by the evidence (c.f. Jullien 1902). It is true that a number of Egyptian temples do contain Christian remains: for example, the massive ritual space of the Temple of Amon at Karnak encompasses a number of small churches, but the fundamental monumentality of the building, the unity of the pre-Christian temple, was not affected by these additions. Church building within Pharaonic sacred space often involved the smallest addition and subtraction of architectural elements to form a basic basilican space; crosses and graffiti carved upon the surfaces hardly constitute a radical reordering of pre-Christian space (Coquin 1972). One could argue that the addition of the mosque at the southern pylon of the Temple of Amon Ra at Luxor offers a far more overt statement of spatial reordering than the rather more fragile efforts of Christians. The latter are hardly shattering rewritings of spatial ritual texts.

The conversion of pagan temple into Christian church is also noted at a number of sites in Nubia (Welsby 2002, 36-7), but in terms of Aksumite archaeology is something that has yet to be recognised. Tradition suggests that the Cathedral Church of Maryam Zion, the most important church in Christian Ethiopia, stands upon the foundations of a pre-Christian temple (e.g. Bent 1896, 193). The church does sit upon a large and well-made podium showing obvious Aksumite-period architectural affinities, but we have no evidence within Aksum itself for a pre-Christian cultic installation, so any statement about the syncretism of space around Maryam Zion is, without further archaeological excavation, purely conjectural. The basilicas excavated on the summit of the hill of Beta Giyorgis, however, are clearly associated with the extensive and newly-uncovered tomb and palace structures there. We also know that the large moon temple nearby at Yeha was converted into a church at some point after the fourth century AD, but this is the only archaeological evidence of a Christian building appropriating the space of a pre-Christian cultic building

(Doresse 1957, 231). It is in the countryside rather than in the major population centres where we see evidence for the siting of churches or monasteries upon sites of probable pre-Christian significance, and this factor would seem to suggest a differential treatment of pre-Christian sacred space in rural areas, unlike in urban areas where – especially at Aksum – the stelae burials were largely respected and untouched.

The post-Aksumite rock-hewn and semi-rock-hewn churches of Tigray – the subject of extensive work by David Buxton and Ruth Plant – appear to be intermediate architectural and chronological forms between the Aksumite basilica of the fourth, fifth and sixth centuries AD, and the *possible* twelfth-century AD monolithic churches of Lalibela in the Lasta highlands far to the south (Buxton 1947). The act of building a church within a natural cave or fissure appears to be a statement of acculturation of a natural space (Heldman 1992); caves were significant cultic locales in highland Ethiopia, as witnessed by the placement of later prehistoric rock art sites within them, and many of these church buildings also enclose a spring. Water sources hold a special significance in the psychogeography of the Ethiopian highlands; here they were reconfigured in a Christian framework and in time became centres of healing cults and pilgrimage. Known as *tsebel*, these holy wells were often directly associated with the identity of a saint (Buxton 1971; Plant 1985, 109-110, 193). At Lalibela many of the monasteries fringing the town are associated with pre-Christian holy mountains. The monastic churches of Na'akweto La'ab and Yemrehane Krestos are also sited in caves beneath old waterfalls; again the association of water is strong, but in all cases the spring head is somehow enclosed, enculturated and made Christian (Finneran and Tribe 2004).

Recent work at Shire, north-western Tigray, has cast light upon another form of psychogeographical association of Christian place, not with a natural place but with a pre-existing, encultured sacred space (Finneran and Phillips 2003). A number of churches and monasteries in this region enclose stelae (this is clear at the church of Weybla Maryam, Semema, which is also situated upon a podium of probable Aksumite date; whether it represents the foundation of a temple is unclear). Scholarly opinion would suggest that these stelae are associated with graves, so it is clear that Christian places of worship seem to respect pre-Christian burial zones, an indication of the strength of social memory within the landscape (Fig. 3). One monastery in the area uses a monolith as a marker to demarcate gendered zones within monastic space. The fact that these stones are regarded by monks, priests and people in general as being pre-Christian does not dim their significance; their meanings and functions have simply been 'rewritten', their role in the psychogeography of the landscape altered. The association of a pre-Christian monolith with a church is something that will be familiar to medieval archaeologists in Britain; one important and obvious, but exceptional, example is the church at Rudston, East Yorkshire, whose

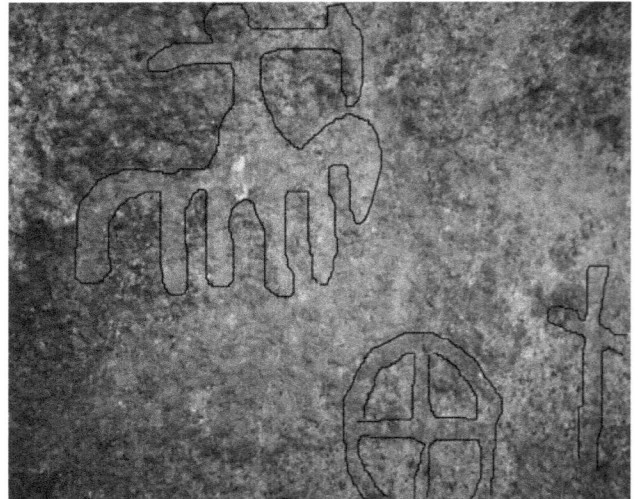

Figure 4 Baahti Shillom, Shire; Christianised art (Niall Finneran).

Figure 3 Standing stone in a church compound at Shire (Niall Finneran).

grounds enclose a monolith not too unlike those found in northern Ethiopia (Morris 1989, 81), but then again it is but a short step, acculturation, to reconceptualise the monolith into the idea of a standing cross such as are found in churchyards in Britain (Henderson 1999, 207).

Another monolith in the Shire region at Adi Hahno is a more effective witness to this idea of syncretism of space and changing psychogeographic roles. According to folk tradition it is Aksumite in date (and pre-Christian), and was moved to its present position by soldiers of the Muslim general Ibadulla, a liege of the Christian king Dawit II, who undertook a ruthless military campaign in the area to bring the Kunama peoples to heel during the fourteenth century AD – the re-erection of the *pagan* stone at a new place served to commemorate the victory of a *Muslim* general, acting on behalf of a *Christian* king, over a *pagan* people. Even today this place is an important meeting point and offering place for the Muslims in the area. An even more overt reconfiguration of a non-Christian sacred place is found at the rock-art site of Baahti Shillom (Fig. 4): here on a very noticeable landscape feature there are a number of depictions of stylised cattle, as can be found all over northern Ethiopia and Eritrea (so-called Bucrania), but these paintings have been systematically defaced by the addition of crude crosses in red paint. It is almost as if the image has been Christianised, the magic removed, and the power of the cattle icons rendered neutral. Baahti Shillom also stands in the grounds of a monastery, another clear association of multi-vocality in sacred place (similar Christianisation

of a pre-Christian motif may be noted on the Lioness at Gobedra Hill, Aksum, where a cross has been carved into the rock behind the tail).

Ideological reinforcement of the landscape

I have argued elsewhere that the development of a monastic system presages a secondary evangelisation process across the landscape; this is a picture noted in late antique Gaul and Germany (James 1981), and is also a feature of the Christianisation of the Ethiopian rural landscape. Arguably the concept of Christian monasticism was introduced to Ethiopia by the Syrian 'Nine Saints' at some point in the sixth century AD (Tamrat 1972, 23); these initial monastic foundations became powerful economic and ideological foci in the landscape and would eventually attract immense imperial patronage (Finneran and Tribe 2004). The first phase of monasticism saw the establishment of important monasteries across the core zone of the Aksumite kingdom; a number of these establishments are attached to foundation legends which explicitly state that the monasteries were built upon sites sacred to pre-Christian belief systems. Legends associated with the founding of the monastery of Debre Damo by Saint Abuna Aregawi state that the place was the abode of a dragon, which was subsequently converted to Christianity and now guards the monastery (Levine 1974, 49), and some scholars have suggested that the existing monastic water cisterns were remodelled from pre-Christian sacred springs (Hein and Kleidt 1998, 95; Matthews and Mordini 1959), although as yet there is no direct archaeological evidence of this. The monasteries of Aba Pantaleon and Aba Liqanos at Aksum have also yielded archaeological evidence of some form of cultic function in pre-Christian times (Munro-Hay 1991, 208), and it is clear that these monastic centres were sited on dramatic rock pinnacles that enabled them to physically dominate the landscape. From a phenomenological perspective the siting of monasteries on rock pinnacles and flat-topped plateaux (*ambas*) makes a very overt statement of domination of space, of monumentality and visual impact (cf. Trigger 1990), yet also simultaneously distances the community from the secular world, a mindset of psychogeography that runs through the ethos of the eremitic monastic movement (e.g. MacGinty 1983). The Byzantine Greek Orthodox monasteries at Meteorea, for example, embody a similar psychogeographical idea of physical distancing combined with visual impact.

A secondary phase of monastic expansion during medieval times after the Solomonic restoration dynasty sought to extend political influence to the pagan lands to the south (Tamrat 1972, 111), saw a similar reconception of psychogeographic space. Monasteries within the landscape respected the earlier spatial rules, often reusing pre-existing sacred places on dominating landscape features or on islands, a strategy that distanced yet simultaneously dominated psychogeographic space. I have noted elsewhere (Finneran and Tribe 2004), that monasteries founded by the famous monk Tekla Haymanot during the fourteenth century AD were also sited upon political boundaries within the landscape, a strategy which enabled the community to exercise control over a number of social groups; in this way the monastery reconceptualised both secular and sacred space. In short, the impact of the monastic system within the Ethiopian landscape was profound: it facilitated an ideological strengthening, the establishment of dedicated Christian communities throughout the core of the Aksumite polity, and in a later, secondary phase effected the means of political control across the landscape until the emergence of a more compliant royal church in the fifteenth century AD (Crummey 2000, 29). The Ethiopian monasteries make a number of visual and sensual statements; they dominate the landscape, frequently built upon visual natural features that may (because of this visuality) have had profound sacred meanings for pre-Christian peoples, but they are also physically distanced. The patterning of Ethiopian monastic places within the landscape had profound ideological and secular consequences for the ordering of socio-economic and psychogeographical space.

Imperial patronage and the secularisation of Christian space

We have now almost come full circle in our narrative; although wary of that teleological concept that is 'Christianisation', we have arrived, in the later middle ages, at a situation where the political power of the imperial dynasty was vested in the monastic system, implanted in the countryside, with a controlled landscape dominated by imperial power through the Church itself. Imperial patronage was the means by which secular authorities were able to control the Church. At the most basic level this manifested itself in donations of luxury goods and paintings (the iconographic schemes of a number of favoured churches juxtapose important political and ecclesiastical leaders with New and Old Testament personalities). A more overt means of secular

control and domination of the church resulted in a reconceptualisation of the landscape, with awards of land (the *gult* system, which remained intact until the 1974 revolution), which made monasteries exceptionally wealthy from the early medieval period (twelfth century AD) onwards. These lands were imperial gifts and were exempt from taxation; favoured monasteries soon found themselves masters of extensive tracts of good farmland, and in all cases the distribution of land was strictly codified in the form of the land charter (see Crummey 2000 for an overview).

In a recent exercise in developing a new landscape archaeology methodology, I have been able to identify and reconstruct the *gult* system of the monastery of Giorgis in Shire on the basis of survey, toponymic study and collation of sources from contemporary manuscripts (Finneran 2003). Although not as explicit as the Anglo-Saxon charter bound descriptions, we can begin to identify specific *gult* awards, assess their productivity potential, and from these data reconstruct the monastic economies of medieval Ethiopia. What we can say at this stage is that in many cases the monastery became the key focus of power within the Ethiopian agrarian landscape from the twelfth century AD onwards, and this power was obviously ideological as well as economic (Pankhurst 1966, 47). Until the seventeenth century AD there was no real centralised political capital in the kingdom; there was a system of peripatetic, wandering imperial encampments, and in many cases these vast tented camps were established (often for a period of ten years) adjacent to favoured monastic communities. The monastery tied in many levels of power in the landscape; it was an important node of domination, both spiritual and secular (Kaplan 1986; Lagopoulos and Stylianoudi 2001).

Political and economic demands also resulted in the explicit creation of sacred places within the landscape. The Zagwe capital at Lalibela (Roha) in the Lasta Highlands is recognised as an important ecclesiastical centre (although we may debate the original functions of some of the buildings that are now churches, which may have originally had a secular role), and was a place of some political and ideological importance. According to legend this place did not grow organically, but was essentially a created sacred place rich in symbolic connotations (Heldman 1995). Tradition says that King Lalibela built his eponymous capital in response to a command from God: he was to create an earthly Jerusalem, and this he did. The place is rich in biblical imagery: the small watercourse that flows through the town was named the Jordan, a carved stone cross there marks the place where John the Baptist baptised Jesus (Fig. 5), there are hills called Golgotha and Olivet – it is a recreation, in miniature, of the holy city in the vastness of the north-central Ethiopian Highlands. However, once again secular concerns played a part in the creation of this holy space in the landscape. At the time of the creation of Lalibela, the real Jerusalem would have been off limits to Ethiopian pilgrims, as the ongoing Crusades and dangers of travel would have made access difficult, so in a sense the king was able, in the creation of his own pilgrim space, to fulfil God's wishes and also take financial advantage of extensive pilgrim interest.

Figure 5   Lalibela: the monolithic cross in the River Jordan denoting the place of 'Christ's' baptism (Nial. Finneran).

It is possible, according to a recent study by David Phillipson, that the construction of the churches should not be attributed to Lalibela alone; the complex developed over a much longer period of time and was centred upon pre-existing 'secular' hypogaea (Phillipson 2004). It is clear that the church architecture here (and at the outlying monastery of Yemrehane Krestos) recalls Aksumite features, such as the wooden beams, horizontal construction and window frames that are skeucmorphically represented on stelae 1 to 3 at Aksum, a testament to a strong thread of social memory and a respect of the past. The idea of building underground is also intriguing; did the church builders attempt to reconfigure existing pre-Christian sacred places, or are these excavations attempts to fabricate a natural cave structure? Can we find a link between the cave churches found in Tigray or, indeed the semi-subterranean tomb structures of Kaleb and Genre Maskel at Aksum? What is clear is that the world below ground may have been as significant as the landscape above. Whatever the symbolic meanings inherent in the psychogeography of the town of Lalibela, it is clear that the town represents a vast and probably expensive exercise in creating monumentality, and bears witness to the power, both secular and ideological, of the Church and its ability to manipulate space.

Conclusion

'...the ancient tissue of Roman sacred space was being picked out of shape by these new foci of the holy among them' (Markus 1990, 147)

The impact of Christianity in Ethiopia was felt at every level of society. The social, cultural and economic implications of this new cosmological order would have ramifications beyond Ethiopia – it facilitated better integration into a wider world of trade and exchange possibilities, and resulted in a new perception of space, and a reordering of psychogeography. Within the urban centres, it appears that Christianity respected pre-Christian space to some degree, a situation generally recognisable throughout the eastern Christian world (cf. Bayliss 1999; Saradi-Mendelovici 1990), yet the countryside was subject to a different set of spatial psychogeographical rules. Here the natural world offered more scope for danger, and we find the Christianisation of rock art sites, and churches and monasteries placed within or upon significant natural features, or enclosing pre-existing sacred sites. The formal urbanised landscapes of control lent themselves to a rapid configuration as Christian space; the countryside was only really 'tamed' in a secondary, monastic-dominated phase of evangelisation. It is also important to recognise that the idea of a syncretism of space extends beyond multiple ideological rewriting of ritual text (cf. Turner 2004). In Ethiopia, Christianity also reconceptualised secular space (Lefebvre's 'material' space); monastic systems within the landscape added a new layer of political as well as ideological control, nodes of secular and economic power within a colonised landscape (the monastery in early medieval Ireland, for instance, reflects this combined role of secular and ideological centre). The creation (or remodelling) of Lalibela integrates both forms of space, a place with undoubted psychogeographic resonance as well as immense political, social and economic significance, especially given the desire of the Zagwe interloper dynasty to appeal to social memory and emphasise their inheritance of the Solomonic, Aksumite Christian imperial tradition forged hundreds of miles to the north. This then is the idea of syncretism of space, a multi-vocality of meanings, feelings and values in places that have resonance both 'imagined' and 'material', psychogeographic or secular, during a period of immense social, economic and cultural change.

Acknowledgements

I should like to thank Dr. Sarah Semple for the invitation to speak at the Institute of Archaeology, University of Oxford (January 2004) as part of the post-graduate seminar series upon which this paper is based. Funding for much of the work outlined herein was provided by The British Institute in Eastern Africa, the Society of Antiquaries of London, SOAS and the British Academy. I would like to thank Professor David Phillipson for highlighting a number of weaknesses in my argument, but any errors remain my sole responsibility.

Bibliography

Anfray, F. 1974. Deux villes Axoumites: Adoulis et Matara. *Atti IV Congresso Internationale di Studi Etiopici*, 745-65. Rome: Academia Nazionale dei Lincei.

Anon. 1958. Preliminary problems in constructing a situation. *Situationiste Internationale* 1, cited in: http://art.ntu.ac.uk/mental/whatisps.htm; accessed 3/11/04.

Barnish, S. 2001. *Religio in Stagno:* nature, divinity and the Christianisation of the countryside in late antique Italy. *Journal of Early Christian Studies* 9(3), 387-402.

Barrot, J. 1987. *What is Situationism? A Critique of the Situationist Internationale.* London: Unpopular Books.

Bayliss, R. 1999. Usurping the urban image: the experience of urban topography and late antique cities of the near east. In Baker, P., Forcey, C., Jundi, S. and Witcher, R. (eds.) *TRAC 98: Proceedings of the Eighth Annual Theoretical Roman Archaeology Conference Leicester 1998,* 59-71. Leicester.

Bent, T. 1896. *The Sacred City of the Ethiopians.* London: Longman, Green and Co.

Blair, J. 1996. Churches in the early English landscape: social and cultural contexts. In Blair, J. and Pyrah, C. (eds.) *Church Archaeology: Research Directions for the Future,* 6-18. Council for British Archaeology Research Report 104. York: Council for British Archaeology.

Bradley, R. 2000. *An Archaeology of Natural Places.* London: Routledge.

Brown, P. 1995. *Authority and the Sacred: Aspects of the Christianisation of the Roman Empire.* Cambridge: Cambridge University Press.

Buxton, D. 1947. The Christian antiquities of northern Ethiopia. *Archaeologia* 92, 1-42.

Buxton, D. 1971. The rock-hewn and other medieval churches of Tigray province, Ethiopia. *Archaeologia* 103, 33-100.

Conti-Rossini, C. 1910. *Liber Axumae.* Scriptores Aethiopici ser. 2 tom. 8. Paris: Corpus Scriptorum Christianorum Orientalum.

Coquin, R. 1972. La christianisation des temples de Karnak. *Bulletin de l'Institute Française Archaeologique Orientale* 72, 169-78.

Crummey, D. 2000. *Land and Society in the Christian Kingdom of Ethiopia from the Twelfth Century to the Twentieth Century.* Addis Ababa: Addis Ababa University Press.

Davies, D. 1994. Christianity. In Holm, J. and Bowker, J. (eds.) *Attitudes to Nature,* 28-52. London: Pinter.

De Contenson, H. 1961. Les fouilles à Ouachété Golo près d'Axoum, en 1958. *Annales d'Ethiopie* 4, 3-16.

Doresse, J. 1957. *L'Empire du Prêtre Jean.* Paris: Plon.

Fattovich, R. 1987. Some remarks on the origins of the Aksumite stelae. *Annales d'Ethiopie* 14, 43-69.

Finneran, N. 2002. *The Archaeology of Christianity in Africa.* Stroud: Tempus.

Finneran, N. 2003. The monasteries of Shire, northern Ethiopia. *Ecclesiology Today* 30, 3-9.

Finneran, N. and Phillips, J. 2003. The Shire region archaeological landscape survey 2001: a preliminary report. *Azania* 37, 139-47.

Finneran, N. and Tribe, T. 2004. Towards an archaeology of kingship and monasticism in medieval Ethiopia. In Insoll, T. (ed.) *Belief in the Past. The Proceedings of the Manchester Conference on Archaeology and Religion,* 63-74. British Archaeological Reports International Series 1212. Oxford: British Archaeological Reports.

Hein, E. and Kleidt, B. 1998. *Ethiopia – Christian Africa: Art, Churches and Culture.* Ratingen: Melina Verlag.

Heldman, M. 1992. Architectural symbolism, sacred geography and the Ethiopian church. *Journal of Religion in Africa* 22, 222-40.

Heldman, M. 1995. Legends of Lalibela: the development of an Ethiopian pilgrimage site. *Res* 27, 25-38.

Henderson, G. 1999. *Vision and Image in Early Christian England.* Cambridge: Cambridge University Press.

Ingold, T. 1993. The temporality of landscape. *World Archaeology* 25(2), 152-74.

Insoll, T. 2001. Introduction: the archaeology of world religion. In Insoll, T. (ed.) *Archaeology and World Religion,* 1-32. London: Routledge.

James, E. 1981. Archaeology and the Merovingian monastery. In Clarke, H. and Brennan, M. (eds.) *Columbanus and Merovingian Monasticism,* 33-55. British Archaeological Reports International Series 113. Oxford: British Archaeological Reports.

Jones, F. 1954. *The Holy Wells of Wales.* Cardiff: University of Wales Press.

Jullien, M. 1902. Le culte Chrétien dans les temples de l'ancienne Égypte. *Les Études* 92, 237-53.

Kaplan, S. 1982. Ezana's conversion reconsidered. *Journal of Religion in Africa* 13(2), 101-9.

Kaplan, S. 1986. Court and periphery in Ethiopian Christianity. *Asian and African Studies* 20, 141-52.

Kilbride, W. 2000. Why I feel cheated by the term Christianisation. *Archaeological Review from Cambridge* 17(2), 1-17.

Lagopoulos, A. and Stylianoudi, M. 2001. The symbolism of space in Ethiopia. *Aethiopica* 4, 55-95.

Lane, P. 1999. Archaeology, non-conformist missions and the 'colonisation of consciousness' in southern Africa c. 1820-1900. In Insoll, T. (ed.) *Case Studies in Archaeology and World Religion*, 153-65. British Archaeological Reports International Series 755. Oxford: British Archaeological Reports.

Lefebvre, H. 1991. *The Production of Space*. Oxford: Blackwell.

Levine, D. 1974. *Greater Ethiopia: The Evolution of a Multiethnic Society*. Chicago: Chicago University Press.

MacGinty, G. 1983. The influence of the Desert Fathers upon early Irish monasticism. *Monastic Studies* 14, 85-91.

Markus, R. 1990. *The End of Ancient Christianity*. Cambridge: Cambridge University Press.

Markus, R. 1994. How on earth could places become holy? Origins of the Christian idea of holy places. *Journal of Early Christian Studies* 2(3), 257-71.

Matthews, D. and Mordini, A. 1959. The monastery of Debra Damo, Ethiopia. *Archaeologia* 97, 1-58.

Milis, L. 1986. La conversion en profondeur: un processus sans fin. *Revue du Nord* 68, 487-98.

Morris, R. 1989. *Churches in the Landscape*. London: Dent.

Moscos, J. 1992. *The Spiritual Meadow (Pratum Spirituale)*. Trans. J. Wortley. Kalamazoo: Cistercian Publications.

Munro-Hay, S. 1991. *Aksum: An African Civilisation of Late Antiquity*. Edinburgh: Edinburgh University Press.

Oubina, C., Boado, F. and Estevez, M. 1998. Rewriting landscape: incorporating social landscapes into cultural traditions. *World Archaeology* 30(1), 159-76.

Padel, O. 2002. Local saints and place-names in Cornwall. In Thacker, A. and Sharpe, R. (eds.) *Local saints and Local Churches in the Early Medieval West*, 303-60. Oxford: Oxford University Press.

Pankhurst, R. 1966. *State and Land in Ethiopian History*. Addis Ababa: Addis Ababa University Press/Institute of Ethiopian Studies.

Paribeni, R. 1907. Richerche nel luogo dell'anticha Adulis. *Monumenti Antichi, Reale Accademia dei Lincei* 18, 438-572.

Parker Pearson, M. 1982. Mortuary practices, society and ideology. In Hodder, I. (ed.) *Symbolic and Structural Archaeology*, 99-113. Cambridge: Cambridge University Press.

Pawlinkowski, J. 1974. The Judaic spirit of the Ethiopian Orthodox Church: a case study in religious acculturation. *Journal of Religion in Africa* 4, 178-99.

Phillipson, D. 1994. The symbolism and significance of the Aksumite stelae. *Cambridge Archaeological Journal* 4, 189-210.

Phillipson, D. 1998. *Ancient Ethiopia* London: British Museum Press.

Phillipson, D. 2000. *Excavations at Aksum 1993-1997* (2 vols.). London/Nairobi: Society of Antiquaries of London/British Institute in Eastern Africa.

Phillipson, D. 2004. Lalibela: Ethiopia's rock-cut churches. Unpublished paper presented at the joint meeting of the Anglo-Ethiopian Society and the British Institute in Eastern Africa, British Academy, London, October 27th, 2004.

Plant, R. 1985. *The Architecture of the Tigre, Ethiopia*. Worcester: Ravens.

Ricci, L. and Fattovich, R. 1987. Scavi archeologici nella zona di Aksum. *Rassegna di Studi Etiopici* 31, 123-97.

Saradi-Mendelovici, H. 1990. Christian attitudes towards pagan monuments in late antiquity and their legacy in later Byzantine centuries. *Dumbarton Oaks Papers* 44, 47-61.

Semple, S. 1998. A fear of the past: the place of the prehistoric burial mound in the ideology of middle and later Anglo-Saxon England. *World Archaeology* 30(1), 109-26.

Sinclair, I. 1997. *Lights out for the Territory*. London: Granta.

Stewart, C. and Shaw, R. (eds.) 1994. *Syncretism and Anti-syncretism: The Politics of Religious Synthesis*. London: Routledge.

Tamrat, T. 1972. *Church and State in Ethiopia 1270-1527*. Oxford: Clarendon.

Tilley, C. 1994. *A Phenomenology of Landscape*, London: Berg.

Trigger, B. 1990. Monumental architecture: a thermodynamic explanation of symbolic behaviour. *World Archaeology* 22(2), 119-32.

Tuan, Y.-F. 1974. *Topophilia: A Study of Environmental Perceptions, Attitudes and Values.* New Jersey: Prentice Hall.

Turner, S. 2004. Christianity and the conversion period landscape of southwest Britain. In Insoll, T. (ed.) *Belief in the Past. The Proceedings of the Manchester Conference on Archaeology and Religion*, 125-36. British Archaeological Reports International Series 1212. Oxford: British Archaeological Reports.

Urbanczyk, P. 2003. The politics of conversion in north-central Europe. In Carver, M. (ed.) *The Cross Goes North: Processes of Conversion in Northern Europe AD 300-1300,* 15-27. York: York Medieval Press.

Van der Veer, P. 1994. Syncretism, multi-culturalism and the discourse of tolerance. In Stewart, C. and Shaw, R. (eds.) *Syncretism and Anti-syncretism: The Politics of Religious Synthesis,* 196-211. London: Routledge.

Welsby, D. 2002. *The Medieval Kingdoms of Nubia.* London: British Museum Press.

Williams, H. 1998. Ancient landscapes and the dead: the reuse of prehistoric and Roman monuments as early Anglo-Saxon burial sites. *Journal of Medieval Archaeology* 41, 1-32.

Connotations of arable land use in landscape archaeology

Helen Lewis

The idea of land use is central to our perception of past cultural landscapes. Despite revisions of landscape concepts in archaeology, very few authors have discussed the role of modern perspectives in the interpretation of ancient land use, or the connotations of land use in landscape archaeology. In this paper some ways in which arable land use has been integral to interpretations of past landscape are discussed by way of a historical review, using what is now a classic Wessex case study demonstrating how connotations attached to land-use practices in landscape archaeology have been fundamental to our understanding of later prehistoric societies.

The importance of arable land use in landscape perspectives

Agricultural land uses and their social connotations play an especially important role in landscape perception. The interpreted divisions between agriculturalist/hunter-gatherer subsistence, and between arable/pastoral farming systems, denote certain types of social organisation linking land use to landscape. Influential ethnographic works, such as Boserup's *The Conditions of Agricultural Growth* (1965), have frequently been cited as providing support for the existence of specific relationships between land use, technology and socio-political organisation, and these relationships have often been used, both explicitly and implicitly, as 'universals' when interpreting past landscapes.

Arable farming is an activity of long-standing interest to archaeologists. The word 'arable' has been related to the Latin word for ard – *aratrum* (Steensberg 1977, 5), and implies cultivation using tillage implements. The adoption or development of cultivation has been seen as one of the markers (and causes) of many cultural changes in prehistoric societies. The degree to which arable land use is both central to modern landscape connotations and to the perspectives of its current practitioners suggests that such land use is likely to also have played a significant role in the perspectives of ancient farming peoples. Many past landscape studies in British archaeology have focused on an architectural (monumental or settlement) landscape. However, it is not only possible, but also valuable and necessary to address landscape perceptions and changes through exploring evidence of prehistoric land use.

Wild and idyllic landscapes

The dichotomy held to exist between settled agricultural and mobile pastoral or hunter/gatherer societies has an extremely long history. It has been omnipresent in landscape archaeology, where a primitive/mobile/wild 'other' has commonly been contrasted with an advanced/settled/'idyllic' 'self' (after Goody 1977, 7-8; Thomas 1996b; Schama 1995; Duncan 1993; Kluckhohn 1953; for alternate perspectives see papers in Descola and Pálsson 1996). The association of mobile or settled lifestyles with particular land-use practices and landscapes has been a fundamental part of archaeological thinking in Europe since the beginning of the discipline. Barker (1985, 1, 3) dates the idea of an evolutionary progression from 'savage' to 'herdsman' to 'agriculturalist' to Nilssen (1868), although the concept of a similar, but cyclical, development is dated to Ancient Greek times at least (Isaac 1970). The idea of progress is still prevalent, despite past suggestions that the concept of a universal and evolutionary opposition between mobile and sedentary communities is often based in ethnocentrism, and is not always appropriate in specific applications (Goody 1977, 8; Clark 1952; Whittle 1997).

Two perspectives on landscape discussed by Schama in *Landscape and Memory* (1995) in regard to art, architecture, ethnicity and history are relevant here: the idyllic Arcadia and the wild Arcadia. These have been seen as being both in conflict and in a symbiotic relationship with each other in landscape perspectives. The idyllic Arcadia represents a 'perfect pastoral state' of 'bucolic contentment' – domesticated, safe, predictable, and inhabited by settled farmers – while the wild Arcadia is said to be the world of 'hunters and gatherers, warriors and sensualists' – it is free, unpredictable, and has an 'integrity' lacking in the idyllic Arcadia (Schama 1995, 522-3; Brody 2000). Schama's discussion of these two perceived landscapes suggests that land-use interpretation, especially as it pertains to the relationship between sedentary-idyllic and mobile-wild may be seen to be an inherent part of modern landscape perception. The dichotomy presented can be linked to the idea that a tension exists between 'the desire…to represent the landscapes of the self…and the desire to represent the spaces of the other' (Duncan 1993, 367).

In archaeology and ethnography, the conflict or relationship between the 'tame' and the 'wild' has been frequently expressed in the past. It is seen, for example, in Hodder's *domus* and *agrios* (1990), in descriptions of the agricultural revolution – '…from a nomadic to a settled life, from a natural to an artificial basis of subsistence' (Frazer 1925, 129) – and in studies of ethnicity and archaeological interpretation: '…the myth of civilization overcoming the barbarian in all of us…' (Jones 1997, 66). This dichotomy is an important construct in landscape studies. These ideals have followed political and social fashions, and have shaped the historic and modern physical landscape, as well as landscape perceptions (Schama 1995; Nissen 1980;

Deneven 1992). Preferences for viewing past landscapes as 'idyllic' or 'wild' can be argued to pervade archaeology, especially in studies of later prehistory, where perceived relationships between settlement patterns and land-use practices are a key part of landscape studies. For example, Schama's idyllic Arcadia sounds very close to some past interpretations of the middle-late Bronze Age landscape in Wessex (e.g. Bradley 1984a, 91), while his wild Arcadia could be seen to be reflected in some landscape studies on the Neolithic and early Bronze Age (Barrett 1994; Whittle 1996). The conflict between the 'wild' and the 'idyllic' has, of course, nowhere been more prominent than in studies of the Mesolithic-Neolithic transition (e.g. Zvelebil 1986; Zvelebil and Dolukhanov 1991; Jones 1996; Janik 1998), where the beginning or adoption of agriculture is linked with landscape changes.

Landscape interpretations are based on complex associations between the archaeological evidence and modern perceptions, and although some past work has addressed this (e.g. Thomas 1991), it has rarely been in terms of land-use types (but see Evans 1987; Cooney 1997). While the concept of Arcadia is not limited to landscape or place, archaeological landscape perspectives have frequently alluded to an idea of Eden, with either an idyllic or (especially more recently) wild Eden in mind.

Landscape and arable land use: ethnographic and historic 'universals'

Assessment of the nature of the presumed relationships between land use and settlement patterns, and exploration of how landscape preferences influence archaeological interpretation of the links between land use and landscape are greatly needed. Regarding agrarian change, the relationships between material culture (usually agricultural technology), land use, land tenure and social organisation have been studied most thoroughly in geography, history and anthropology. Probably the most familiar topics in this regard have been the changes associated with historical developments such as enclosure and shareholding (e.g. Dodgshon 1981; Chambers and Mingay 1966), as well as political and economic approaches to rural settlement and land use (Chisholm 1962; Goodman and Redclift 1981; Marsden 1988; 1989; Jones and Woolf 1969). A great deal of past research has also focused on social changes related to the movement from small-scale family-based farming to industrialised farming and agribusiness. This work has largely dealt with the rise of industrialism, capitalism and urbanism in societies around the world (e.g. Moran *et al.* 1993). A review of these bodies of literature is not presented here, although they have been used in past archaeological interpretations of land use (e.g. Fleming 1985), and still hold much pertinent information for those studying the role of land-use connotations in landscape archaeology.

A further body of theory on agrarian change based on cross-cultural comparisons of ethnographic data has focused on issues of cultural complexity and development associated with agricultural change in 'primitive'

societies. These ethnographic studies have had an enormous influence on archaeological landscape perspectives, especially regarding relationships between prehistoric land-use practices, social organisation and cultural change. Although earlier authors (e.g. Frazer 1925) noted widespread links between these factors, perhaps the most influential work for archaeology has been that of Boserup (1965; 1970) and Goody (1976), who conducted systematic ethnographic studies of these relationships. These studies, and the evolutionary perspectives in which they are founded, tend to be associated with processual archaeology, although their influence has arguably been stronger in post-processual archaeological work, which rarely investigated the claims of the 'universal' models developed, but frequently used the underlying modelled relationships as a backdrop. Some archaeological authors who have explicitly acknowledged the impact of these models on landscape studies include Barrett (1994), Cooney (1997) and Evans (1987). See Morrison (1994) for one review of the impact of Boserup's ideas in archaeology in general.

At issue here are the following, rather simplified and occasionally paraphrased aspects of these models. Boserup (1965, 12-13) identified several arable systems based upon length of fallow time (frequency of cropping). This was taken to be a measure of the intensity of arable land use. Boserup's study suggested that subsistence farmers are conservative: they have a limited production level, and will resist changes to their system of production and technology for as long as possible. They may, however, be forced by pressures such as population growth to increase their agricultural output by intensifying production. A cycle of resistance-'change under duress' carries on over time, with farmers continually attempting to augment output efficiency to meet increasing demand. Under the model, ever-increasing intensification of land use (through shortening of fallow time) and change in agricultural technology were related to and resulted from this cycle, creating a dynamic evolution to increasingly productive, but also more labour-intensive, methods of farming (Boserup 1965, 58-9, 66-7; Barker 1985, 259).

Boserup distinguished two main types of agrarian systems: long-fallow and short-fallow (Table 1), which lie along a continuum of land-use types from virgin land to continuous cropping (when a new crop is sown immediately upon harvest of the last crop on a given piece of land) (Boserup 1965, 13, 15). This continuum is evolutionary or progressive in nature, with a progression over time from extensive arable to increasingly intensive arable land use, or to arable-associated nomadic pastoralism once grasslands have been created by clearance and cultivation (*ibid.* 17-8, 20-1).

Boserup correlated fallow systems with arable technology, land tenure, the sexual division of labour, and marriage systems by dividing arable practices into two major types: shifting and plough cultivation. These were roughly equated to female and male farming, and extensive and intensive agriculture (Boserup 1970, 50),

Table 1 Boserup's fallow types (after Boserup 1965, 15-6)

Fallow length	Description
Long – forest-fallow (20-25 years)	New plots are cleared for planting each year, used for a year or two, and then left fallow for forest regeneration. Root crops.
Long – bush-fallow (6-10 years)	As above, but left for bush regeneration. If plots are cultivated non-intensively, cropping length can be extended from 1-2 years up to the length of the fallow period (6-10 years).
Long – grass-fallow	Regeneration to wild grassland.
Short fallow (1-2 years)	Regeneration to wild grassland. Cereal crops.
Short – annual cropping (several months)	Includes systems with annual crop rotation. Usually seasonal fallow. Cereal crops.
Short - multicropping	May have no fallow. At least two crops are grown per year.

Table 2 Boserup's evolutionary sequence of arable systems (after Boserup 1965; 1970)

Fallow type	Tools and methods	Other	Increasing			
Forest-fallow (shifting)	Axes or burning/ringing for forest clearance. No tillage tools or just digging sticks. No weeding necessary.	Low land tenure Female tillage labour Polygamy/polygyny Bridewealth	intensification	division of labour	population	land productivity
Bush-fallow (shifting)	As above, but need hoe for weeding. Burning or additions of turf to sustain fertility.	Low land tenure Female tillage labour Polygamy/polygyny Bridewealth				
Grass-fallow (plough)	Plough becomes indispensable – hoe cannot effectively remove roots. Burning not normally used, as not effective against grass roots.	Nomadic invasions Herbivorous animals Cereal and fodder crops High land tenure Male tillage labour Polygamy rare Dowry				
Short grass-fallow	As grass-fallow. Manuring to sustain fertility.	As grass-fallow	↓	↓	↓	↓

and were related to fallow sequences in the manner set out in Table 2. Although Boserup suggested a tendency to follow this progressive sequence over time, there is no actual requirement in the model that technology must change when fallow length is either decreased or increased. Intensification of the fallow system may occur in a regime using any type of implement (Boserup 1965, 58).

Boserup's discussion of agrarian systems and how they change is very important for the incorporation of ancient arable land use into landscape archaeology. She suggested that there is a correlation between the evolution of fallow length, technology and certain aspects of social organisation. For example, the use of digging sticks and hoes in long-fallow systems is generally associated with female agricultural labour. Long-fallow (extensive) systems require access to a relatively large area of land, which in turn implies weaker social ties to each plot (mobility and low tenure). Short-fallow (intensive) systems generally correlate with traction tillage (ard/plough) and male tillage labour (although much of the rest of agricultural labour is female). They are associated with long-term investment of labour in a particular area of land (high tenure and sedentism and sometimes private land ownership), a greater investment in agricultural technology, and an increase in the division of labour (specialisation). Both systems correlate with various marriage and kinship practices (Table 2). The main impetus for change from one system to another was suggested to be population pressure and its impact on soil fertility. Other possible factors were briefly mentioned, such as climate or availability of secondary forest (Boserup 1965, 16, 34, 117; 1970, 33, 35, 50).

In *Production and Reproduction* (1976) Goody took the relationships discussed by Boserup somewhat further. Through cross-cultural analysis of ethnographic data from Eurasia and Africa, he suggested that the type of agriculture practised correlates not only with male/female labour, familial land tenure and marriage, but, through these, also with inheritance systems and power organisation. He noted that hoe-based arable farming is associated with female agricultural labour and with exogamous marriage systems. These correlate with the presence of bridewealth and inheritance patterns whereby male and female property is transmitted to members of the same sex on each individual's side of the family (homogeneous inheritance). Many of these societies are matrilineal. Plough-based farming is associated with male tillage labour and endogamous marriage systems, which are related to the presence of dowry, and to a transfer of marriage property to children regardless of sex (diverging devolution) (Goody 1976, 7). These societies tend to be politically complex and to have a high population density.

Goody (1976) discussed the spatial distribution of plough-based agriculture as correlating with that of highly socially stratified and populous societies with strong land tenure (found in Eurasia, and in those parts of Africa in which Islam had an early influence). This geographic outline echoes that for plough distribution given by Glob (1951, 109). Hoe-based farming is said to be predominantly found in 'less class-ridden societies' with lower population densities, and which have access to a large area of land (although it may be relatively poor land) (Goody 1976, 33, 35). These systems mirror Boserup's model and were placed along an evolutionary continuum. Goody did not discuss reasons for agrarian change, except to say that population pressure may be one reason. He did, however, examine the effects of such change regarding interactions between the factors listed above. For instance, in a plough-based system good land is a valuable asset – 'capital' – while in a hoe-based system land is plentiful and there is not such pressure to own. Land tenure is strengthened when plough-based arable farming is adopted. As plough-based farming can produce more crop than is needed by the farming family, a market is stimulated. This leads to population growth, and increasing social stratification is supported by this growth and by surplus production. Marriage systems can be seen to reflect the ability of women to inherit land (as in many societies with diverging devolution). The emergence of diverging devolution may be related to intensification, as there is a tendency to keep resources within the nuclear family (Goody 1976, 13, 20).

Boserup and Goody proposed relationships between land use, land tenure and the sexual division of certain aspects of agricultural labour, and suggested correlations between arable systems and levels of social stratification and inheritance patterns. These are evolutionary, following a progression said to be taken from archaeological thought (the sequence hunting-farming-industrialism) (Goody 1976, 3), although the influence of conquest and conversion on the spatial distribution of practices was also noted (*ibid.* 25). Other evolutionist work following along the lines of Boserup and Goody has been reviewed by Pimental and Hall (1989) and Netting (1974).

The Boserup model has been criticised from many perspectives. Some arguments (Grigg 1979; Hunt 1997) suggested that there were intrinsic errors, and that the model may only apply to certain restricted situations even in modern studies. Most criticism was directed towards Boserup's insistence on using the decline theory regarding labour productivity (Boserup 1965, Chapters 3-5, 117-8). This, it has been suggested, was not supported as a universal by the extant body of ethnographic or historic data (Hunt 1997). Other critiques focused on causes of and paths to intensification, and the relationship between these and population and social changes (Datoo 1978; Netting 1993; Bender 1978, 204-214), and the assumption that technology was related to intensification (Bray 1986). In addition, the picture of pastoralists as mobile, 'simple' or 'egalitarian' societies has seen revision (Sutter 1987; Gibson 1988). Despite these and later critiques, the Boserup-Goody model has seen continued and often uncritical use in landscape archaeology.

The main point here is that what began as social connotations associated with land-use practices became correlations when presented by Boserup and Goody. These correlations link types of land use that can be identified in the archaeological record to variations in social organisation. Although these links were not claimed to hold in all cases or all places (Goody 1976, 118-9; Boserup 1965, 17), the implied fundamental relationships between land use and social organisation appear to have been applied (often subconsciously) in many prehistoric landscape studies. It is probably not surprising that these models have been so widely accepted, as these ethnographic studies claimed to take their ideas of social evolution from archaeology itself (Goody 1976, 3; Boserup 1965, 16-8). The archaeological record, however, holds many indicators that these relationships may not be easily applicable to all prehistoric farming societies. A brief survey of the occasionally confusing influence of so-called 'ethnographic universals' in one region may be illuminating in this regard.

Land-use connotations in landscape archaeology: an example from Wessex

The importance of the ideas behind the Boserup-Goody model for landscape archaeology cannot be overstated. The apparent universality of the model implies that if any one aspect of the relationships presented above were found, the presence of the others might be inferred. In prehistoric archaeology the components of the model which are most regularly found are those material cultural remains relating to agrarian technology and fallow length, or possible indications of land tenure and social stratification. The model presented an evolutionary framework that relates arable agricultural technology to land-use practices, and then to social structure, meaning that it could be used to relate land use to landscape over time. The fundamental premises represented by this model do not, however, necessarily rest easily with much archaeological evidence, nor with modern landscape preferences. For example, in Wessex, despite decades of discussion and archaeological investigations, there still remain two major viable, but in the context of modern urban landscape perspectives and ethnographic universals, opposing models of the relationships between agricultural systems, settlement patterns and landscape during the Neolithic and Bronze Age – these have been called the 'sedentary model' (Whittle 1997, 19; see also Thomas 1991) and the 'mobility orthodoxy' (Cooney 1997, 24). These variations in opinion relate specifically to connections held to exist between arable land use and residential settlement patterns, and the preference for one or the other model changes over time, not mainly on evidence-based re-assessment, but apparently reflecting swings in landscape preferences in modern archaeology and society (e.g. compare Whittle 1985 with Whittle 1996; 1997, 19; see Schama 1995 for a study of these changing attitudes in general).

The archaeological record of southern England has proven to be especially fruitful for theoretical model development regarding Neolithic and Bronze Age landscapes. The impact of land-use perceptions has had a particularly interesting history in landscape studies of ancient Wessex, partly because of a major juxtaposition in the archaeological data from this region: although there is a relative plethora of information on ancient monumental landscapes, standard archaeological methods and approaches have produced relatively little contemporaneous settlement and land-use evidence for the periods up to at least the middle Bronze Age, and particularly for the middle-later Neolithic and early Bronze Age, the periods at which some of the most important monument groups and types were constructed and re-constructed (although this negative picture is changing, e.g. French *et al.* 2007; Richards 1990; Parker Pearson *et al.* 2006). Despite this unbalanced record, and evidence at variance with it from other regions in the British Isles, Wessex has traditionally served as the basis for models of cultural change in prehistoric Britain (Bradley 1984b; 1992; Cooney 1997, 22, 27).

The two positions that have been opposed in studying land use and landscape in Neolithic and Bronze Age Wessex are both based on Boserupian-style concepts of agrarian change. Links between land use, settlement patterns and the monumental landscape in this region have conventionally been inferred through a strong reliance on interpreted 'universal' evolutionary relationships between subsistence, settlement and social organisation developed through ethnographic research (e.g. Barrett 1994; Thomas 1996b). Evidence that arable agriculture has been regularly present in the region in some form or other since at least the middle Neolithic (e.g. Helbaek 1952; Moffett *et al.* 1989; Smith *et al.* 1981; Smith 1971, 101-2; Jones 1980; McInnes 1971, 126) has been alternately interpreted as indicating either the presence of permanent settlement and intensive cultivation patterns, or as showing the existence of mobile settlement and extensive arable practice (see e.g. reviews in Thomas 1999; French *et al.* 2007). Land use was explicitly linked to landscape in southern England by Barrett in *Fragments from Antiquity* (1994), and his example provides a useful summary of the issues.

Barrett (1994, 135) related changes in ritual practice and settlement patterns in southern England during the second millennium BC to issues of land tenure, by addressing the relationship between the 'sequence of ritual practices' seen in the monumental evidence and day-to-day 'economic' activities. Barrett supported the view that the adoption of farming at the end of the fifth to the early fourth millennium BC (early Neolithic) was not the 'agricultural revolution' described by earlier writers (e.g. Childe 1949, 187), but the beginning of a long period of mobile settlement patterns with extensive mixed farming and hunting/gathering. Through the Neolithic and into the early Bronze Age, land tenure was suggested to slowly increase in strength, primarily related to the repeated use of monuments, with a 'true agricultural revolution' occurring in the second millennium BC (middle Bronze Age). This was marked in the landscape by the proposed development of intensive, more predominantly arable farming in permanent fields, associated with permanent domestic settlement patterns (Barrett 1994, 143-51). According to this scenario, an evolving sense of land tenure precipitated the beginnings of permanent settlement and intensified arable land use proposed to be seen during the later Bronze Age.

This model was opposed to the 'traditional' idea that the adoption of agriculture in the early Neolithic was a major transformation (part of the 'Neolithic revolution'). The latter scenario suggests that the Neolithic marked the beginning of long-term progressive forest clearance for the purposes of intensive cultivation (with short-fallow systems and, usually, ard traction tillage), associated with a change from Mesolithic mobile hunter-gatherer to Neolithic sedentary agricultural societies (Barrett 1994, 146-7). In the 'traditional' view, while domesticated animals are seen as a main food staple, early Neolithic people have been envisioned to be growing barley and wheat (variously using hoes, digging sticks or ards), and residing in permanently or regularly occupied settlements. Contemporaneous monuments were 'family vault(s), correspond(ing) to…area(s) of arable land and pasture' (Childe 1949, 34, 77). Settlement by these Neolithic arable or mixed-regime farmers has been suggested to be in locations which would be relatively good for cultivation, areas of 'easy settlement', such as the chalklands of southern England. Communities have been suggested to have used tracts of land running between the valley floors and upland plateaux, with these two areas being used for grazing while soils in between them were tilled for crops – emmer on loamy soils, and barley on lighter soils on the edges of downs and in downland valleys (Dennell 1976; Childe 1949, 33).

An extension of this settled-arable pattern into the later Neolithic and early Bronze Age is a variant which became popular in the late 1970s and early 1980s (Whittle 1997, 16). The monumental evidence, taken to indicate social complexity, coupled with the continuing (if low) presence of indicators of cereal cultivation (ard marks, cereal-type pollen, seeds and grain impressions), was used to infer a sedentary and farmed settlement landscape – '...these monuments established by agrarian communities betoken the success of a way of life based on mixed farming...' (Fowler 1983, 5) (see also Renfrew

1973; Burgess 1980; Case 1977, 76). This idea was repeatedly criticised for not dealing with the scarcity of evidence for sedentism, and the apparently relatively low importance of agrarian farming (Darvill 1982, 90; Thomas 1996b). Assessment of the latter is, however, directly related to the former, as much evidence for later 'intensive' arable farming is found exactly on settlement sites, which are rare for the Neolithic-early Bronze Age in Wessex. As such, gauging the amount, type or intensity of agrarian activity during these periods remains seriously problematic for approaches based mainly on remains from 'domestic' structures; this includes many environmental archaeological approaches used as standard in the investigation of ancient land use, such as the study of macrobotanical and faunal remains.

Despite finds of arable crop remains in Wessex and evidence of soil tillage from the earlier Neolithic onwards (see Lewis 1998 and French *et al.* 2007 for reviews), the settlement pattern expected for an agrarian-based society – one with permanent fields associated with domestic site remains ('houses') – is not in evidence in the region, with rare exceptions (e.g. Green in French *et al.* 2007), until the middle Bronze Age at least. This, coupled with evidence suggesting gathering, hunting and herding were of great importance (Moffett *et al.* 1989; Bradley 1994, 95), led many authors to suggest the existence of a Neolithic and early Bronze Age mobile or nomadic lifestyle with mixed farming, but only a minor and/or semi-permanent arable component (Whittle 1977a and b; Childe 1949, 98-9; Entwistle and Grant 1989, 208; Fleming 1971; 1972). Variations on this theme have included a mixture of a farmstead-dwelling population and mobile groups interacting in the landscape, and the existence of an annual cycle of population movement which included locations where cereals were grown (Brück 1997; Thomas 1991, 20-1; 1996a, 317-18; 1999; Bradley 1978c; Fleming 1988, 100-3).

Barrett stated that the evidence available from the fourth to the second millennia BC does not suggest a 'predominant concern with the social control of portions of land surface' (1994, 143) (*i.e.* there is little evidence for permanent fields, settlement, land holding), which should be associated with farmers focused on arable production. It was held to reflect instead a period of primarily seasonal movement, with minimal land tenure and long-fallow cultivation systems. Following earlier ideas on land tenure (e.g. Fleming 1985; 1989a and b; Ingold 1986), and using the Boserup-Goody model, Barrett associated long-fallow systems with digging sticks and hoes, mobility and 'land held in trust by the community itself' (1994, 143-4). Arable agriculture would play only a minor role in a mixed subsistence economy dominated by herding and the exploitation of wild resources. The evidence for such a model was somewhat sparse, as '…(archaeological) traces of these long fallow systems, other than the negative trace of no surviving early field boundaries and no enclosed settlements, cannot be identified on the Wessex chalk' (Barrett 1994, 144).

Barrett saw the major transformation in Wessex prehistory occurring in the second millennium BC, with changes in burial practices and settlement patterns related to a change to short-fallow arable farming systems. These short-fallow systems were associated with annual or multi-cropping, controlled access to land and strong tenure, more permanent settlement (greater investment in a smaller, specific area of land), and traction-based tillage technology (Barrett 1994, 143-4, after Boserup 1965).

The appearance of recognisable field boundaries and enclosed settlement forms in southern England (e.g. Dorset group 5, Black Patch, Beacon Hill, South Lodge, Itford Hill – Fleming 1989b, 65; Bradley 1978a; Drewett 1978; 1982), was linked to this agrarian change. Although some authors (Fowler 1981, 45-6; Pryor 1996; 2006), have questioned the association of many middle-late Bronze Age field systems with arable land use, suggesting that stock-rearing is more likely, the presence of these first clear indicators of land division and (in some cases) their associated settlement remains has frequently been related to either a consolidation or intensification of arable systems already in existence in the region (Fleming 1989b, 78; Barrett 1994; Bradley 1980). An alternate explanation has suggested a movement of arable/mixed farmers into the area from elsewhere, either from abroad (Childe 1949, 187; Curwen and Hatt 1953, 76, 78), or from some agricultural hinterland into the Wessex core (Bradley 1978b and c). The evidence of enclosed settlements has been interpreted as representing the first recognisably 'permanent' 'domestic' settlement in the region, and the middle Bronze Age has been described as the point at which the historical and present-day rural idyllic landscape can be seen to have begun in southern Britain (Thomas 1991, 10), although some would move this into the Iron Age (e.g. Barker 1985, 218).

Barrett (1994) suggested that permanently-settled arable or mixed farming systems held by some to exist prior to this middle Bronze Age land division are absent, and not simply archaeologically invisible due to erosion, later land use or insubstantial house forms (Gibson 1982, 42-3; Simpson 1971, 131; McInnes 1971, 128). While evidence demonstrates that arable farming was known of throughout the entire time range discussed, the introduction of this practice in the Neolithic was seen to have had a minimal impact on settlement patterns (although settlement patterns are notoriously hard to pin down for this region for that time). 'Permanent' settlement was thus not related to the introduction of cultivation, but to the change from long- to short-fallow agrarian systems. Interpreted land tenure transformations during the Bronze Age were associated with slow cumulative changes in the already-existing agrarian system. These culminated in middle Bronze Age 'indications of technological change, a more intensive use of the land with short fallow, a concern for the division and demarcation of the land, and possible changes in the definition of settlement locations' (Barrett 1994, 147).

In this example from southern England, a wild-to-tame landscape evolution, once firmly placed at the Mesolithic-Neolithic transition, was moved to the middle Bronze Age, if not later (Brück 1997; Whittle 1997, 22). All sides to this debate have been grounded in the same basic body of evidence. The ambiguity of this evidence regarding land use and settlement during the Neolithic period and early Bronze Age has, however, meant that both interpretations of settled agrarian or mixed farmers – the 'sedentary model' (Whittle 1997, 19) – and models of mobile mixed farmers or herders with a strong hunter/gatherer component – the 'mobility orthodoxy' (Cooney 1997, 24) – have found support. One of the most interesting and intractable issues of Neolithic and Bronze Age landscape studies in southern England has been the attempt either to wed or to extricate these apparently contradictory ideas.

The connotations of residential settlement patterns for land-use interpretations

The apparent impasse in model development in the Wessex region was partly a result of two elements. First, there has been difficulty in obtaining the type of data needed to directly assess the land use-landscape link. Specifically, until recently efforts have concentrated on locating settlement sites and on excavating monumental evidence, while it is information on land-use patterns that may be more easily forthcoming and ultimately more useful in this regard (French et al. 2007; Smith 1984). Second, and perhaps more important, specific sorts of land use carry certain landscape connotations, and modern preferences have been attributed to the past with little exploration of how land use is perceptually linked to landscape. The belief that land-use types, social systems and landscapes evolve into one another and can be held in opposition to each other (as in shifting vs. plough agriculture, or mobile vs. sedentary settlement patterns, or idyllic/rural vs. wild landscapes), for example, may be a hindrance to the interpretation of archaeological evidence. There is no theoretical or practical reason why several systems of land use and settlement could not be operating in tandem in southern Britain from the fourth millennium BC onwards, at least on a small scale (see Whittle 1997). In addition to the non-exclusivity of mobile and sedentary practices, at least regarding land-use activities (Harlan 1995, 112), there is regional and local variability to consider (Cooney 1997; Bradley 1984b; 1992, 18; French et al. 2007). There is a great deal of variation seen in past ethnographic and historical studies of agricultural practices, suggesting that the prediction of patterns of land use, the relationship of land use to social organisation, and the stability of landscape types may be more complicated than many authors appear to believe, or, at least, choose to present (see Morrison 1994, 144-146 for discussion of the impact of Boserupian ideas in this regard).

A key feature of the land use-landscape relationship in archaeological interpretation is the problematic inferred link between agrarian communities and permanent settlement patterns. Where there is evidence of arable farming, the ancient society may immediately be placed into the 'settled-intensive-stratified-endogamous' category, even if no evidence of strong agricultural or domestic land tenure exists. Thomas (1996b), for example, noted that many authors assume that Neolithic mixed agricultural societies must have been sedentary and should have had houses (also see Whittle 1997, 16). Alternately, where 'permanent' domestic settlement structures (houses) are not found, there has been the assumption that not only residential, but also agricultural land tenure was low, and that arable farming cannot have been of great significance, even if evidence of such land use is present. The association of permanent residential settlement with agrarian land use has been partly based on the relationship between domestication and houses (creation of a domesticated and domestic setting vs. an untamed, wild setting – Hodder 1990, 44-5; Thomas 1996b). For example, Brown (1997, 125) states that a 'domestic' landscape (a settlement as opposed to a 'ritual' landscape) 'can also be said to be a…landscape where…wild resources…were replaced by domesticated plants and animals'. This conceptual relationship is also partly based on ethnographic work, which suggests that where 'agriculture is the predominant activity, the crucial factor becomes ownership of the land' (Guidoni 1975, 12, in Roberts 1996, 71). It has normally been encapsulated in the notion of 'farmstead' or 'homestead', which comprises buildings and 'bounded open spaces' (Roberts 1996, 15-6). In addition to the association with land tenure and domestic architecture, sedentary living has been seen as being favourable for cereal-farming communities for various practical reasons: cereals do not move, the labour requirements for successful harvesting and processing of large crops are more easily attained by a stationary population, crop losses are high and yields low during the first few years of cultivation on an area, storage facilities are needed for grain, crops need protection, etc. (Barker 1985, 43; Roberts 1996, 21, 23; Doolittle 1984, 127-8; Case 1969). Issues have also been raised regarding animal training where traction is in use (Coles 1973, 33; Hansen 1969), as it was from the early Neolithic in Wessex (see Lewis 1998 and French et al. 2007 for reviews of the evidence for arable land use from the region, and issues regarding the interpretation of that evidence).

If we look at modern, ethnographic and historic examples, it is difficult to cite many cases of annual or multi-cropping systems whose farmers do not possess permanent domestic architecture, suggesting that some general correlation between short-fallow and locally-intensive agrarian land use, 'permanent' houses and sedentism might perhaps exist. However, there are numerous variations in links between land-use and settlement patterns. Many non-agrarian peoples and even non-agriculturalists live in what are normally called 'permanent' substantial structures and villages (e.g. Harlan 1995, Chapter 1), and pre-agricultural sedentism has been said to play an important role in the development and adoption of farming at the end of the Palaeolithic or Mesolithic, a key issue in some regions (e.g. McCorriston and Hole 1991, 29-50; Sauer 1952;

Price 1996, 359). There are many examples of past and present hunter-gatherer and pastoral groups with a strong sense of tenure regarding certain types of land and land-use (hunting grounds, burial grounds) (Roberts 1996, 124), and Barrett's model (1994, 141, 143-4) suggested that land tenure with regard to monumental places in the Neolithic landscape of Wessex was strong enough to culminate in permanent settlement patterns by the middle Bronze Age. On the other hand, some mixed farmers with permanent arable fields have been seen to follow seasonally mobile residential settlement patterns, the classic ethnographic example being that of the Cheyenne in North America (Hodges 1957, 143; Whittle 1996; Brück 1997; Whittle 1997, 21 also cites the Penobscot, after Speck 1940). Even where permanent domestic settlement patterns and permanent arable fields exist in a modern, urbanised industrial society, this does not imply individual or familial land ownership (such as the recent example of communal farms). In addition, if farmers in Wessex during the Neolithic and early Bronze Age were relatively mobile, actually locating the residential sites of mobile agriculturalists in the landscape may be very difficult, especially in areas with contemporaneous and, especially, later cultivation. It has been suggested that, if found, such sites would have features that are common to the settlement sites of both sedentary agriculturalists and mobile hunter-gatherers (Graham 1994, 95, 100-1; Roberts 1996, 123-4).

Extensive agricultural systems have often been associated with frequent settlement abandonment; indeed, either abandonment or intensification is held to be the main option when sustainability is threatened. This dichotomy also fits into the sedentary/mobile divide – there are said to be two types of agriculturalists: intensifiers and abandoners. These are traditions that are integrated into the organisation and the history of any given group (Stone 1993). Using Barrett's (1994) model, one might suggest that Wessex farmers who were traditionally abandoners evolved into intensifiers. Some studies of ethnographic and historic comparatives, however, have suggested that both may exist in any one region simultaneously, and that they do not normally tend to change pattern, even in the long-term (see Stone 1993).

Brück (1997) argued that the apparent absence of settlement during the early Bronze Age in the Wessex region is neither an actual lack, nor a factor of archaeological visibility. Archaeologists simply expect to find certain types of domestic structures in a landscape with an arable farming component, such as rectilinear timber buildings or stone houses, as are seen in other parts of Europe and Britain (Thomas 1991; Childe 1949, 77). (Note, however, that certain authors have related the earliest houses in central Europe to horticultural and not arable farming – e.g. Sherratt 1995, 250.) Brück (1997) agreed with a model of short-term settlement patterns related to pastoral land use. While there was some basis presented for the argument for short-term settlement, the association of this to yet another type of land use (pastoralism) simply perpetuates the original impasse of the arable=sedentary and pastoral=mobile landscape

dichotomy (Cooney 1997, 26). It is clear that there is arable agriculture in southern England during the Neolithic and early Bronze Age, although minimal evidence of its actual specific locations has been found, relative to that of other areas, or from later periods in this area. As noted above, the 'negative' evidence argument is unfortunately rather circular, since there is a clear depositional and survival relationship between, for example, macrobotanical assemblages and domestic sites and structures. Regarding the remains of arable land use on sites, if we have few residential 'houses' in evidence, we should expect to have relatively fewer crop remains compared to periods or locations where 'dwellings' are regularly found archaeologically, not least because residential locales appear to have been the location of much crop processing, consuming and storage activity in prehistoric societies with arable agriculture.

The fact that certain types of structural evidence are expected to be associated with this type of agriculture, such as permanent field boundaries and domestic settlement remains, may be a reflection of modern archaeological preconceptions of what arable land use is, and may reveal nothing about the practice or importance of cultivation in prehistoric southern England. Recognising these evolutionary expectations regarding arable landscapes, as with residential settlement landscapes, does not solve the evidential or methodological problems. It does, however, highlight certain preconceptions brought to bear on prehistory. With a concentration on an architectural landscape it will remain difficult to see arable landscapes if they do not include the anticipated structural elements (surviving boundaries and settlements). The focus on boundaries which have a strong survival potential, for example, has perhaps led to a distorted view of agrarian prehistory, the timing and importance of land division, and the development of land tenure in prehistoric southern England.

The land use/landscape conundrum is far more complex than the discussion presented here. The links between domestic settlement patterns and arable practices are as yet under-studied and unclear in archaeology, as are those between agricultural land tenure and arable and pastoral land use. What the settlement record of southern England demonstrates is that the universal relationships assumed to exist between various types of land use and settlement landscapes do not necessarily hold (c.f. Whittle 1997). They are, as noted by Thomas (1996b, 1) a 'series of expectations and prejudices', and they can be seen to be based on an acceptance of evolutionary land-use connotations which relate to evolutionary landscape types. Is later prehistoric Wessex an exception to the generalised rule, or the exception that proves the rule?

Linking land use and landscape
Despite the confidence with which scholars have related agricultural to social changes in ancient Wessex, the archaeological evidence of land-use practices remains ambiguous from this region. Bradley's previous

contention that the 'evidence for agricultural change (during the Bronze Age in Wessex) is so well known that a detailed account is not needed' (1984a, 107) is patently untrue. The agricultural prehistory and the relationship of land use to the prehistoric landscape of this region in particular remain very poorly conceptualised. In addition, the importance of agriculture and land use to recent archaeological perspectives on Neolithic and Bronze Age landscapes has rarely been addressed. As such, the region presents an ideal case study for the role of land use in landscape archaeology, and should continue to be a prime candidate for the systematic application of new methods of investigation.

A recent case study from Wyke Down, Dorset (French *et al.* 2007) focused specifically on the issue of whether or not there is evidence for a major change in land use during the Bronze Age in Wessex, through a systematic landscape study of the upper Allen River valley (Cranborne Chase) exploring soil and sedimentary history, past vegetation and site-specific land-use indicators in buried soils under and within monuments, as well as in the wider landscape. This study was established to address exactly the issues raised here, from an environmental archaeological perspective that did not rely on 'domestic' architecture or land division evidence to address land-use history. An extensive review of land-use evidence from the Wessex region reveals a great variety of local land-use histories from all of later prehistory, and that a focus on large-scale evidence, such as pollen, in regional models of landscape change, at the expense of the numerous and diverse pictures presented by site-specific and landscape-scale evidence, has resulted in a rather simplified overarching model of agriculture in the Neolithic and Bronze Age (*ibid.*). It is also significant that in the Wyke Down study of a Wessex chalk downland landscape, there was no evidence found of a substantial shift to arable land-use practices in the middle Bronze Age. Indeed, the land-use data suggested relative stability in the landscape regarding land use from the early Neolithic through to at least the Iron Age, despite the construction over time of many monuments and the development of what has been considered a classic Wessex-type archaeological landscape. This led the project to suggest a de-coupling of concepts that automatically link land use and monumental landscape change, and that archaeologists should focus instead on the development of landscape interpretations from a perspective that both integrates and actively explores land use as central to landscape prehistory (*ibid.*). The project also suggested that the variation seen in specific landscapes in Wessex does not reflect exceptions to the wider regional picture, but demonstrates that Neolithic and Bronze Age Wessex includes a patchwork of land-use histories, and that the implications of 'universal' models assumed by archaeological landscape studies cannot adequately reflect the complexity of ancient Wessex societies.

From a theoretical perspective, the idea of universal or generalised relationships between land use, settlement, technology, social organisation and landscapes is both interesting and frequently drawn upon. However, there are indications that the perspectives underpinning such models cannot account for the archaeological record, at least in regions such as Wessex, and this should lead us to question these evolutionary assumptions (see also Bradley 1972; McGlade 1995; Morrison 1994). The regional and local spatial and temporal variation known to exist from ethnographic and historic work also suggests that explorations of these relationships should be carried out at a site or landscape, and not regional or 'universal' scale. Instead of relying on coincidences in ethnographic data or upon our own acknowledged landscape perceptions (and preferences), it must be more profitable to explore the links between land use and landscape using the archaeological record itself. One part of the evidence required to do this is that which produces information on land-use patterns.

Generating and addressing evidence for land uses during the Neolithic and Bronze Age can provide another means of exploring ancient landscapes and landscape perspectives. In Wessex, buried soils are the most readily available and widespread reservoirs of evidence for local prehistoric land use. In addition, they contain time-depth information in terms of landscape and land-use change. Systematic examination of this record would provide an opportunity to address not only land-use practices themselves, but also how land-use change reflects and is reflected in landscape changes and perceptions. Land-use connotations are integral to archaeological perceptions of past landscapes. In certain regions, such as Wessex, where existing land-use evidence is understudied relative to monumental and, later, settlement evidence, it is especially important to address modern biases relating to land-use connotations when interpreting ancient landscapes. These perceptions may be best explored through an examination of land-use evidence, as opposed to a concentration on the evidence of architectural remains.

Acknowledgements
Thanks to Vladislav Stukalov, Vladimir Olkhovoi and Natalya Rostovsteva, Charles French, Dorian Fuller, Chris Stevens, Queens' College Cambridge, and the British Federation of University Women.

Bibliography
Barker, G. 1985. *Prehistoric Farming in Europe*. Cambridge: Cambridge University Press.

Barrett, J.C. 1994. *Fragments from Antiquity: An Archaeology of Social Life in Britain, 2900-1200 BC*. Oxford: Blackwell.

Bender, B. 1978. Gatherer-hunter to farmer: a social perspective. *World Archaeology* 10(2), 204-22.

Boserup, E. 1965. *The Conditions of Agricultural Growth: the Economics of Agrarian Change under*

Population Pressure. Chicago: Aldine Publishing.

Boserup, E. 1970. *Woman's Role in Economic Development*. London: George Allen and Unwin.

Bradley, R. 1972. Prehistorians and pastoralists in Neolithic and Bronze Age England. *World Archaeology* 4, 192-204.

Bradley, R. 1978a. Prehistoric field systems in Britain and north-west Europe – a review of some recent work. *World Archaeology* 9(3), 265-80.

Bradley, R. 1978b. *The Prehistoric Settlement of Britain*. London: Routledge, Kegan and Paul.

Bradley, R. 1978c. Consolidation and land-use in the late Neolithic and early Bronze Age. In Limbrey, S. and Evans, J.G. (eds.) *The Effect of Man on the Landscape: The Lowland Zone*, 95-103. Council for British Archaeology Research Report 21. London: Council for British Archaeology.

Bradley, R. 1980. Subsistence, exchange and technology – a social framework for the Bronze Age in southern England c. 1400-700 bc. In Barrett, J. and Bradley, R. (eds.) *Settlement and Society in the British Later Bronze Age*, 57-75. British Archaeological Reports, British Series 83. Oxford: British Archaeological Reports.

Bradley, R. 1984a. *The Social Foundations of Prehistoric Britain: Themes and Variations in the Archaeology of Power*. Harlow: Longman Group.

Bradley, R. 1984b. Regional systems in Neolithic Britain. In Bradley, R. and Gardiner, J. (eds.) *Neolithic Studies: A Review of Some Current Research*, 5-14. British Archaeological Reports British Series 133. Oxford: British Archaeological Reports.

Bradley, R. 1992. The gravels and British prehistory from the Neolithic to the early Iron Age. In Fulford, M. and Nichols, E. (eds.) *Developing Landscapes of Lowland Britain. The Archaeology of the British Gravels: A Review*, 15-22. London: Society of Antiquaries of London.

Bradley, R. 1994. Symbols and signposts – understanding the prehistoric petroglyphs of the British Isles. In Renfrew, A.C. and Zubrow, E.B.W. (eds.) *The Ancient Mind: Elements of Cognitive Archaeology*, 95-106. Cambridge: Cambridge University Press.

Bray, F. 1986. *The Rice Economies: Technology and Development in Asia*. New York: Blackwell.

Brody, H. 2000. *The Other Side of Eden. Hunters, Farmers and the Shaping of the World*. New York: North Point Press.

Brown, K. 1997. Domestic settlement and the landscape during the Neolithic of the Tavoliere, S. E. Italy. In Topping, P. (ed.) *Neolithic Landscapes*, 125-37. Oxbow Monograph 86. Oxford: British Archaeological Reports.

Brück, J. 1997. *The Early-middle Bronze Age Transition in Wessex, Sussex and the Thames Valley*. Unpublished Ph. D. Thesis. University of Cambridge.

Burgess, C. 1980. *The Age of Stonehenge*. London: Dent.

Case, H.J. 1969. Neolithic explanations. *Antiquity* 43, 176-86.

Case, H.J. 1977. The Beaker culture in Britain and Ireland. In Mercer, R. (ed.) *Beakers in Britain and Europe*, 71-84. British Archaeological Reports S26. Oxford: British Archaeological Reports.

Chambers, J.D. and Mingay, G.E. 1966. *The Agricultural Revolution 1750-1880*. London: BT Batsford.

Childe, V.G. 1949. *Prehistoric Communities of the British Isles*. Third Edition. London: W. and R. Chambers.

Chisolm, M. 1962. *Rural Settlement and Land Use*. London: Hutchinson.

Clark, G. 1952. *Prehistoric Europe – The Economic Basis*. London: Methuen.

Cooney, G. 1997. Images of settlement and the landscape in the Neolithic. In Topping, P. (ed.) *Neolithic Landscapes*, 23-31. Oxbow Monograph 86. Oxford: British Archaeological Reports.

Coles, J M. 1973. *Archaeology by Experiment*. London: Hutchinson University Library.

Curwen, E.C. and Hatt, G. 1953. *Plough and Pasture: the Early History of Farming*. New York: Henry Schuman.

Darvill, T. 1982. *The Megalithic Chambered Tombs of the Cotswold-Severn Region: An Assessment of Certain Architectural Elements and their Relation to Ritual Practice and Neolithic Society*. Highworth: Vorda.

Datoo, B.A. 1978. Towards a reformulation of Boserup's theory of agricultural change. *Economic Geography* 54, 135-44.

Denevan, W.M. 1992. The pristine myth: the landscape of the Americas in 1492. *Annals of the Association of American Geographers* 82, 369-85.

Dennell, R.W. 1976. Prehistoric crop cultivation in southern England: a reconsideration. *Antiquaries Journal* 56(1), 11-23.

Descola, P. and Pálsson, G. (eds.) 1996. *Nature and Society: Anthropological Perspectives*. London: Routledge.

Dodgshon, R. 1981. The interpretation of subdivided fields: a study in private or communal interests? In Rowley, T. (ed.) *The Origins of Open-field Agriculture*, 130-44. London: Croom Helm.

Doolittle, W.E. 1984. Agricultural change as an incremental process. *Annals of the Association of American Geographers* 74(1), 124-37.

Drewett, P. 1978. Field systems and land allotment in Sussex, 3rd millennium B.C. to 4th century A.D. In Bowen, H.C. and Fowler, P.J. (eds.) *Early Land Allotment*, 67-80. British Archaeological Reports British Series 48. Oxford: British Archaeological Reports.

Drewett, P. 1982. Late Bronze Age downland economy and excavations at Black Patch, East Sussex. *Proceedings of the Prehistoric Society* 48, 321-400.

Duncan, J.S. 1993. Landscapes of the self/landscapes of the other(s): cultural geography 1991-92. *Progress in Human Geography* 17(3), 367-77.

Entwistle, R. and Grant, A. 1989. The evidence for cereal cultivation and animal husbandry in the southern British Neolithic and Bronze Age. In Milles, A., Williams, D. and Gardner, N. (eds.) *The Beginnings of Agriculture*, 203-15. British Archaeological Reports International Series S496. Oxford: British Archaeological Reports.

Evans, C. 1987. Nomads in 'Waterland'? Prehistoric transhumance and Fenland archaeology. *Proceedings of the Cambridge Antiquarian Society* 76, 27-39.

Fleming, A. 1971. Territorial patterns in Bronze Age Wessex. *Proceedings of the Prehistoric Society* 37 (1), 138-66.

Fleming, A. 1972. The genesis of pastoralism in European prehistory. *World Archaeology* 4, 179-91.

Fleming, A. 1985. Land tenure, productivity and field systems. In Barker, G. and Gamble, C. (eds.) *Beyond Domestication in Prehistoric Europe*, 120-6. London: Academic Press.

Fleming, A. 1988. *The Dartmoor Reaves: Investigating Prehistoric Land Divisions*. London: BT Batsford.

Fleming, A. 1989a. Coaxial field systems in later British prehistory. In Nordström, H.-Å. and Knape, A. (eds.) *Bronze Age Studies*, 151-62. Transactions of the British-Scandinavian Colloquium in Stockholm, May 10-11, 1985. Statens Historiska Museum, Stockholm, Studies 6. Stockholm: Statens Historiska Museum.

Fleming, A. 1989b. The genesis of coaxial field systems. In van der Leeuw, S.E. and Torrence, R. (eds.) *What's New? A Closer Look at the Process of Innovation*, 63-81. London: Unwin Hyman.

Fowler, P.J. 1981. Wildscape to landscape: 'enclosure' in prehistoric Britain. In Mercer, R. *Farming Practice in British Prehistory*, 9-54. Edinburgh: Edinburgh University Press.

Fowler, P.J. 1983. *The Farming of Prehistoric Britain*. Cambridge: Cambridge University Press.

Frazer, J.G. 1925. *The Golden Bough. Part V. Spirits of the Corn and of the Wild.* Volumes I-II. Third edition. London: MacMillan.

French, C., Lewis, H., Allen, M. J., Green, M., Scaife, R. and Gardiner, J. 2007. *Prehistoric landscape development and human impact in the upper Allen valley, Cranborne Chase, Dorset.* Cambridge: McDonald Institute for Archaeological Research.

Gibson, A. 1982. *Beaker Domestic Sites: A Study of the Domestic Pottery of the Late Third and Early Second Millennium BC in the British Isles.* British Archaeological Reports, British Series 197. Oxford: British Archaeological Reports.

Gibson, D.B. 1988. Agro-pastoralism and regional social organisation in early Ireland. In Gibson, D.B. and Geselowitz, M.N. (eds.) *Tribe and Polity in Late Prehistoric Europe: Demography, Production and Exchange in the Evolution of Complex Social Systems*, 41-68. New York and London: Plenum Press.

Glob, P. V. 1951. *Ard og Plov i Nordens Oldtid* (in Danish with English summary). Jysk Arkæologisk selskabs Skrifter Bind 1. Aarhus: Universitetsforlaget i Aarhus.

Goodman, D. and Redclift, M. 1981. *From Peasant to Proletarian. Capitalist Development and Agrarian Transitions.* Oxford: Basil Blackwell.

Goody, J. 1976. *Production and Reproduction. A Comparative Study of the Domestic Domain.* Cambridge: Cambridge University Press.

Goody, J. 1977. *The Domestication of the Savage Mind.* Cambridge: Cambridge University Press.

Graham, M. 1994. *Mobile Farmers. An Ethnoarchaeological Approach to Settlement Organization among the Rarámuri of Northwestern Mexico.* Ann Arbor: International Monographs in Prehistory.

Grigg, D. 1979. Ester Boserup's theory of agrarian change: a critical review. *Progress in Human Geography* 3, 65-84.

Guidoni, E. 1975. *Primitive Architecture: History of World Architecture.* Milan: Faber and Faber/Electra.

Hansen, H.-O. 1969. Experimental ploughing with a Døstrup ard replica. *Tools and Tillage* 1 (2), 67-92.

Harlan, J.R. 1995. *The Living Fields: Our Agricultural Heritage*. Cambridge: Cambridge University Press.

Helbaek, H. 1952. Early crops in southern England. *Proceedings of the Prehistoric Society* 18, 194-233.

Hodder, I. 1990. *The Domestication of Europe: Structure and Contingency in Neolithic Societies*. Oxford: Basil Blackwell.

Hodges, H.W.M. 1957. Braves, Beakers and battle-axes. *Antiquity* 31, 142-6.

Hunt, R.C. 1997. Boserup revisited: a comparative study of technology and labor productivity in rice agriculture. Unpublished lecture given at the Department of Social Anthropology, University of Cambridge, February 14, 1997.

Ingold, T. 1986. *The Appropriation of Nature: Essays on Human Ecology and Social Relations*. Manchester: Manchester University Press.

Isaac, E. 1970. *Geography of Domestication*. Englewood Cliffs: Prentice-Hall.

Janik, L. 1998. The appearance of food procuring societies in the southeastern Baltic Sea region. In Zvelebil, M., Domańska, L. and Dennell, R. (eds.) *Harvesting the Sea, Farming the Forest. The Emergence of Neolithic Societies in the Baltic Region*, 237-43. Sheffield: Sheffield Academic Press.

Jones, A. 1996. Food for thought: material culture and the transformation in food use from the Mesolithic to Neolithic. In Pollard, T. and Morrison, A. (eds.) *The Early Prehistory of Scotland*, 291-300. Edinburgh: Edinburgh University Press.

Jones, E.L. and Woolf, S J. 1969. *Agrarian Change and Economic Development: The Historical Problems*. London: Methuen.

Jones, M. 1980. Carbonised cereals from Grooved Ware contexts. *Proceedings of the Prehistoric Society* 46, 61-3.

Jones, S. 1997. *The Archaeology of Ethnicity: Constructing Identities in the Past and Present*. London: Routledge.

Kluckhohn, F.R. 1953. Dominant and variant value orientations. In Kluckhohn, C., Murray, H.A. and Schneider, D.M. (eds.) *Personality in Nature, Society and Culture*, 342-57. New York: Knopf.

Lewis, H.A. 1998. *The Characterisation and Interpretation of Ancient Tillage Practices through Soil Micromorphology: A Methodological Study*. Unpublished Ph.D. thesis, University of Cambridge.

Marsden, T. 1988. Exploring political economy approaches in agriculture. *Area* 20, 315-22.

Marsden, T. 1989. Restructuring rurality: from order to disorder in agrarian political economy. *Sociologia Ruralis* 29, 312-17.

McCorriston, J. and Hole, F. 1991. The ecology of seasonal stress and the origins of agriculture in the Near East. *American Anthropologist* 93(1), 46-69.

McGlade, J. 1995. Archaeology and the ecodynamics of human-modified landscapes. *Antiquity* 69, 113-32.

McInnes, I.J. 1971. Settlements in later Neolithic Britain. In Simpson, D.D.A. (ed.) *Economy and Settlement in Neolithic and Early Bronze Age Britain and Europe*, 113-30. Leicester: Leicester University Press.

Moffett, L., Robinson, M. A. and Straker, V. 1989. Cereals, fruit and nuts: charred plant remains from Neolithic sites in England and Wales and the Neolithic economy. In Milles, A., Williams, D. and Gardner, N. (eds.) *The Beginnings of Agriculture*, 243-61. British Archaeological Reports, International Series S496. Oxford: British Archaeological Reports.

Moran, W., Blunden, G. and Greenwood, J. 1993. The role of family farming in agrarian change. *Progress in Human Geography* 17(1), 22-42.

Morrison, K.D. 1994. The intensification of production: archaeological approaches. *Journal of Archaeological Method and Theory* 1 (2), 111-59.

Netting, R. McC. 1974. Agrarian ecology. *Annual Review of Anthropology* 3, 21-56.

Netting, R. McC. 1993. *Smallholders, Householders: Farm Families and the Ecology of Intensive, Sustainable Agriculture*. Stanford: Stanford University Press.

Nilsson, S. 1868. *The Primitive Inhabitants of Scandinavia*. London: Longmans.

Nissen, H.J. 1980. The mobility between settled and non-settled in early Babylonia: theory and evidence. *Colloques Internationaux du C.N.R.S. No 580 - l'Archéologie de l'Iraq: Perspectives et Limites de l'Interprétation Anthropologique des Documents*, 285-90. Paris: CNRS.

Parker Pearson, M., Pollard, J., Richards, C., Thomas, J., Tilley, C., Welham, K., Allen, M., Bennett, W., Field, D., French, C., Linford, N., Payne, A., Robinson, D. and Ruggles, C. 2006. The Stonehenge Riverside Project. Summary interim report on the 2006 season. http://www.shef.ac.uk/content/1/c6/02/21/27/summary-interim-report-2006.pdf (online at January 14, 2009).

Pimental, D. and Hall, C.W. 1989. *Food and Natural Resources*. New York: Academic Press.

Price, T.D. 1996. The first farmers of southern Scandinavia. In Harris, D.R. (ed.) *The Origins and*

Spread of Agriculture and Pastoralism in Eurasia, 346-62. London: University College London Press.

Pryor, F. 1996. Sheep, stocklands and farm systems: Bronze Age livestock populations in the Fenlands of eastern England. *Antiquity* 370, 313-24.

Pryor, F. 2006. *Farmers in Prehistoric Britain*. Second edition. Stroud: History Press.

Renfrew, A.C. 1973. Monuments, mobilization and social organisation in Neolithic Wessex. In Renfrew, A.C. (ed.) *The Explanation of Culture Change – Models in Prehistory*, 539-58. London: Duckworth.

Richards, J.D. 1990. *The Stonehenge Environs Project*. English Heritage Archaeological Report 16. Edinburgh: Historic Buildings and Monuments Commission (England).

Roberts, B.K. 1996. *Landscapes of Settlement: Prehistory to the Present*. London and New York: Routledge.

Sauer, C.O. 1952. *Agricultural Origins and Dispersals: The Domestication of Animals and Foodstuffs*. Cambridge: Massachusetts Institute of Technology Press.

Schama, S. 1995. *Landscape and Memory*. London: Harper Collins.

Sherratt, A. 1995. Instruments of conversion? The role of megaliths in the Mesolithic/Neolithic transition in north-west Europe. *Oxford Journal of Archaeology* 14(3), 245-60.

Simpson, D.D.A. 1971. Beaker houses and settlements in Britain. In Simpson, D.D.A. (ed.) *Economy and Settlement in Neolithic and Early Bronze Age Britain and Europe*, 131-52. Leicester: Leicester University Press.

Smith A.G., Grigson, C., Hillman, G. and Tooley, M. J. 1981 The Neolithic. In Simmons, I.G. and Tooley, M.J. (eds.) *The Environment in British Prehistory*, 125-209. London: Duckworth.

Smith, I.F. 1971. Causewayed enclosures. In Simpson, D.D.A. (ed.) *Economy and Settlement in Neolithic and Early Bronze Age Britain and Europe*: 89-112. Leicester: Leicester University Press.

Smith, R.W. 1984. The ecology of Neolithic farming systems as exemplified by the Avebury region of Wiltshire. *Proceedings of the Prehistoric Society* 50, 99-120.

Speck, F.G. 1940. *Penobscot Man: the Life History of a Forest Tribe in Maine*. London: Oxford University Press.

Steensberg, A. 1977. Stone shares of ploughing implements from the Bronze Age of Syria. *Det Kongelige Danske Videnskabernes Selskab Historisk-filosofiske Medælelser*, 47/6.

Stone, G.D. 1993. Agricultural abandonment: a comparative study in historical ecology. In Cameron, C.M. and Tomka, S.A. (eds.) *The Abandonment of Settlements and Regions: Ethnoarchaeological and Archaeological Approaches*, 74-81. Cambridge: Cambridge University Press.

Sutter, J.W. 1987. Cattle and inequality: herd size differences and pastoral production among the Fulani of northeastern Senegal. *Africa* 57(2), 196-218.

Thomas, J. 1991. *Rethinking the Neolithic*. Cambridge: Cambridge University Press.

Thomas, J. 1996a. The cultural context of the first use of domesticates in continental central and northwest Europe. In Harris, D.R. (ed.) *The Origins and Spread of Agriculture and Pastoralism in Eurasia*, 310-12. London: University College London Press.

Thomas, J. 1996b. Neolithic houses in mainland Britain: a sceptical view. In Darvill, T. and Thomas, J. (eds.) *Neolithic Houses in Northwest Europe and Beyond*, 1-12. Oxbow Monograph 57. Oxford: Oxbow.

Thomas, J. 1999. *Understanding the Neolithic*. London and New York: Routledge.

Whittle, A. 1977a. *The Earlier Neolithic of Southern England and its Continental Background*. British Archaeological Reports Supplementary Series 35. Oxford: British Archaeological Reports.

Whittle, A. 1977b. Earlier Neolithic enclosures in northwest Europe. *Proceedings of the Prehistoric Society* 43, 329-48.

Whittle, A. 1985. *Neolithic Europe: A Survey*. Cambridge: Cambridge University Press.

Whittle, A. 1996. *Europe in the Neolithic: The Creation of New Worlds*. Cambridge: Cambridge University Press.

Whittle, A. 1997. Moving on and moving around: Neolithic settlement mobility. In Topping, P. (ed.) *Neolithic Landscapes*, 15-22. Oxbow Monograph 86. Oxford: Oxbow.

Zvelebil, M. 1986. Mesolithic prelude and Neolithic revolution. In Zvelebil, M. (ed.) *Hunters in Transition: Mesolithic Societies of Temperate Eurasia and their Transition to Farming*, 5-15. Cambridge: Cambridge University Press.

Zvelebil, M. and Dolukhanov, P. 1991. The transition to farming in eastern and northern Europe. *Journal of World Prehistory* 5, 233-78.

Sustaining prehistoric agricultural landscapes in southern Spain, highland Yemen and northern New Mexico: the geoarchaeological perspective

Charles French

Introduction

This paper addresses issues of stability and sustainability of agricultural landscapes in some semi-arid regions of the world, namely south-eastern Spain, the highlands of western Yemen and northern New Mexico. The emphasis will be on the recognition of land use in palaeosol and erosion sequences, especially in prehistoric times.

Stung by several archaeologists' criticism, notably Evans' (2003) and Redman and van der Leeuw's (2002) remarks that environmental archaeologists rarely ever put their knowledge and ideas back into the system, nor demonstrate that their work has relevance to the modern social dimension of agricultural landscapes, this is my attempt to begin to address that imbalance. This approach is especially applicable to those landscapes that are viewed as marginal and prone to erosion, and therefore rather unproductive today.

To do this, I will look at the results of the Aguas and Archaeomedes projects in south-eastern Spain near Almeria, the Dhamar Highlands project in Yemen and a collaborative project with the Rocky Mountain Research Station in the Rio Puerco basin of northern New Mexico northwest of Albuquerque, in all of which I have been a team member as a geoarchaeologist. These projects explore the critical factors which make semi-arid and marginal landscapes suitable for agricultural use, despite inevitable and/or unstoppable degradation processes, and investigate methods of land use which allowed the land to remain productive and sustaining of local communities in the past. In addition, all are interested in how those observations might inform our management of these landscapes today.

Traditionally in geoarchaeological studies in the United Kingdom, a major emphasis has been on the recognition of fields and agriculture in the landscape. Past agricultural field systems are often readily visible in the landscape as either cropmarks or lynchets, such as the rectilinear systems of 'Celtic fields' on Gussage Down, southwest of Salisbury (Green 2000, fig. 92), or as ditch and bank systems in buried landscapes such as at Fengate (Pryor 1980, fig.18) and Welland Bank Quarry (French 2003, 152-7). Fields are also recognised from plough, ard or spade marks in buried soils in excavations (Lewis 1998; 2002), and as particular features in soil thin section, such as at Welland Bank Quarry (French 2003, 49-53). In the damp and temperate landscapes of England, burial of old land surfaces and palaeosols containing the imprint of past activities in the soil tends to occur gradually over time and is rarely affected by destructive erosive forces, thus giving both relatively good preservation and time-depth to the imprint of past land-use activities.

In contrast, in semi-arid parts of the world, landscapes are dominated by rapid and often brief periods of incision, erosion and aggradation, events which often occur repeatedly and violently. Soils rarely have time to become fully developed, often with only incipient soil formation (or organic accumulation) occurring on recently stabilised surfaces of eroded sediments such a colluvium or alluvium. There are often secondary deposits of calcium carbonate and/or amorphous iron and clay intercalation, and silty clay or calcitic crusts which both obscure and alter soil development. Also, there is often not the luxury of large-scale rescue excavations being undertaken which would allow whole field systems to be investigated and sampled. Instead, to understand these ancient farming landscapes one has to rely on geoarchaeological survey for deposit mapping, using any and all available exposed sections, backed up by soil and sediment characterisation, aerial, archaeological and augering surveys, pollen analysis and a combination of radiometric and luminescence dating.

The case studies

The lower Aguas valley of south-eastern Spain

A geoarchaeological survey of the lower Aguas valley was undertaken with Dr. David Passmore and Professor Tony Stevenson under the auspices of the Aguas project (Castro *et al.* 1994; 1998; 2000) (Fig. 1). Today this is an area with 200-800mm of annual rainfall. The large meandering river bed of the Aguas only holds water briefly, after seasonal thunderstorms. Its floodplain area is dominated by repeated episodes of thick alluvial deposition, with *c.* four metres of accumulation occurring in pre-Roman times. The tributary valleys, emerging from the Sierra Cabrera mountains just inland, are dominated by debris flow and colluvial slumping, infilling the valleys by depths of up to 10m, as well as repeated and deep gully and channel incision and avulsion (Figs. 2 and 3). Despite this, there were several well-established proto-urban sites flourishing in the Copper Age, such as Gatas and Las Pilas (Chapman 1990) (Fig. 1).

Based on the initial work of Courty *et al.* (1994) for the Archaeomedes Project, and augmented by the detailed Aguas sequencing work of Bukistra *et al.* (1998), French *et al.* (1998) and Rodriguez Ariza and Stevenson (1998), five major periods of incision and erosion events were observed in this valley system, as follows:

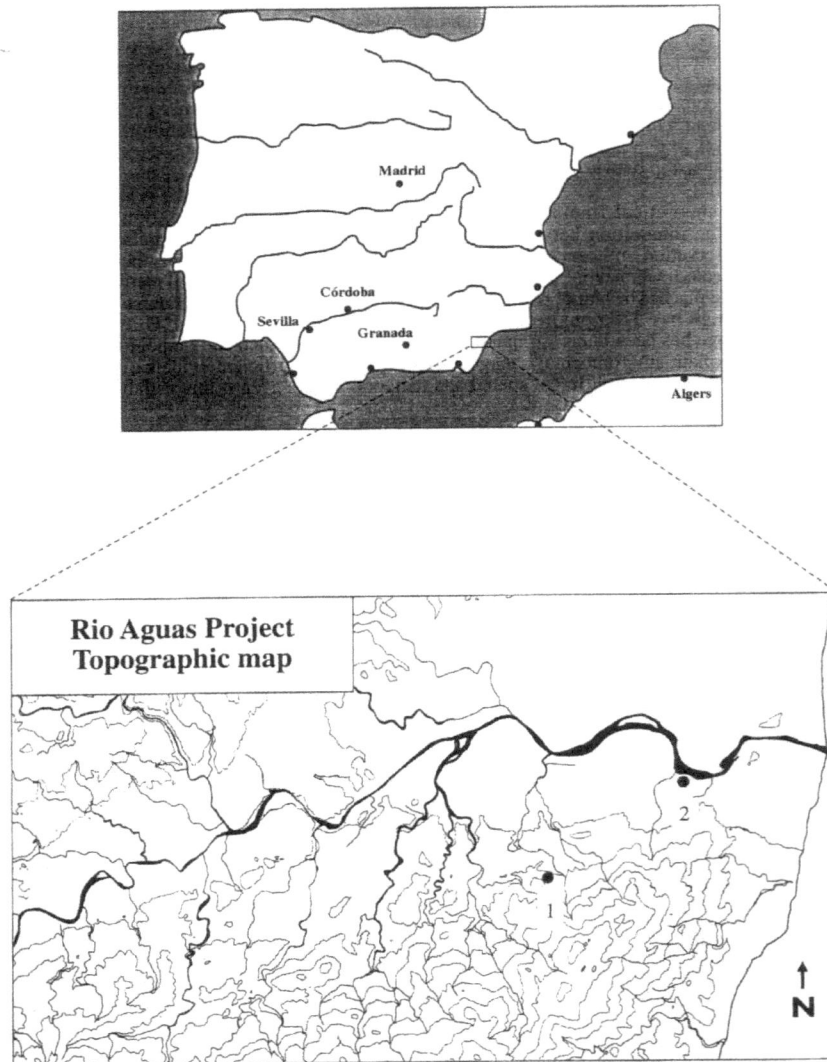

Figu-e 1 Location map of the Aguas valley study area in south-eastern Spain (note: 1 is the site of Gatas and 2 is Las Pilas) (after Castro et al. 1998, map 1).

- deep incision and infilling during the late Quaternary, c. 17,000-13,000 BP, in the tributary valleys,
- a slowing of erosion, except in the main valley floor in the Chalcolithic, Copper and Early Bronze Ages and a long-term degree of stability in the tributary valleys,
- a return to incision and erosion in the tributary valleys, and aggradation in the valley floor during the earlier half of the second millennium BC,
- destruction of pine, oak and olive trees and the concomitant expansion of cereal crops since the Bronze Age (second millennium BC), and over much wider areas of the valley-scape,
- incision and erosion in the Roman period in the tributary valleys and main valley floor,

- incision and erosion in the ninth and tenth centuries AD (Andalusian) in the tributary valleys and main valley floor,
- incision and erosion in the last 500-600 years, which has become especially marked in the last 20 years, in both the tributary valleys and main valley floor, with many new gullies forming, colluvial infilling of tributary valleys, and deep incision in the valley floor.

This gives a picture of strongly punctuated equilibrium occurring over the last 4,000 years against the backdrop of longer-term desertification or aridification, the destruction of maquia (open scrub of olive and pine trees) and expanding cultivation of cereal crops, and more and more parts of the valley system being exploited on an increasingly intensive and extensive scale. In recent times, these factors have been exacerbated by uncontrolled water abstraction associated with urban and tourism developments, as well as terrace destruction and the creation of new large fields on hill-slopes without soil conservation measures.

Wherever the geoarchaeological survey team looked, with coverage of all landscape zones in the study area possible due to the amount of gullying and exposed sections to record, the only surviving buried soils of the Bronze Age and later periods were thin organic A horizons developed in the top of stabilised, calcareous colluvial sediments. This was a poor soil resource, which needed careful husbanding to be of use in any agricultural system.

Today, the well-established terrace system that developed over the past 500 years or so is subject to a variety of pressures. Irrigation, over-cropping, mono-cropping, uncontrolled grazing, primarily by goats, and the lack of terrace wall maintenance is leading to the washing out and drowning of vegetation root systems, the formation of calcitic and gypsum-rich crusts on field surfaces, the blowing out and collapse of terrace walls, and localised but extensive colluvial fan formations (Fig. 2). Also, the advent and uptake of European Union agricultural subsidies is leading to the amalgamation of many small terraced fields into much larger fields situated across slopes, often with quite steep gradients. In combination, these land-use events are leading to increased amounts of calcitic, silt sized, material entering the colluvial and alluvial systems of the tributary and main valleys (respectively), effectively causing the collapse of the formerly quite stable medieval and post-medieval terraced agricultural system. At the same time, the increasing violence and frequency of the thunderstorms that punctuate the otherwise very dry climate of the area trigger new gully incision, almost overnight in some cases (Fig. 3).

The answer to sustaining this collapsing and drying system is sometimes seen in the actions of individual small land owners in the Aguas valley. Unfortunately, this is not common, and is undermined by government policies and the encroachment of urban and tourism developments. The small fields remain terraced, small amounts of well-derived irrigation water are channelled at a trickle morning and evening to all fields, and each terrace enjoys a multi-crop usage, for example with wheat grown around olive trees one year, and a vetch or glover-type crop grown the next, with goats grazed on that briefly. The secret is retaining the soil and its moisture content through the use of terrace walls and root systems, keeping the soil surface covered by vegetation, and adding organic matter and manure to the soil to maintain the nutrient base and binding/structural qualities of the soil. The palaeosols observed in the survey were few, thin and under-developed organic A horizons formed on weathered colluvial deposits.

The Dhamar Highlands of western Yemen
The Dhamar Survey Project in western Yemen (Fig. 4) was directed by Tony Wilkinson (then of the University

Figure 2   A view of denuded and colluviated former terraces in the Barranco de Gatas.

Figure 3 New gully incision as a result of thunderstorms over a two-year period (1994-6) above Las Pilas.

of Chicago). It involved a combination of broad sweep, prehistoric archaeological survey with palaeo-environmental and geoarchaeological investigations, specifically concentrating on the earlier-middle Holocene period (Wilkinson 1997; 2005). The Dhamar Highlands are dominated by high volcanic mountains (up to 3,000 metres), fertile tributary valleys (Fig. 5) and wide, high (2,000 metre) alluvial valleys or plains, with 200-700 millimetres of rainfall annually today (*ibid.*).

It appears that there were the following major events in this system:
- a rain-fed system with a higher groundwater table with large, shallow, calcareous lakes situated in the alluvial valleys from *c.* 10,000-7,000 BP (Acres 1982; Wilkinson 1997),
- two major periods of substantial soil development in the Neolithic, in the sixth-early fifth and the earlier fourth millennia BC, separated by fine colluvial material (Wilkinson 1997); erosion and colluviation were certainly underway shortly after *c.* 4,500 BC and 3,600 BC (Wilkinson 2005, 174). The earlier prehistoric soil appears to have been rain-fed, and developed a very thick organic A horizon over a well-developed B horizon with

some suggestion of once more wooded conditions existing at some time; this brown earth soil was developed in both the tributary valleys and the alluvial plains, but had a longer survival in the tributary valleys. The later soil developed during this time can be associated with episodic rainfall, flood run-off agriculture and a very thick organic or mollic A horizon, probably associated with long-term grassland development, but developed on a calcitic, weathered B horizon,

- disruption of the stable soil system in the later third-second and in the later first millennia BC and renewed colluviation, with attempts via early terracing to combat this instability from *c.* 2,000 BC (Wilkinson 1997), and
- the deliberate damming of tributary valleys with substantial stone dam constructions from about 1000 BC (Wilkinson 1997), possibly as a response to the decline of the rain-fed system and the need to conserve diminishing water resources to support settlement and agriculture.

One suggestion here is that the shrinking use of the alluvial plains subsequent to the drying up of the lakes enabled an apparently large number of smaller Neolithic and Bronze Age settlements to become established in the highlands themselves, and this is certainly demonstrated by the archaeological survey results. This is probably set, as for southeast Spain, against a back-drop of long-term aridification or desertification, with a lessening of rainfall occurring over the last 4,000 years. Certainly, deep sea cores obtained from off the south-western Arabian coast and in the adjacent Indian Ocean suggest that monsoonal circulation was stronger, and therefore there was greater rainfall in this part of Yemen in the early-middle Holocene (Sirocko 1996; Sirocko *et al.* 1991; Zonnenveld *et al.* 1997; Cullen *et al.* 2000). From the third millennium BC, there were steady but oscillating drying conditions (Lemcke and Sturm 1997), which may have led to greater susceptibility to soil erosion and flash flooding. In terms of the archaeological record, there appears to have been population dispersal from the alluvial plains into the upland valleys from about 3,000 BC, taking advantage of the slower desiccation in the highlands than on the plains, and of the more episodic rainfall.

Today, the whole system survives through irrigation from deep wells (often 100+ metres in depth). In particular, the large irrigated areas of the alluvial plains are marginal and fragile; the small, terraced fields of the tributary hill valleys are by contrast lush and productive. The use of soil conservation measures, small contained or terraced fields, manuring, trickle irrigation and minimal plough intervention are all practised (Fig. 5), and help to make this a sustainable system for the present-day small rural population.

The Guadalupe area, Rio Puerco, northern New Mexico
Geoarchaeological survey developed in collaboration with Richard Periman of the USDA Rocky Mountain

Research Station focused on a 5 kilometre stretch of the Rio Puerco valley either side of Guadalupe (Pueblo ruin), near Cuba in northern New Mexico (Fig. 6). A combination of geoarchaeological, palaeobotanical and dating approaches were used to investigate Holocene fire and erosion history, with the aim of suggesting land-use

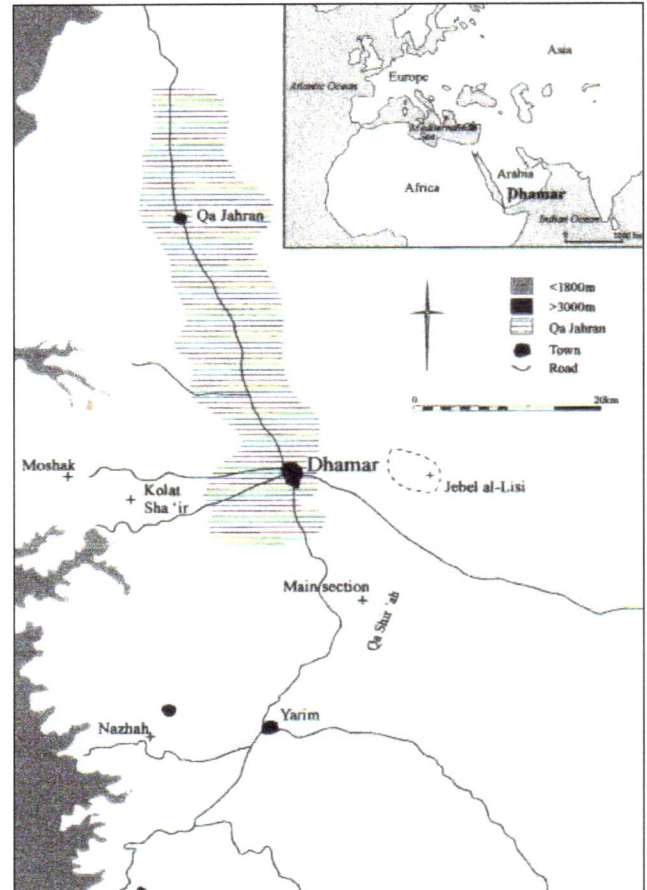

Figure 4 Location map of the Dhamar highlands survey area in west-central Yemen (based on Wilkinson 1997, fig. 1).

Figure 5 Modern, small terraced and irrigated fields in an upland valley, Sedd Adhriah, Yemen.

strategies to combat the frequency and spread of fire in this semi-arid national forest landscape.

The existing valley floor is believed to represent the *c.* AD 1000-1400 valley floor, contemporary with the surviving Anasazi Pueblo occupation sites in the area. This valley floor would have had a relatively shallowly incised, meandering channel system flowing within it, forming a braid plain. The modern channel bed in the Rio Puerco is cut to a level of *c.* 11-12 metres below this valley floor level (Fig. 7). This incision and down-cutting has been caused by thunderstorm events and associated sediment run-off from the immediate valley catchment, associated with sparse vegetation cover and semi-arid climatic conditions, and aggravated by intensive livestock grazing and lightning-strike fires. In places it has resulted in some infilling and the creation of broad terrace benches within the valley floor, defined about 4 metres above the river's base. This dramatic incision is believed to have occurred within the last 120 years or so, a process possibly related to a return to greater run-off erosion, with more intense grazing pressures associated with Navajo sheep rearing and 'Texan–style' cattle ranching (Nials and Durand 2003). Climatic factors, such as drier conditions, need not be the sole cause of this phenomenon. Rather, mismanagement of this marginal landscape by over-intensive grazing is a more likely cause of the recent and intensive destabilization of the Puerco drainage system. In the last few years, incision and the cutting of new gullies through the Pueblo period valley base is continuing, and this could have been exacerbated by the ten-year drought period that the area was experiencing at the time of investigation (with 200-700 millimetres of rainfall per year).

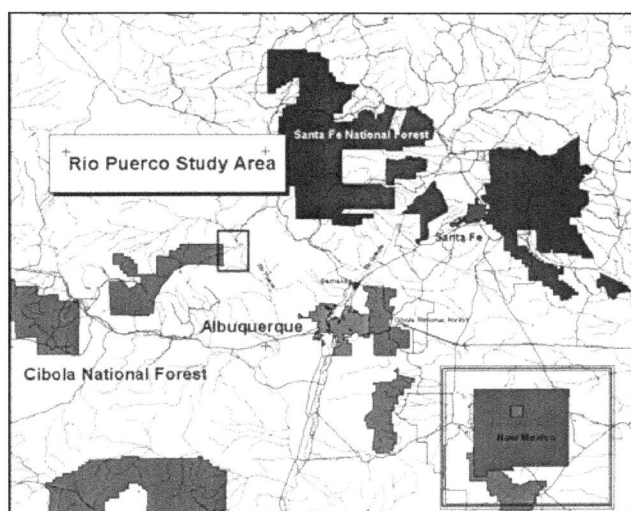

Figure 6 The Rio Puerco study area in north-central New Mexico (R. Periman).

The valley infills in the Rio Puerco, and the associated Arroyo Tapia, Guadalupe and Salado tributaries, are composed of finely bedded sediments varying in composition from clay to silty clay to silts and very fine

sands. In particular, there were four major standstill zones or periods of incipient soil formation which have been radiocarbon dated by Beta-Analytic Inc. to: pre-5,750 BC, *c.* 2,600-2,200 BC, AD 350-550 and AD 1000-1400 (Fig. 7). The period between the first two stabilisation zones is dominated by frequent fire signatures, both of derived or washed-in burnt material, and from *in situ* burnt surfaces indicative of longer and more intense burns of a more substantially wooded environment than today. During this period there were sparse pinyon-juniper woods with willow, and a diverse non-arboreal flora in the floodplain, with maize present and local fires in evidence (Scott Cummings 2004). What has not been established is whether these fire signatures in the alluvial record relate solely to lightning-strike fires, or also to fires deliberately set to encourage grass growth and shrubby plant production as a food resource for a variety of game animals, or to the burning of specific plant communities to increase the production of cultigens and other economic plants.

The most well-developed, middle stabilisation zone is in fact composed of at least three superimposed, but interrupted (by fine alluvial silty clay sediments), episodes of incipient soil formation. These soils were essentially associated with a slowly aggrading, seasonal flood-meadow type of environment, along with localised pinyon-juniper woods with some oak, willow and mesquite, and with common grasses and moist areas (Scott Cummings 2004). Similar interrupted alluvial/ incipient palaeosol sequences were observed in the Rio del Oso study (Periman 2005). At this stage, the river consisted of several medium-sized braided channels. In addition, this zone of soil development is characterised by the presence of man-made, re-cut ditch features set at right angles to the floodplain. The occurrence of these ditches at several locations in the study area suggests that they represent a wider archaeological phenomenon, showing some degree of land management, drainage control and/or water storage at about 4,500-4,000 years ago (in the middle-later Archaic period). It remains to be seen whether this alluvial floodplain was only supporting scrubby grassland, or was deliberately managed and irrigated for maize agriculture. *Zea* or maize pollen has been extracted from the base of these ditch fills in the Rio Puerco, and is suggestive of some maize agriculture at about 2,500 BC. Similarly positioned ditches in an alluvial infill sequence have been observed near the Zuni Pueblo on the Colorado Plateau some 100km to the southwest, where they are also associated with maize agriculture dated to about 3,000-4,000 years ago (Damp *et al.* 2002). This would be consistent with Matson's (1991, 252-8) model for early floodwater farming and the introduction of maize into the American southwest, as well as the management of grasses and shrubs for game animals.

Following this, there was a return to a phase of increased erosion and run-off, marked by the deposition of alluvial fine sand and silt. This phase is associated with a substantial meandering channel system and repeated signatures of past fire events. There was another brief stabilisation zone marked by incipient soil formation and organic accumulation at about AD 370-540, followed by renewed alluvial aggradation.

Figure 7 The main Rio Puerco alluvial and incipient soil sequence beneath the Anasazi valley floor, with the major standstill zones visible as darker bands in the sections, and the nineteenth-twentieth century AD incised river floor of today.

Just before AD 1000, there was a final return to a slower aggradational dynamic, with the deposition of overbank flood deposits of silty clay, the accumulation of some organic remains, and incipient soil formation. This was associated with numerous small and shallow stream channels in a seasonally active braid plain. From about this time and the development of the Pueblo period settlements (to the fourteenth century AD) until the late nineteenth century AD, alluvial aggradation slowed dramatically, and the drainage system appears to have reached a lengthy period of relative stability. There was a wide valley floor and a single large meandering river channel system. This system appears to have become rapidly infilled by some major erosive events from time to time, probably quite late in this period, resulting in major channel avulsion across the floodplain.

Thus, the sedimentary and soil record in the Rio Puerco valley acts as a sensitive record of changing vegetation, fire history and human exploitation over time. Large areas of the valley bottom were affected by major periods of relative instability and alluvial deposition, with periods of relative stability and incipient soil formation. But the latter situation, which certainly existed for the bulk of the later half of the Holocene, changed irrevocably in the nineteenth to twentieth centuries AD, with over-intensive livestock grazing leading to very sparse scrub vegetation unable to resist thunderstorm-induced run-off, erosion and channel incision on a catastrophic scale. This situation may also be aggravated by increased thunderstorm frequency, if not intensity with respect to the dewpoint, and the declining influence of snowmelt in the last 4000 years or so, leading to an increased fire hazard for the study area (Scott Cummings 2004).

Conclusions

Despite all three study areas being in different parts of the world, there are many similarities in terms of the climatic and sedimentary records, and the response of the landscape systems to the combined effects of human actions and long-term climatic change.

In each there is a long-term trend towards greater aridification, which in southern Spain and New Mexico is associated with an increased frequency and intensity of thunderstorm events, especially in the last 4,000 years. This has the effect of creating new gullies and arroyos almost overnight, and the considerable loss of soils and sediments downslope and downstream. For example, it is estimated that the Rio Puerco delivers on average 78% of the total suspended sediment load of the Rio Grande, although it drains only 26% of that basin and provides only 4% of the run-off (Aby *et al.* 2005). The inability of the landscape system to retain soil and sediment is often compounded by modern agricultural practices, such as the destruction of terraced fields in southern Spain, and over-grazing in the last century associated with an increased and continuing fire hazard in New Mexico. It is only in the upland valleys of highland Yemen that a sensitive form of terraced and irrigated small-field arable agricultural system is practised that is capable of being sustained. In this region of Yemen, it is soil conservation with a diverse multi-use of small fields that is seen as a sustainable way forward in these semi-arid, marginal landscapes. Modern agricultural practices, such as those currently seen in the Aguas valley of southern Spain, featuring the removal of small-field terrace systems and the creation of larger, open fields with few boundaries, irrigation via deep wells, and mono-crops of grain and/or tomatoes only compound the problems, and make the landscape more prone to salt crusting, poor crop returns, soil erosion and gully incision.

In each all three study areas, a greater frequency of thunderstorms only compounds the problems coincident with present-day land use. Moreover, the trend to aridification is further exacerbated by water abstraction on a grand scale, associated with modern urban development. This particularly applies to southern Spain with its tourism developments, and to New Mexico, where sprawling cities such as Albuquerque are dependent on water and fuel resources to maintain western living standards. It is only in highland Yemen where the rural population is sufficiently small and the demands of modern society are growing only very slowly, that water abstraction on a detrimental scale is not yet occurring.

Despite the evident and extensive erosion records, the Holocene soil and sediment records suggest that a system of punctuated equilibrium has pertained in each study area. There are quite long phases of stability indicated by soil formation phases, interrupted by shorter to longer phases of colluvial and/or alluvial deposition. For example, the earlier-middle Holocene phase in the Rio Puerco seems to be one of gradual, long-term, seasonal alluvial deposition associated with fire, at least partially related to human manipulation of that landscape. In contrast, the similar earlier Holocene period in the Aguas system seems to be one of long-term stability, which becomes interrupted on a widespread and repeated scale from the second millennium BC onwards. This is as much associated with intensifying human exploitation for settlement and agriculture since the Copper Age as with long-term desertification. Finally, in Yemen there are substantial periods of long-term soil development and stability throughout the earlier-middle Holocene. Despite the aridification trend in the highlands of Yemen over the Holocene, and especially in the last 4,000 years, soil conservation has apparently been practised long-term, at least in the upland valleys, unlike in the other two study areas. This allowed the formation and retention of thick, organic soils on valley slopes in the Neolithic, which appear to have been artificially enhanced and thickened by the addition of organic material, and possibly irrigated in the past. These soils were not subjected to continuous arable agriculture, and were retained by terraces believed to have existed for about the last 4,000 years (Wilkinson 2005). This demonstrates what can be done with sensitive and small-scale exploitation despite the apparent marginality of the landscape.

Acknowledgements

I would like to especially thank my principal colleagues and collaborators who have made these studies possible: Professor Bob Chapman (University of Reading), Dr. David Passmore (University of Newcastle-upon-Tyne), Dr. Richard Periman (Rocky Mountain Research Station, Albuquerque), and Professor Tony Wilkinson (Durham University). The funding that made the geoarchaeological work possible was from the European Union for the Aguas project, National Geographic for the Dhamar project, and the United States Department of Agriculture for the Puerco study.

Bibliography

Aby, S., Gellis, A and Pavich, M. 2005. *The Rio Puerco arroyo cycle and the history of landscape changes.* www:htttp://geochange.er.usgs.gov/sw/impacts/geology/puerco1/

Acres, B.D. 1982. *Yemen Arab Republic Montane Plains and Wadi Rima Project: Soil Classification and Correlation in the Montane Plains.* Project Record, 72.

Surbiton: Land Resources Development Centre.

Bukistra, J., Dever, L., Hagedorn, Ch., Hoshower, L., Patzold, J., Schulte, L. and Wefer, G. 1998. Climate change. In Castro, P.V., Chapman, R.W., Gili, S., Lull, V., Mico, R., Rihute, C., Risch, R. and Sanahuja, M.E. (eds.) *Aguas Project: Palaeoclimatic Reconstruction and the Dynamics of Human Settlement and Land Use in the Area of the Middle Aguas (Almeria), in the South-east of the Iberian Peninsula,* 38-45. Luxembourg: European Commission.

Castro, P.V., Colomer, E., Courty, M-A., Fedoroff, N., Gili, S., Gonzalez Marcen, P., Jones, M.K., McGlade, J., Mico, R., Monton, S., Rihuete, C., Risch, R., Ruiz Parra, M., Sanahuja, M.E and Tenas, M. (eds.). 1994. *Temporalities and Desertification in the Vera Basin, Southeast Spain.* Archaeomedes Project, Vol. 2. Unpublished report to the European Union.

Castro, P.V., Chapman, R.W., Gili, S., Lull, V., Mico, R., Rihute, C., Risch, R and Sanahuja, M.E. (eds.). 1998. *Aguas Project: Palaeoclimatic Reconstruction and the Dynamics of Human Settlement and Land Use in the Area of the Middle Aguas (Almeria), in the South-east of the Iberian Peninsula.* Luxembourg: European Commission.

Castro, P.V., Gili, S., Lull, V., Mico, R., Rihuete, C., Risch, R., Sanahuja, M.E and Chapman, R.W. 2000. Archaeology and desertification in the Vera Basin (Almeria, South-east Spain). *European Journal of Archaeology* 3, 147-66.

Chapman, R.W. 1990. *Emerging Complexity.* Cambridge: Cambridge University Press.

Courty, M-A., Fedoroff, N., Jones, M.K. and McGlade, J. 1994. Environmental dynamics. In Castro, P.V., Chapman, R.W., Gili, S., Lull, V., Mico, R., Rihute, C., Risch, R. and Sanahuja, M.E. (eds.) *Temporalities and Desertification in the Vera Basin, Southeast Spain.* Archaeomedes Project, Vol. 2, 19-84.

Cullen, H.M., deMenocal, P.B., Hemming, S., Hemming, G., Brown, F.H., Guilderson, T. and Sirocko, F. 2000. Climate change and the collapse of the Akkadian empire: evidence from the deep sea. *Geology* 28, 379-82.

Damp, J.E., Hall, S.A and Smith, S. J. 2002. Early irrigation on the Colorado Plateau near Zuni Pueblo, New Mexico. *American Antiquity* 67, 665-76.

Evans, J.G. 2003. Book review of "Geoarchaeology in Action: Studies in soil micromorphology and landscape evolution." Unpublished review manuscript for *Landscape Studies.*

French, C. 2003. *Geoarchaeology in Action: Studies in Soil Micromorphology and Landscape Evolution.* London: Routledge.

French, C., Passmore, D. and Shulte, L. 1998.

Geomorphology, erosion and soil formation processes. In Castro, P.V., Chapman, R.W., Gili, S., Lull, V., Mico, R., Rihute, C., Risch R. and Sanahuja, M.E. (eds.) *Aguas Project: Palaeoclimatic Reconstruction and the Dynamics of Human Settlement and Land Use in the Area of the Middle Aguas (Almeria), in the South-east of the Iberian Peninsula*, 45-52. Luxembourg: European Commission.

Green, M. 2000. *A Landscape Revealed: 10,000 Years on a Chalkland Farm*. Stroud: Tempus.

Lemcke, G. and Sturm, M. 1997. 18O and trace element measurements as a proxy for the reconstruction of climate changes at Lake Van (Turkey): preliminary results. In Nuzhet Dalfes, H., Kukla, G. and Weiss, H. (eds.) *Third Millennium BC Climate Change and Old World Collapse*, 653-78. NATO ASI Series, Global Environmental Change, Volume 49. Berlin: Springer.

Lewis, H. 1998. *The characterisation and interpretation of ancient tillage practices through soil micromorphology: a methodological study*. Unpublished PhD thesis, University of Cambridge.

Lewis, H. 2002. An investigation of ancient cultivation at Hengistbury Head Site 6, Christchurch, Dorset. *Proceedings of the Prehistoric Society* 68, 83-102.

Matson, R.G. 1991. *The Origins of Southwestern Agriculture*. Tuscon: University of Arizona Press.

Nials, F.L. and Durand, S.R. 2003. Environmental change in the middle Rio Puerco valley. In Baker, L.L and Durand, S.R. (eds.) *Prehistory of the Middle Rio Puerco Valley, Sandoval County, New Mexico*, 35-54. Archaeological Society of New Mexico Special Publication No. 3. Portales: Archaeological Society of New Mexico.

Periman, R. 2005. Modeling landscapes and past vegetation patterns of New Mexico's Rio Del Oso valley. *Geoarchaeology* 20, 193-210.

Pryor, F. 1980. *Excavation at Fengate, Peterborough, England: The Third Report*. Toronto: Royal Ontario Museum.

Redman, C. and van der Leeuw, S. 2002. Placing archaeology at the centre of socio-natural studies. *American Antiquity* 67, 597-605.

Rodriguez Ariza, M.O. and Stevenson, A.C. 1998. Vegetation and its exploitation. In Castro, P.V., Chapman, R.W., Gili, S., Lull, V., Mico, R., Rihute, C., Risch, R. and Sanahuja, M.E. (eds.) *Aguas Project: Palaeoclimatic Reconstruction and the Dynamics of Human Settlement and Land Use in the Area of the Middle Aguas (Almeria), in the South-east of the Iberian Peninsula*, 62-8. Luxembourg: European Commission.

Scott Cummings, L. 2004. Pollen and charcoal analysis of stratigraphic samples from Tapia Arroyo and Rio Puerco, New Mexico. Paleo Research Institute Technical Report 02-08. Unpublished report to USDA Forest Service.

Sirocko, F. 1996. The evolution of the monsoon climate over the Arabian Sea during the last 24,000 years. *Palaeoecology of Africa* 24, 53-69.

Sirocko, F., Sarntheim, M., Lange, H. and Erlenkeuser, H. 1991. Atmospheric summer circulation and coastal upwelling in the Arabian Sea during the Holocene and the Last Glaciation. *Quaternary Research* 36, 72-93.

Wilkinson, T.J. 1997. Holocene environments of the high plateau, Yemen, recent geoarchaeological investigations. *Geoarchaeology* 12, 833-64.

Wilkinson, T.J. 2005. Soil erosion and valley fills in the Yemen Highlands and southern Turkey: integrating settlement, geoarchaeology and climate change. *Geoarchaeology* 20, 169-92.

Zonneveld, K.A.F., Ganssen, G., Troelstra, S., Versteegh, G. and Visscher, H. 1997. Mechanisms forcing abrupt fluctuations of the Indian Ocean summer monsoon during the last glaciation. *Quaternary Science Reviews* 16, 187-201.

'Where the cattle went, they went': towards a phenomenological archaeology of cattle mustering in the Kunderang ravines, New South Wales, Australia

Rodney Harrison

Introduction

This paper describes the results of a project which sought to record and understand the heritage landscapes associated with cattle mustering in the Kunderang Ravines, an area now managed as a national park and World Heritage Wilderness Area in north-eastern New South Wales, Australia. In addition to drawing on established archaeological, historical and architectural heritage recording techniques, the project employed a range of less conventional methods to map the 'landscape biographies' of both indigenous and non-indigenous former pastoral workers and their families, in the form of both mapped oral history, and of 'story-trekking' (Green *et al.* 2003) along remembered narrative paths. Such an approach allows a more embodied understanding of the archaeology of cattle mustering to emerge. By riding and walking along familiar pathways and mustering routes, pastoral workers and their kin created a familiar sense of being-in-the-landscape (Bender 2001), while simultaneously creating that landscape. In many ways, the work at Kunderang can be understood as a response to Gaston Bachelard's call for 'each one of us [to] speak of his roads, his crossroads, his roadside benches; each one of us should make a surveyor's map of his lost field and meadows' (1969, 11) and to understand those habits which he describes in the same work as the 'passionate liaison of our bodies' with a space or landscape (Wise 2000).

Context and description

East Kunderang pastoral station is located in the upper Macleay River valley, approximately 100 kilometres southeast of Armidale in north-eastern New South Wales in Oxley Wild Rivers National Park, south-eastern Australia. It is situated in rugged gorge country, on the site of part of an earlier sheep station established in 1841. East Kunderang was established as an owner-occupied run in 1892, and for the next 100 years its cattle, horses and stockmen established an impressive reputation, which was influenced by the rugged grandeur of the country in which it was located. A workshop was run on site to discuss options for the conservation and management of the former pastoral station buildings and associated historic landscape as part of the Conservation Management Plan that was being prepared for the site. Research project aims and methodology were also discussed. Workshop participants focussed on the more ephemeral places in the landscape where workers congregated and lived, such as mustering huts and camps, rather than the prominent built structures associated with the station homestead, which tended to be the focus of conservation and management efforts. The way in which these places could be linked together to evidence a system of mustering in the gorge country was also seen to be important. The archaeological and oral history project thus developed around mapping both indigenous and non-indigenous people's memories of the landscape and places in it, focussing on trails and patterns of movement.

Oral histories

The oral histories of former pastoral station workers associated with East Kunderang are rich with details of mustering, riding and walking through the gorge country. A major theme of the oral histories was mapping former mustering routes associated with Kunderang and neighbouring pastoral stations, and discussing the appreciation of the landscape that people developed as a result of their passage through it. All mustering was done on horseback, and it was only in the 1950s and 1960s that motor vehicle access was made available at East Kunderang homestead. Even during the 1990s, when Kunderang cattle were being mustered out of Oxley Wild Rivers and Werrikembe National Parks, this was done predominantly on horseback.

Former Kunderang pastoral station workers who were interviewed spoke at length about their experiences in and around the Kunderang Gorges. Mustering cattle was a major component of the pastoral work of most of the men employed at East Kunderang. Les O'Neill, who started working for Alex Crawford at Kunderang in 1962, recalls the annual round of mustering Kunderang cattle in detail:

> 'Generally around about January they would do it. We would do the mustering on the top first, that would take a couple of weeks, and then we would go down the gorges towards the end of January…coming out of winter they would do a little bit of weaning them down there…out to Moona Plains, bring them up there and wean them and take them back again in a few weeks time.' (interview, 27 February 2001).

Les would also often muster at West Kunderang, at that time under the management of Claude Ciccolini, and for the Crawfords at Moona Plains. Unlike East Kunderang, mustering for the Crawfords at Moona Plains was done using up to five packhorses, to allow them to stay up in the gorges for three or four weeks at a time. The packhorses would carry food and swags with tarpaulins to camp under. Les describes the daily routine:

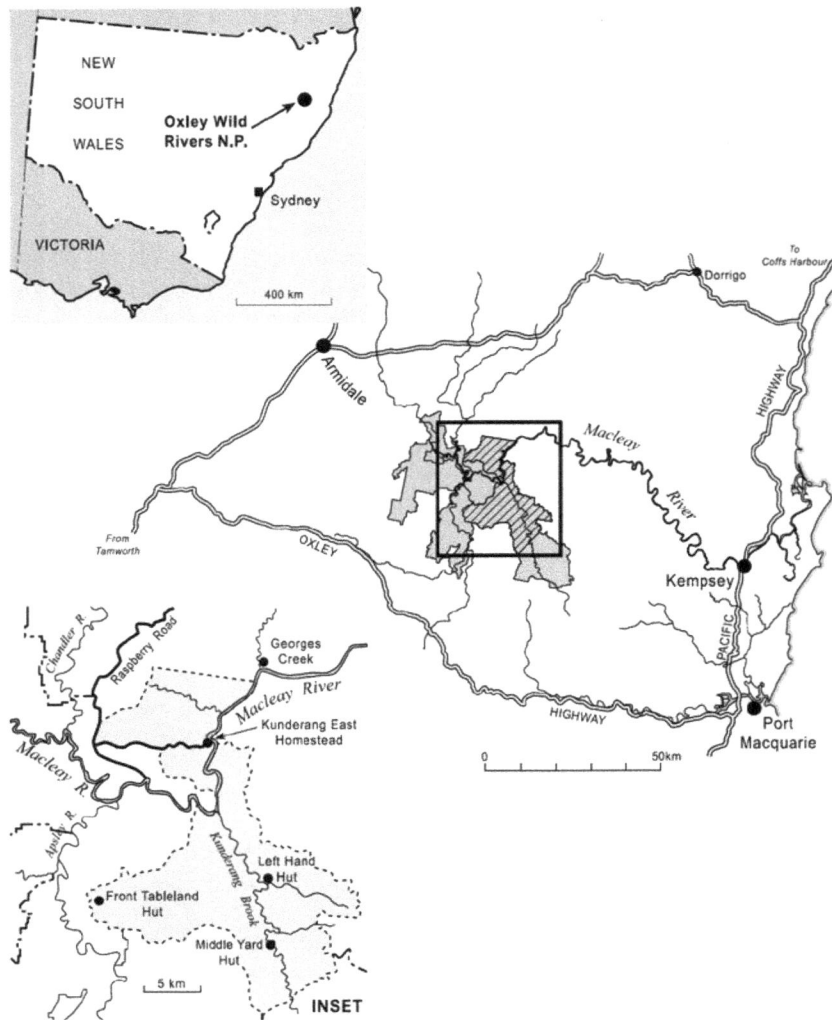

Figure 1 Map showing the location of Oxley Wild Rivers National Park, and the former Kunderang pastoral property.

'Well you'd be out of bed about daylight and then go and catch the horses. When we were down in the gorges it was only the one paddock, so we used to have to wait until everybody was ready to get the horses in. And we just all saddled up and moved off together along the river. But on the top it was different. When they had the horses in a bigger paddock, we kept the night horse out at night and one fella would get the night horse and go and run them all into the yard there each morning.' (interview, 27 February 2001).

Mustering in this deeply dissected landscape was hard work. Stockmen would have to muster cattle up and down creeks and river systems, and up and down spurs from the tablelands into the gorges. Finding and then mustering cattle in such a rugged landscape was incredibly difficult and time-consuming. Tactics included

waiting until there had been a dry period, so the cattle would congregate down in the creeks:

'We liked to get down there before the rains came, when it was reasonably dry. If it was a bit of a dry period then the cattle would come down to the rivers or the creeks for water, off the steep sides. But if it had been raining for two or three days or a week they'd climb up the sides and they wouldn't come back near the bottom until they had to come back for water...Early spring, some time before the spring rains, was good. The cattle weren't really strong and they were a bit easier to handle. From then right up until the storms started in January/February. Then it got pretty hard because there was water everywhere. And it made it harder even just to get up and down the Brook...there was just too much water.' (Maurice Goodwin interview, 1 March 2001).

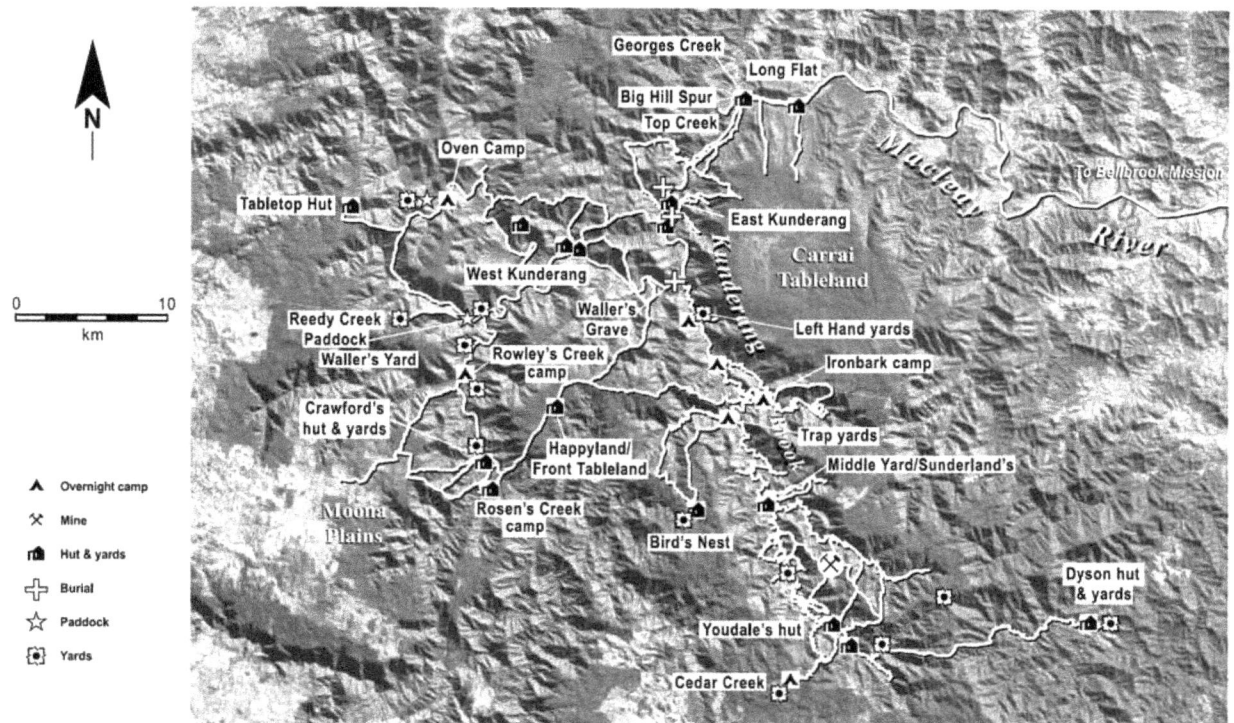

Figure 2   Mustering and travel routes associated with East Kunderang. Different informants' records appear here as a single line. Mustering huts, camps and yards are labelled.

Sometimes dogs were used to help in mustering wild cattle:

> 'You had to be pretty quiet and let the dogs find them because even if they smelled you when the wind changed, they were gone. It's just instinct with them. They would plant, they'd lay down once you put the dog round them, tried to work them, they were like little wood ducks, they'd just crawl in under the bushes and lie down and wouldn't move. You could get right up within a few feet of them they wouldn't come out, unless they come out to chase you…we'd try and get the dogs round them before they saw us, get the dogs to slow them up or circle them in a little mob before they actually saw us, stay out of sight if you could and just let the dogs do most of the work. And then if they busted or split up, which they did pretty often, you'd just get into them and just get what you could…catch calves or a cow or whatever, tie them up as quick as you could, and go and help the dogs, go and get the next one.' (Les O'Neill interview, 27 February 2001).

Food at such mustering camps and huts consisted largely of tinned meat and vegetables, supplemented with the meat of wild ducks and occasional kangaroos:

> 'We would have our vegetables, potatoes and pumpkin and onion was the main thing. Corned meat for the first few days then we would be on

to the tinned meat … [if we were out there for a long time] Alex Crawford would come out every four or five days or so with a packhorse and bring some fresh stuff for us.' (Les O'Neill interview, 27 February 2001).

Mustering tracks and landscape biographies
'Landscape biographies' map the way people's lives were lived in and through the landscape of the Kunderang ravines. The regular seasonal pattern of movement involved in the muster became, for the interviewees, a focal point for discussing the nature of work, their perception of the landscape, and changes in the environmental health of the gorges. Those who were interviewed were keen to pass on their recollections of mustering in the gorge country. Their stories illustrate the processes, as well as the storylines, that mark their own passage through, and hence knowledge of, the rugged landscape.

Interviewees were encouraged to make use of maps and aerial photographs at different scales to mark the locations of events and places to which they referred during oral history interviews (Fig. 2). What many of the men and women drew was a series of lines that marked both physical tracks and pathways. These reflect the linearity of their history as it was lived in and through the landscape. The pathways and mustering tracks indicated by the different former pastoral workers represent both different periods in time, as well as the different

47

mustering activities associated with East Kunderang and its neighbours.

Jeff O'Keefe's recollections revolve around mustering Alan Youdale's country in the 1960s, and are intermingled with his more recent experiences, with Maurice Goodwin and Ken O'Keefe, mustering cattle out of the park for NPWS in the early 1990s. This pattern of mustering took him from the headwaters of Kunderang Brook all the way north to its junction with the Macleay. Like Les O'Neill, Ken recalls the locations of yards and overnight camps at Left Hand, Trap Yard, Iron Bark, Cedar Creek, and huts at Bird's Nest, Sunderland's (Middle Hut), Youdale's and Dyson's. The act of telling these mustering paths and representing them on maps produced recollections and memories that, for him, are intimately tied to his understanding of the landscape:

> 'It was the mouth of Small's Creek. It was about '65 and it was very dry. There wasn't much water in Kunderang Brook but there was a little puddle of water at the mouth of Smalls Creek, about 8 or 10 inches deep and we had a pretty good mob of cattle we were bringing up. We were going to pull the weaners off the land to try and give the cows a better go, it was getting pretty dry and it was sort of getting to the stage that if we didn't do something we'd start to lose some cows. So we were bringing them up there and Alan was riding along on a horse he used to call 'the Donk'. He had a big loose rein and he bent down to look up under the tea trees at Smalls Creek to see whether any cattle had gone up the creek or not. We'd had a pretty good mob of cattle and they'd all walked through this puddle of water and when he went to straighten up a tea tree limb poked him in the ribs and half pushed him off the horse. Before he could regain his reins, he only got one rein gathered up, and all that did was circle the Donk round and round and he'd half fallen off, and he nearly got back on the horse, and the Donk was still going round and round in a circle. When he had almost gotten back in the saddle, the limb poked him in the ribs again and pushed him off. He couldn't hang on any longer and he fell off. Flop. Fell on his butt in this puddle of water. It was dirty green slimy water that the cattle had all walked through, and I couldn't help but laugh. And I never forget he got up and he wasn't real happy about it and I couldn't help but laugh. There were some pretty funny things that did happen. Little simple things like that, but they were funny at the time.' (interview, 1 March 2001).

Women's landscape biography
Unlike the men who had worked and mustered on Kunderang and neighbouring properties, Christine Kim, an Aboriginal woman whose father had worked on Kunderang, chose to mark the pathways between Bellbrook Aboriginal mission and Georges Creek, a camp near Kunderang where Aboriginal people would come for holidays, as important linear storylines in her landscape biography. Although Ms Kim and another Aboriginal woman, Irene Lockwood, were the only women who chose to be involved in mapping their oral history, this raises tantalising questions about gender differences in mapping memories of Kunderang. It is likely that this reflects the different working lives of men and women after the 1950s at Kunderang, when the property itself became largely a masculine space. Aboriginal women valued their time at the Georges Creek 'holiday camp' where they were beyond the surveillance of Bellbrook mission managers.

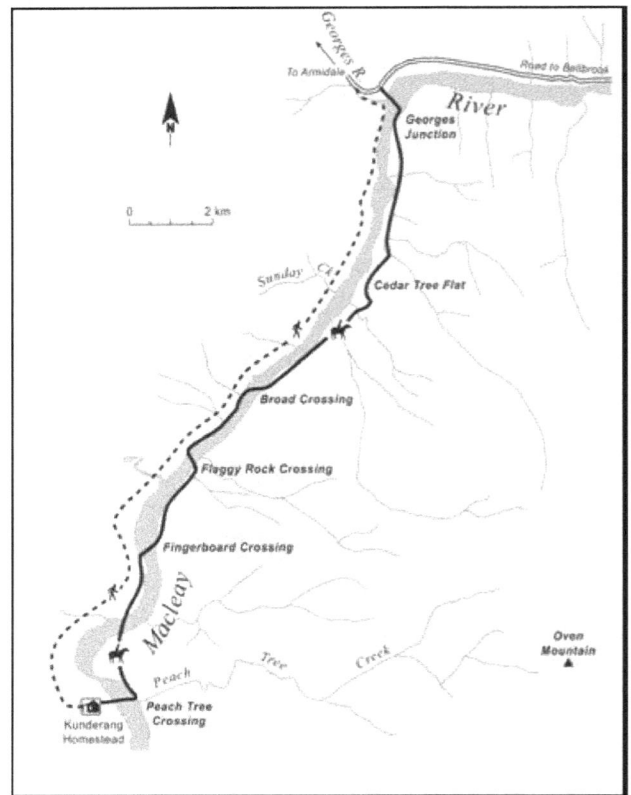

Figure 3 Walking and horse-riding pathways between the East Kunderang homestead, Georges Creek and Bellbrook were an important aspect of the landscape biographies of the women who were interviewed.

Irene Lockwood also recalled the pathway that linked Georges Creek with Kunderang as an important path in her landscape biography:

> 'Georges Creek...that's where we all used to come down from Bellbrook for a holiday...everybody would meet there at Georges Creek and they used to have good time. There would be a camp-fire and singing and story-telling. The old people used to come from Armidale, everywhere...they used to have their holidays there too. They used to build these big tin huts, tin camps. When we were young girls,

and Bruce was working at Kunderang, we used to walk up to Kunderang from Georges Creek with our aunties. We just walked along and went up, no horse, just walking and fishing and going along.' (interview, 21 March 2001).

This track would have also been an important pathway for Thelma McDonell, Alec McDonell's wife, who often had to make the journey between Georges Creek and Kunderang on horseback.

It is possible to represent all of these mustering tracks and pathways, along with the locations of huts and yards, on a map of the area now covered by Oxley Wild Rivers National Park. This map (Fig. 2) illustrates the patterns of pastoral land use in the Kunderang Gorges at a landscape scale. A visual picture is conjured up of generations of history lived in and through the landscape of the gorges. This map also demonstrates that the area now managed by the National Parks and Wildlife Service as 'wilderness' has had a long history of thorough infiltration by Aboriginal people, cattle and pastoralists that has played a fundamental role in forming the landscape.

A heritage of mustering in the gorge country
'Story trekking', visiting and mapping places mentioned in oral histories with those same story tellers (Green *et al.* 2003, 378), formed an important way of both tapping into deep, embodied memories about relationships to place, as well as gaining a more thorough, phenomenological understanding of these places. Many of the features recorded during these site visits were ephemeral traces, unlikely to have been given significance except in dialogue with the lived memories of the former pastoral workers and their families. The fact that these traces are so ephemeral is often the reason for proclaiming the areas as National Parks with relatively unmodified 'natural' landscapes; this makes it even more important to record these places and features in conjunction with people who have lived experience of them. While leaving traces may be 'the primal phenomenon of all the habits that are involved in inhabiting a place' (Benjamin 1999, 472), the experience of dwelling in space (c.f. Ingold 2000) creates a link between stories and spatial practices (de Certeau 1984, 121). As the influential spatial thinker Merleau-Ponty argues (1962), the 'human body provides the fundamental mediation point between thought and the world' (c.f. Tilley 1994, 14).

The archaeological traces associated with mustering in the gorge country consist of clearings and huts, and the remains of mustering camps and yards. As indicated above, mustering camps with yards formed an important focus of the work of mustering in the gorges. My objective when recording these sites was to document and record the material evidence associated both with pre-contact Aboriginal uses of the site (part of the broader set of objectives for this project involved a consideration of the relationship between pre- and post-contact Aboriginal people's use of this landscape), as well as any pastoral

infrastructure that remained. Informants greatly assisted in identifying and fleshing out many of the details of the use and function of both places and the material objects that remained at them. Most of these site visits were made under time constraints, and visibility at all sites was variable. While this does not constitute a 'complete' survey of these sites, this method was considered to be appropriate to this study, which was as interested in the 'sites' themselves, as in the way in which they were linked by both stories and physical pathways to other places in the Gorge country. I will present two examples from the much more detailed set of places documented in Harrison (2004).

'Happy Land': Front Tableland
Front Tableland (or 'Happy Land' as it was euphemistically known) is a clearing at the top of one of the spurs that formed one of the main travel routes from the Kunderang ravines up to the tablelands and on to Moona Plains (Fig. 4). A hut and yards were built here some time prior to the 1890s. When Les O'Neill first went to Front Tableland in the 1960s, there was a cleared horse paddock and a very dilapidated set of yards, which Alec McDonell and he repaired. The hut of the Fitzgeralds, who purchased the original Kunderang run in partnership with the McDonnells, and who were resident at Kunderang from 1889-1928, was not extant, but there was a slab-lined well and a bark lean-to that had been built by George Cohen. They would muster at Front Tableland for up to two weeks at a time, then return to East Kunderang homestead to change horses and take a few days rest before returning to finish the job. Up to 100 head of cattle would be mustered for branding from the creeks and gorges into the yards at Front Tableland before being driven down into the valley to the bullock paddock at Kunderang Creek.

When the property was under the management of Kellion Estates, a new mustering hut was built at Front Tableland in 1967. This timber-framed corrugated-iron building is located on a small rise above a large fenced paddock and stockyards.

The fabric of the yards at Front Tableland documents over 100 years of progressive alterations to their function and form, although the remains are the most substantially intact of the Fitzgerald period stockyards in Oxley Wild Rivers National Park. Les O'Neill explains:

> 'Well there had been a fairly big set of split-rail and post yards. When they'd fallen down and they repaired them, they used the old rails again, put some new posts in but mainly all new posts and the old rails. And I think it was either three or four yards, it wasn't a bad set of yards in those times...there was a receiving yard and a drafting yard, which they used to use for the branding yard. I don't know whether there were only the three or four yards there. There might have been four yards. (interview, 27 February 2001).

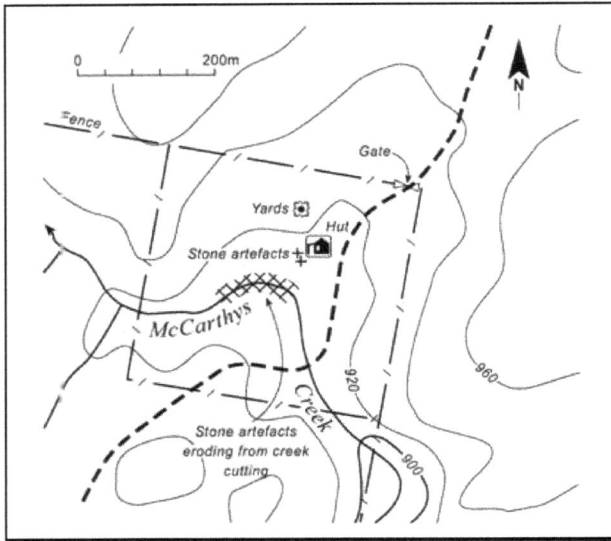

Figure 4 Site plan, Front Tableland ('Happyland').

The yards show evidence for several periods of construction. The earliest parts are constructed of split rails and posts, while later round posts and rails either replaced or were wired onto the earlier ones. The final phases of repair, most likely dating to the Kellion period, show the use of star pickets (again often wired against earlier posts) with wire and metal railing. The layout of the yards is now difficult to interpret, but there appears to have been three of four holding yards, plus a receiving and drafting yard as explained by O'Neill.

Aboriginal archaeology at Front Tableland

Aboriginal stone artefacts are exposed in two locations at Front Tableland: in the dripline of the hut itself, and in exposures along the creek that runs through the block. These artefacts occur in eroding clay exposures and indicate that there are areas of potential pre-European archaeological deposit at this site. Artefacts noted were predominantly flakes and debitage (flaking debris) of chert and mudstone. Les O'Neill recalls George Cohen constructing a bark shelter at the site, which, although no longer extant, relates to a long tradition of Aboriginal people, and then settlers after them, constructing bark shelters in this area:

> '...every night after you had your tea, old George had his little bark hut that he built there and he'd stroll off with his little bag of flour and away he'd go and cook a damper for the next day, and come back with it the next morning. No camp oven or anything, he'd just cook it in the ashes. You would see him going off with [just] a bag of flour and a billy-can of water.' (interview, 27 February 2001).

The use of bark in the construction of huts and shelters was widespread amongst Aboriginal communities on the north coast. Although they varied in size and sturdiness

of construction, they were generally built on a frame of saplings, with cured bark sheets lashed on to the frame (Morris 1989, 77). These shelters were reputedly widely adopted by European cedar getters, and variations on them often formed the first huts in which a pioneering Macleay pastoralist would live while awaiting construction of a more elaborate dwelling. The use and method of cutting sheets of bark was probably one of the earliest technologies adopted from Aboriginal people by European settlers in this area.

Rusdens Creek campsite

In addition to mustering huts with yards, a number of areas that contained just yards in the gorges formed the basis for makeshift mustering camps, which were used when mustering cattle out of the surrounding creeks for several days at a time. Les O'Neill and Maurice Goodwin took me to one such camp at Rusdens Creek (Fig. 5), where the Crawfords (who owned Moona Plains, which abutted the western boundary of Kunderang on the tablelands) built a set of branding yards down at the base of the spur some time prior to the 1950s. This camp replaced an earlier pair of huts and yard at Riverside, which may have been built before the turn of the twentieth century:

> 'There was only one yard there when the Crawfords were there, but there's two yards there now and the paddock has fallen down. The Crawfords only had the small horse paddock and one yard. The yard was built like a pig sty. It had only little small rails in it and every time a rail would break they'd put another one in and the cattle couldn't see through it, that's how they kept them in there. But all they had to do was make a hole and they'd knock the whole yard down...you've never seen yards like it ...'(Les O'Neill interview, 27 February 2001).

The site is located on gently sloping ground at the base of the 'Riverside spur' on a bend in the Apsley River:

> 'There were three spurs that the Crawfords had, they had the 'Riverside spur', which they didn't travel very much. The older Crawfords used to travel it all the time, I think that's where they [NPWS] have the road down now. They had the one they call the 'Horse spur', that's where the walking track is and they had another one they called the 'Cattle spur'. It was a longer spur but it wasn't much of a climb for the cattle [because] it was on the side of the spur instead of on top of it...' (Les O'Neill interview, 27 February 2001).

The site contains a small fenced paddock and set of timber stockyards, plus the remains of domestic materials associated with camping activities further up the incline from the yards. The yards had been ingeniously constructed using the trunks of several conveniently placed trees as posts. At least two periods of construction are evident: the first includes the use of round posts and wire, the second the use of star pickets. The yards also possessed a roughly circular branding yard with a crush (constructed more recently than the branding yard itself) and a sorting yard.

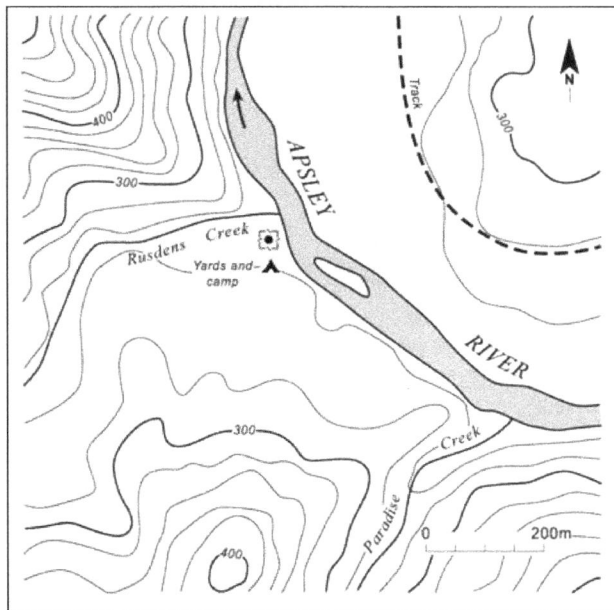

Figure 5 Site plan, Rusdens Creek campsite.

During my visit to the Rusdens Creek campsite in 2001, I recorded the yards and the remains of camping equipment stored there. This included billies and kerosene lanterns stored underneath a tree, as well as other domestic items such as a meat safe and the remains of tarpaulin stretched over posts. Also discovered were shovel handles and a sledge-hammer head. Les O'Neill remembers the hearth being used for cooking, and a 'fish smoker' built by Max Duval into the side of the hill, although only a depression remains in the location indicated by him. The remains of posts, some of which had been used for firewood, and a bed frame and tarpaulin, were scattered across the site.

Aboriginal archaeology at Rusdens Creek
Just above the yard at Rusdens Creek is a natural spring, around which is a low-density scatter (less than 5 per square metre) of flaked stone artefacts (not shown on map due to scale). These include several large multi-platform chert cores and flakes. The spring and the flat clearing near a spur would have made this a favourable location for camping by Aboriginal people in the past. The site has been disturbed by cattle trampling and was not recorded in any further detail.

The archaeology of mustering in the Kunderang ravines: a summary
There is a pattern and rhythm to the location of yards and huts in the Kunderang Gorges that can only be read and recognised at a particular spatial scale. This pattern would

have been the one most easily recognised by the men and women who worked mustering cattle on Kunderang for over 100 years. Although Kunderang was the head station, yards and huts to house mustering teams were located at strategic points throughout the gorge country, generally on the tablelands near good access spurs. Cleared paddocks would be established around a simple hut and yards. There are three of these huts associated with Kunderang still preserved in Oxley Wild Rivers National Park, although during the Fitzgerald period there were four or five huts.

Further down the hierarchy of places there were numerous, less frequently used yards and paddocks where the mustering team would occasionally camp as they worked their way down the rivers and creeks to find and muster wild cattle. There were no structures built at these locations, although canvas tents were sometimes erected. Often stores of cooking equipment and canvas for shelter were left at these mustering camps. These sites were ephemeral and would be difficult to locate if they were not pin-pointed by someone who has knowledge of working at them, but they demonstrate clearly the system of pastoral land use in the gorge country. As archaeological sites, these places preserve information about the ways of life of former pastoral workers, but taken together with the oral history they build a powerful picture of the pastoral industry as a land-use strategy that was highly adaptable to the varied landscapes of New South Wales.

The scatters of stone artefacts recorded at every one of the mustering hut, camp and yard sites most likely represent the remains of successive camping episodes carried out by small groups of Aboriginal people, who moved into the gorge country in the warmer months. Following the results of Godwin's research on the Macleay (1983; 1985; 1990; 1997; 1999), these sites probably date to within the last 2000 years. All sites occur within the contexts suggested by Godwin's model, close to watercourses on flat ground or near semi-permanent water sources and good access spurs to the tablelands. Flaked glass pieces and scarred trees with evidence of steel axe marks provide tantalising hints of post-contact use of the sites by Aboriginal people, or the transferral of Aboriginal techniques of hut construction to settler pastoralists. The co-occurrence of Aboriginal and pastoral sites is significant as it suggests that settlers 'learned' to use the landscape in similar ways to Aboriginal people in the deep past, and that there was a transference of environmental knowledge from the Aboriginal people who worked in the industry in the recent past to European settlers.

Knowing the country
Human pathways often make use of trails formed by animals, such as kangaroos and wild horses and cattle, which travel the easiest routes between tableland and river valley floor. Early pastoralists in search of a route between the valley and tableland discovered Aboriginal footpaths and cleared tracks that they came to use as

stock-routes and roads. There is certainly very good evidence for the continuous re-use of several of these much older Aboriginal pathways over 160 years of European settlement.

The interviews collected for the project are rich with places that constitute landscapes of dwelling, working, walking and riding. These landscapes have a personal character, but also reflect wider shared notions of cultural and natural landscapes in the pastoral industry. For the former pastoral workers and their descendents, the landscape of the Kunderang ravines is understood in profoundly different ways to the way it is now understood by the Department of Environment and Conservation, which manages the national park. Recollections of the country emphasise particular kinds of places, such as clearings on the tablelands and river flats, on the river itself, and the ever-important spurs, those escalators of the gorge-lands. The linearity and seasonality of movement between tableland and gorges forms a moving landscape, a construction within which people's memories can be articulated and made to speak in profoundly personal ways.

Making places at East Kunderang
The relationship between work and people's understanding and appreciation of the landscape of the gorges is of critical importance. Jeff O'Keefe noted when describing a particular creek while he was mapping his landscape biography:

> 'Steep hard creek but amazingly enough we used to have very good luck because the sides were so steep, the cattle wouldn't climb out of them easily. They always used to sidle around the sides and then they'd come down again. Over the time we had a lot of success in it. Early in the piece we got every beast out of Blacks Camp. Some of the creeks, even Left Hand and Thread Needle, still have got a handful of cattle in them, but Blacks Camp, quite early in the piece we had every beast out of it.' (interview, 2 March 2001).

Jeff's knowledge of Black's Camp Creek is profoundly phenomenological; his understanding of the creek is as part of a wider lived and working mustering landscape. There is a relationship here between the movement of people and cattle which is important in understanding the way in which stockmen came to know and appreciate this landscape:

> 'We used to say 'If the cattle can get there, follow that track because you'll get there'. The cattle were wise enough to know that if they couldn't get round the side or over a steep bank or something they wouldn't go, so if the cattle went around a steep incline or something we'd follow their tracks because they knew where they were going. And that proved pretty well all the time. If the cattle didn't want to go there you

had to be careful because it was probably too steep, or too shaley or the water was too deep. But a lot of it is probably common sense, if it gets too steep you get off and lead your horse. You don't go scrambling around where you're going to get it busted.' (Maurice Goodwin interview, 1 March 2001).

Bruce Lockwood echoed this sentiment when he remarked on the courage of Aboriginal people mustering in the Kunderang Gorges: 'where the cattle went, they went'. Indeed, cattle provide a wide range of metaphors for understanding human experience, particularly travel, in the Kunderang ravines. Such observations have been made regarding pastoralists in other parts of the world (e.g. Tilley 1999, 51). The use of human/cattle metaphors is shared by both Aboriginal and settler pastoralists. This is part of the shared working language which developed through living and working together in the gorges over 150 years.

The way in which people move about in this highly dissected environment is not only reflected in people's language, but is inscribed on the very landscape itself. The named features in the gorges all focus on spurs and creeks, reflecting the broader pattern of movement both to muster cattle and to move across the land from the tableland to the valley. The landscape is described and named as a working, moving landscape. This in turn represents a profoundly landscape-oriented body of lore, which documents the long history of people and cattle in the gorges.

The 'short cut'
For landscape philosopher Michel de Certeau, it is people's interlinked paths and pedestrian movements that form 'real systems whose existence in fact makes up a city' (1984, 97). The history of the city begins at ground level, with people's footsteps. In the Kunderang Gorges, it is not pedestrian movement but the movement of horses and riders along pathways, and cattle across their daily and seasonal 'beat', that constitutes the social face of the country. We can inscribe these movements and pathways as lines on maps, but to do so would miss the practices of starting and stopping, walking, crossing rivers, roping and throwing wild cattle, and incidents that occurred along the way (Pearson and Shanks 2001, 148). De Certeau distinguishes tricks in the 'ways of doing' (1984, xviii,), the ways in which people continually subvert the constraints of landscapes.

One such trick is the 'short cut', a frequent inclusion in both Aboriginal and non-Aboriginal men's oral histories which stress moving through space, constituting a focal point for the intersection between history, event, people and landscape (Fig. 6):

> 'Yes it's not very far from the mouth of Thread Needle [Creek]. Well, actually you don't come out the mouth of Thread Needle with cattle, you short cut over a bank and cross to Middle Yard.

And it's a steep little climb up and a steep little climb down and, in the dark, at night coming back with tired cattle, it was a great place where years ago they used to lose a lot of them. So we decided we'd take the portable yards, to a place where there was a bit of a track where they used to cut posts years ago. We would just put them in to the portable yards without the hassle of losing them or widening the yard and we'd go back next morning, either take the 'Blitz' [truck] over and put them on, or drive them across next morning when we had plenty of time.' (Maurice Goodwin interview, 1 March 2001).

Similarly, I discussed earlier the short cut between East Kunderang and Georges Creek used by both Aboriginal and non-Aboriginal women and men to move between the homestead and settlement at Georges Creek, and the short cut between Georges Creek and the mission at Bellbrook, which was emphasised by Aboriginal women in their interviews.

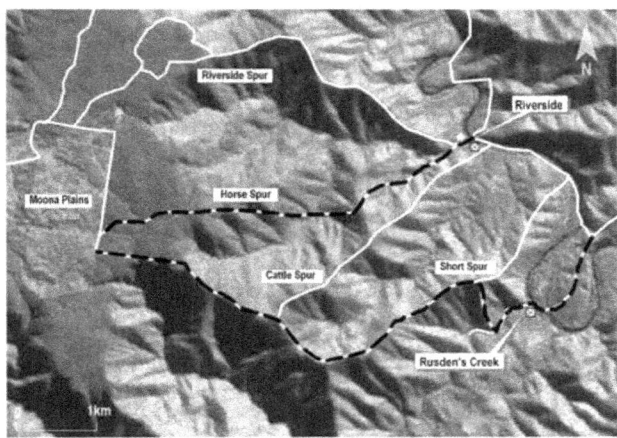

Fig. 6 The 'short' and 'horse' spurs: short cuts used by the Crawfords to travel between Moons Plains, Rusden's Creek and Riverside.

Like the short cut, the detail of embodied landscape biographies can be lost in the broad stroke of the line on the page. The Kunderang narratives seem to support Gibson's 'theory of reversible occlusion', which describes the way in which the environment is known by humans along a path of observation of surfaces which move in and out of view in a particular order along a pathway or route of travel (1979, 198; see discussion in Ingold 2000, 238). These stories relive and recreate the landscape by recalling the routes along which it was experienced and known. The 'ways-of-doing' associated with mustering in the Kunderang ravines form part of the collective experience from which former pastoral workers constitute their sense of collective identity, and sense of place (e.g. papers in Feld and Basso 1996). 'Places not only *are*; they *happen*' (Casey 1996, 13).

Conclusion

A focus on the material remains of mustering may have revealed details of the 'system', but the accounts of former pastoral workers has allowed a more profound understanding of both the relationship between people and landscape in the gorges, as well as the *experience* of walking and riding what we recorded as narrative paths during oral history recordings. The stories, a series of named places linked by narratives, pay testament to an involvement with the landscape (Tilley 1994, 27; Pearson and Shanks 2001, 135). The constraints formed by this rugged, dissected landscape, the river itself, and the shared experiences of huts and mustering camps form the basis for the active creation of the cultural landscape of the Kunderang ravines. Riding and walking constitute a kind of spatial acting-out, choreographed by pathways of movement, and the constraints formed by the landscape. Living and working in the Kunderang ravines meant an active and constant engagement with the landscape. For the former Kunderang pastoral workers, to travel the landscape is to 'remember it into being' (Pearson and Shanks 2001, 138).

Bibliography

Bachelard, G. 1969. *The Poetics of Space*. Jolas, M. (trans.). Boston: Beacon Press.

Bender, B. 2001. Introduction. In Bender, B. and Winer, M. (eds.) *Contested Landscapes: Movement, Exile and Place*, 1-18. Oxford and New York: Berg.

Benjamin, W. 1999. *Selected Writings*. Jennings, M., Bullock, M., Eiland, H., and Smith, G. (eds.), Livingstone, R. (trans.), Vol. 2. Cambridge: Belknap Press of Harvard University.

Casey, E.S. 1996. How to get from space to place in a fairly short stretch of time: phenomenological prolegomena. In Feld, S. and Basso, K.H. (eds.) *Senses of Place*, 13–51. School of American Research Press/ University of Washington Press.

de Certeau, M. 1984. *The Practice of Everyday Life*. Berkeley: University of California Press.

Feld, S and Basso, K.H. 1996. *Sense of Place*. Santa Fe: School of American Research Press.

Gibson, J.J. 1979. *The Ecological Approach to Visual Perception*. Boston: Haughton Mifflin.

Godwin, L. 1983. Archaeological site surveys on the eastern margin of the New England Tablelands. *Australian Archaeology* 17, 38–48.

Godwin, L. 1985. A report on the archaeology of the Apsley-Macleay Gorge System. Appendix 9, Macleay-Apsley natural resources and land-use study: the case for a National Park. Unpublished report by NPWS to Department of Environment and Planning.

Godwin, L. 1990. *Inside information: settlement and alliance in the late Holocene of north-eastern New South Wales*. Unpublished PhD thesis, University of New England, Armidale.

Godwin, L. 1997. Little big men: alliance and schism in north-eastern New South Wales during the late Holocene. In McConvell, P. and Evans, N. (eds.) *Archaeology and Linguistics: Aboriginal Australia in Global Perspective*, 297–310. Oxford: Oxford University Press.

Godwin, L. 1999. Two steps forward, one back: some thoughts on settlement models for the north coast of NSW. In Hall, J. and McNiven, I. (eds.) *Australian Coastal Archaeology*, 211–218. Canberra: ANH Publications, Department of Archaeology and Natural History, RSPAS, Australian National University.

Green, L.F., Green D.R. and Neves, E.G. 2003. Indigenous knowledge and archaeological science: the challenges of public archaeology in the Reserva Uaçá. *Journal of Social Archaeology* 3(3), 366–98.

Harrison, R. 2004. *Shared Landscapes: Archaeologies of Attachment and the Pastoral Industry in New South Wales*. Sydney: UNSW Press.

Ingold, T. 2000. *The Perception of the Environment: Essays in Livelihood, Dwelling and Skill*. London and New York: Routledge.

Merleau-Ponty, M. 1962. *Phenomenology of Perception*. London: Routledge.

Morris, B. 1989. *Domesticating Resistance: The Dhan-Gadi Aborigines and the Australian State*. Oxford: Berg Publishers.

Pearson, M. and Shanks, M. 2001. *Theatre/Archaeology*. London: Routledge.

Tilley, C. 1994. *A Phenomenology of Landscape: Places, Paths and Monuments*. Oxford and Providence: Berg.

Tilley, C. 1999. *Metaphor and Material Culture*. Oxford and Massachusetts: Blackwell.

Wise, J.M. 2000. Home: territory and identity. *Cultural Studies* 14(2), 295–310.

The nature and distribution of early medieval woodland and wood-pasture habitats

Della Hooke

This study looks at the nature of the 'wild wood' and subsequent changes due to human intervention and methods of land management, emphasising the importance of wood-pasture in early medieval England. The place-name and charter evidence for woodland usage and the distribution of tree species, and the role of woodland in landscape evolution are investigated. A further aspect briefly covered is the iconography of woods and trees in early medieval tradition, folk legend and literature.

The nature of early woodland

Research over the last few decades has contributed greatly towards an understanding of the nature of early woodland in Britain, and has brought into question the conception that 'a squirrel might cross England from tree to tree without ever touching the ground' – the traditional image of the 'wildwood', a view that perhaps became entrenched when Sir Cyril Fox's *The Personality of Britain* was first published in 1932. Oliver Rackham (1998) was amongst those who first suggested that ancient woodland was not dense 'forest' but more like open savannah, and Franz Vera (2000) has also argued plausibly that browsing wild animals would have kept woodland open wherever they were able to get access to it.

Vera bases his ideas on the changes witnessed in the Serengeti at the end of the nineteenth century AD, when rinderpest wiped out 95% of the wildebeest and buffalo populations, in comparison to the situation in the early 1960s, when vaccination removed this danger from the national park's livestock. Climatic fluctuation also played a part, as there was more rain in the dry season and less in the wet season at the end of the 1960s, ensuring good grass growth which increased the food supplies of the herbivores. The actual mechanisms of change were surprisingly complex: wildebeest ate the plants; few plants grew old and withered; there was less fuel for fires; more acacia seedlings survived, but this led to an increase in giraffe numbers and these kept the acacias at shrub size; seedlings were eaten, herbs failed to flower or set seed. This reminds one of the Dorset blue butterfly that needs both ants and a particular plant for a successful life cycle (Thomas and Elms 1998). However, the Serengeti showed how strongly wild herbivores can affect the landscape, and especially the trees.

In the past in Europe, the European bison and the auroch had a role similar to the African wildebeest. The bison, in particular, inhibited succession in the gaps in the forest caused by storms, and created small open spaces. Within the forest, they stripped bark from the trees in winter. The aurochs grazed in the open spaces, and kept them open only where plants with good defensive qualities could become established, such as gorse, hawthorn and juniper. Only when scrub offered protection could trees become established. According to Vera's hypothesis, the trees re-grow but, as the shrubs are closed out by the tree canopy, the herbivores return and prevent regeneration, starting the cycle again. In the open phase, the landscape has a park-like or savannah-type appearance, with a thin scatter of trees left across grasslands and heathlands. These views have been questioned by ecologists, but now seem to be generally accepted, although the favoured scenario (Kirby 2004) is a mosaic of open land, shrub and woodland, with all phases of the cycle present in different areas – the woodland being thickest on steep slopes, for example, where animals found it harder to browse (for additional discussion see Hodder *et al*. 2009).

This is significant in three ways:

1. 'Primeval' woodland in Britain was not dense and impenetrable except in specific locations. It was heavily grazed and browsed by wild cattle and horses, red deer, elk and roe deer, and also uprooted by wild boar. It could, therefore, be more easily cleared by people. It is now known that Mesolithic peoples used fire to create open spaces to which the animals they wished to hunt would be attracted. There may be evidence of this from areas of former hazel woodland at Fawr Forset in South Wales, where raised bog began to form *c*. 8000 BC (Evans 1999, 24-6). Subsequently, early farmers were able to extend the open land with their flint tools. In wetter upland areas, clearance of the tree cover, probably combined with a worsening climate, provided conditions for increased peat formation, inhibiting tree regeneration, a process perhaps beginning in the Bronze Age (Walker and Taylor 1976; Chambers *et al*. 299). Tree leaves were also collected as fodder, especially when cut from regenerating stumps. These practices left many areas, even upon fertile soils, virtually devoid of woodland, or with very patchy woodland, by the end of the prehistoric period.

2. Woodland is not a 'naturally' sustainable habitat, but needs to be protected from animals for adequate regeneration.

3. The habitat has been constantly changing throughout prehistoric and historic times and is far more dynamic than it was once considered to be (I refer to the views being taught in British universities into the 1950s and 1960s, in which woodland clearance was seen as a gradual change effected by people through from

prehistory to well into the medieval period – Thorpe 1971). Returning to the Vera model, scrub is often found fringing more open areas, with such shrubs and trees as the blackthorn, hawthorn, guilder rose, privet, rowan, dogwood, hazel and wild fruit trees (apple, pear and cherry). Within these patches of scrub, oak, beech, aspen, ash, elm, lime and hornbeam are able to become established – a single hawthorn might provide protection for an oak. Many of these shrubs produce little pollen and do not always show up in the pollen record. This sequence generally produces a type of wood-pasture habitat.

The latter is of particular importance because, by late Iron Age times in England, wood-pasture had become one of the most significant resources available, particularly where pastoralism played a significant, if not a dominant, role. Many regions of wood-pasture are likely to have been visited on a seasonal basis and cross-country links of this nature were probably fundamental in defining territories by the late Iron Age, and continued to influence later territorial organisation.

The early medieval evidence
Various factors influenced land use in England in the pre-Conquest period, and among the most important were the natural background (including geology, topography and soils), climatic fluctuations, and use of the land by people. Away from the uplands, woodland tended to be most plentiful, by this period, in areas that were relatively infertile, or were vulnerable and lightly settled frontier regions, or in areas where both of these factors were involved. It was also a valuable resource in several different ways: it provided timber for building, fuel etc., and this led to its protection and management; it was used widely as a wood-pasture resource; and within wooded regions areas might be set aside for hunting, which might include the protection of woodland within deliberately constructed wood banks, possibly topped with dead or living hedges (Hooke 1989). The evidence for woodland usage in this period is largely derived from place-names, pre-Conquest charters, historical narrative, the Domesday Book, and environmental archaeology.

One basic issue regarding this time is whether or not there was substantial woodland regeneration in the immediate post-Roman period. In the mid-1990s, Petra Dark examined all the radiocarbon-dated pollen sequences for Britain spanning the period AD 400–800 and found, not surprisingly, that the situation varied not only across the country, but sometimes within the area of one county (Dark 2000, 130-56). Crop growing was declining as the demands of the Roman army and towns were withdrawn.

This was not necessarily the result of agricultural stagnation – merely a return to farming systems which included more livestock rearing. On the chalklands of southern England, such as the Wessex downlands, fields used until at least the fourth century AD can still be detected in fields under pasture, and many more survived

until the ploughing-up campaigns of the second half of the last century. Although pollen sequences show that there was little change in the upper Thames valley at Barton Court near Abingdon, or around Dorchester (Miles 1986), pre-Conquest charter evidence shows that it was usually open pasture that replaced the arable fields on the downs. There were limited areas of woodland on the upper slopes of the chalk escarpments by the later Anglo-Saxon period, producing woods like those of Groveley Forest above the Wylye valley (Hooke 1988).

Reduction in the amount of arable in the early medieval period did not, therefore, inevitably lead to increased woodland: in Somerset, arable land was abandoned on parts of Exmoor and returned to woodland, but on the Somerset Levels at Meare Heath it was open land that was expanding between the fifth and eighth centuries AD (Beckett and Hibbert 1979). There are regions, however, where a return to a wood-pasture habitat is attested. Woodland regeneration took place at Bignor on the South Downs in Sussex, at Snelsmore on the Berkshire Downs (Waton 1982; 1983), and at Thetford in Norfolk (ex. inf. J. Greig). There is also more evidence for woodland regeneration in northern England and southern Scotland, but even here this may have been part of a traditional cycle of land use (Higham 1992, 77-8).

Two other marginal areas also provide clear evidence of such a change. On the Birmingham Plateau, an open wood-pasture habitat near the former Metchley Roman fort appears to mark a return to more traditional land use (Greig 2005). Scrub, mainly *Crataegus* (hawthorn) and *Prunus* (sloe), had been present alongside arable, pasture and heath land while the fort was in active use, but scrub was spreading before the end of the Roman period, with increasing numbers of woodland species present, especially *Quercus* (oak), *Corylus* (hazel) and *Alnus* (alder). By the post-Roman period, the oak woodland was well established, but rye was being cultivated on a small scale at a distance from the site (probably *c*. AD 600). In a later phase, probably dating to the medieval period, the presence of more *Betula* (birch) and *Ilex* (holly) indicates more open woodland that was being used as wood-pasture, holly in particular being useful as a source of leaf fodder in spring. However, this usage is likely to have begun before this date: *léah* place-names are common in the area and are likely to have indicated open wood-pasture regions (see below). Woodland dominated by birch, alder, oak and holly – all trees of wood-pasture – continued to characterise the environment of this part of the Birmingham Plateau in medieval times. Similar pollen sequences have been found in the West Midlands at Cookley (Worcestershire) and Stafford (Staffordshire) (ex. inf. J. Greig).

A second region in which woodland appears to have regenerated in the post-Roman period over former arable fields is suggested by soil composition in profiles studied in parts of the south-eastern Weald. Some have suggested that this occurred in the immediate post-Roman period, although there must have been sufficient woodland elsewhere (mainly in the east) to provide the fuel needed to support a thriving iron industry in Roman times. By the eighth century AD, charters clearly show that the inner Weald was wooded and being used as seasonal pasture. At first, the wood-pasture was held in common but was later to be appropriated by individual manors as estate fragmentation progressed (Hooke 1989, 113-14). By the later Anglo-Saxon period the Weald could be described as a *mycclan wuda* – 'great wood' – said to be 'a hundred-and-twenty miles long or longer from east to west, and thirty miles broad' (Swanton 1996, 84, ASC 893 for 892).

The links between lowland estate foci and distant woodlands are clearly represented in both the Weald and on the Birmingham Plateau (see below). Some (e.g. Ford 1976) have argued that they originated in the late Iron Age, when woodland was at a premium, reflecting the use of wooded regions as seasonal pastures; others (Klingelhöfer 1992, 44), however, have argued for the origin of such links in the administrative arrangements of the later part of the early medieval period.[1]

Woodland uses and their influence upon land use
Archaeological evidence has shown that woodland has been managed since prehistoric times, with probable evidence of coppicing seen in the charcoal associated with Bronze Age burnt mounds in the Birmingham area, for instance (Hodder 2004, 33), or the coppiced alder found in the buildings of Glastonbury 'lake village' in the Iron Age (Dark 2000, 78). Woodland was carefully managed in Roman times and the oak/hazel woodland at Sidlings Copse that supplied the kilns of the Oxford pottery industry was probably coppiced; the willow that increased significantly in this period may have been deliberately planted as a renewable source of fuel (*ibid.* 120-1). Coppice woods were frequent in Roman Britain and appear to have been cut in some areas at less than ten year's growth (*ibid.* 122). Several Roman writers, like Cato, note how many different kinds of woodland could be managed – willow beds, coppice woods, orchards and 'mast-woods' – the latter providing beech-mast or acorns for herds of swine. Poplars and elms might be planted as a source of leaf fodder, and the leaves of rowan and ash were also used in this way. Columella noted how chestnut was the best wood for cropping, and a medieval chestnut wood on the eastern fringe of the Forest of Dean, a tithe of its chestnuts granted to Flaxley Abbey, just happens to be near the site of a Roman villa – it was probably the Romans who introduced this tree (Columella IV.xxxiii: Ash 1941, 456-7; Hooke forthcoming).

It has been argued that there is less evidence for woodland management at the beginning of the early medieval period, and more environmental evidence is urgently needed. Certainly, timber was essential for building and was highly valued – protected in the seventh century AD laws of Ine, for instance, which laid down heavy fines for unlawfully felling timber (Attenborough 1922, 50-1; Hooke 1998a, 165). This resource is not infrequently noted in charter grants like that of Wolverley in north Worcestershire, which in AD 866 allotted to the recipient of the grant rights to take 'one oak and other timber necessary for building' (Sawyer 1968, S 212; Hooke 1990, 120-1). Carpentry tools have been widely found. Moreover, there are signs that the woodland was managed, for many buildings show the use of small timbers that were probably obtained from coppiced trees. Wood was equally necessary for fuel – both for domestic and industrial usage. One of the main users in the Midlands was the Droitwich salt industry, which used wood to heat the 'ovens' over which salt was evaporated in leaden pans. Indications of the use of trees in areas grazed by stock may be found in the reference, amongst others, to the *coppendan ac*, 'the copped oak-tree', in a boundary clause of Stoke by Hurstborne, in Hampshire (Sawyer 1968, S 276), for this is probably a reference to a pollarded tree: the adjective means 'polled, without a top' (the name appears in a few place-names), a means of providing timber grown out of the reach of animals (Hooke 2003a, 22).

It is the wood-pasture regions that had a profound effect upon the Anglo-Saxon landscape, for they were extensive across marginal areas throughout England and appear to have had a fundamental influence upon the delineation of territories, possibly as early as the Iron Age. There is evidence to suggest that the hill-forts of the Welsh Borderland, for instance, were often sited to control wood-pasture resources in what was predominantly a pastoral economy. Tribal boundaries, too, seem often to have been delineated to run through the most marginal zones of upland moorland or densest woodland. Both the central Weald and the Birmingham Plateau appear to have been frontier regions by the late Iron Age. In early medieval times, the Weald formed the boundary between the men of Kent and the south Saxons, while various folk groups from north and south appear to have inter-commoned on the high ground of the Birmingham Plateau, on the northern frontier of the Hwiccan kingdom (Hooke 1985, 85-6). The lands of the Pencesætan, based in the Penk valley of Staffordshire, and the Tomsætan, based along the valley of the River Teme, met the boundary of Hwiccan estates in this area (far within what appears to have been the line of the seventh-century AD Hwiccan boundary).

In the early medieval Hwiccan kingdom, one can identify links from intensively cultivated regions to the seasonal pastures of woodland/wood-pasture regions, and these influenced the demarcation of the folk regions that were to be subsumed into the Anglo-Saxon kingdoms (Hooke 1985, 75-88). The links that grew out of this utilisation of complementary resources were to influence manorial and ecclesiastical organisation into medieval times. In Kent, the woodland dens were linked by observable drove-ways to estate centres on the coast or the lowland plains, and the woods provided valuable seasonal pasture for pigs, cattle, horses and possibly also sheep (Everitt 1986) (Fig. 1a).

The dens seem to have been communally owned by the folk territories – the basis for the later lathes – before being appropriated by individual manors: a system which

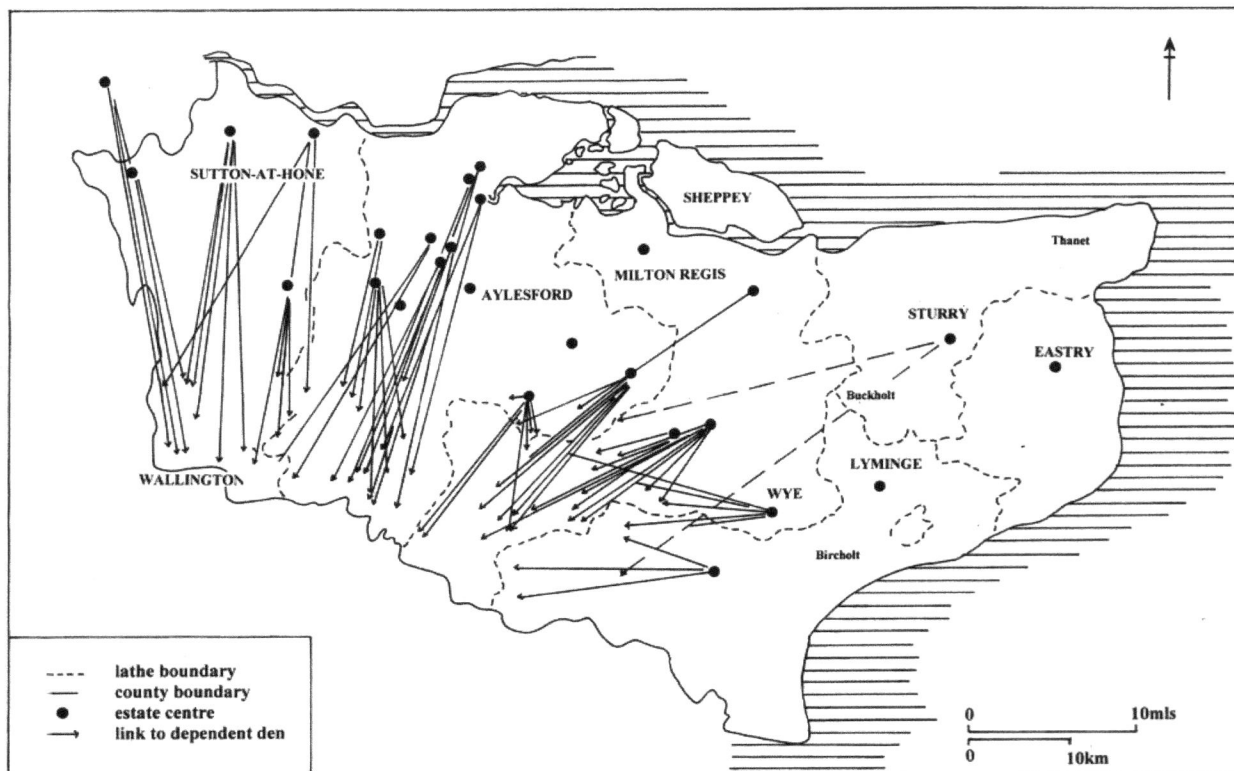

Figure 1a Estate linkages in the Kentish Weald (after Hooke 1998a, 143, fig. 48).

takes the droves back to the early part of the period at least (swine-pastures added to an eighth-century AD charter include 'the wood of the men of the Lympne district [*i.e.* the area based upon the River Limen]' (Sawyer 1968, S 1180; Hooke 1998a, 144)). In the Midlands, estates in the intensively cultivated Avon valley region held land in the woods of north Worcestershire, and the Warwickshire Arden and a similar system of routes linking these regions appear to be fossilised in many of today's roads and bridleways, and may also have influenced the delineation of parish boundaries (Fig. 1b).

Finally, there is increasing evidence for woodland regeneration in the later part of the Anglo-Saxon period, particularly in southern England, and there is reason to believe that this was, at least in part, due to the increased interest in hunting shown by the Anglo-Saxon kings. Forests were recognised in the seventh century AD within the Frankish kingdoms, and English leaders were seldom slow to follow their cultural practices. Hunting rights are included in pre-Conquest charters, and areas of woodland appear to have been physically demarcated by wood banks topped with hedges or fences. The resultant enclosures, some of them extensive, are referred to by the Old English term *haga*, and many lay upon royal estates (for an explanation of the interpretation of this term, see Hooke 1989). The Anglo-Saxon *haga* became the *haia* of Domesday Book, a feature which was described as a place to 'take deer' (perhaps implying an element of 'protection'). Some pre-Conquest charters reveal estates that, in the ninth century AD, were being relieved of the

duty of maintaining the king's huntsmen, falconers and dog-handlers (*ibid*). It is clear that many of the Norman forests that were to be designated after the Conquest were to lie in areas that had already been used for hunting in Anglo-Saxon times (Hooke 1998b, Fig. 2). It may be significant that woodland regeneration seems to have been late at Sidlings Copse, and that this, too, was later to form part of the royal Forest of Stowood.

Place-name evidence
When one examines the terms used for woodland and wood-pasture in the early medieval period there seems to be adequate evidence for the uses outlined above: small woods, probably protected within wood banks, were the 'groves' (Old English *gráf*), and places with 'wood' in their name, like Wootton Wawen in Warwickshire, may have had a special function in relation to the exploitation of the wood and its products (Gelling 1984, 227). *Hangra* was a 'wood on a slope', *hyrst* one on a hillock. But the wider areas of woodland were described by other terms.

Much has been written about the interpretation of *wald* but this appears to have signified a landscape of both grassland and a light cover of trees and shrubs with isolated stands of wood – it also indicated a place with tree fodder (Trier 1963), in some places associated with largely uncultivated land (Vera 2000, 112), and is likely to have been loosely wooded countryside with much open grassland (Fox 1989, 84-5). This kind of land was used for pasture, as in the Gloucestershire Cotswolds, a region well stocked with sheep and already noted for wool production in early medieval times (Hooke 1978). Eventually, as 'wold', the term came to refer to largely open country. Was there then a term for wood-pasture, a landscape of grasslands, scattered trees and woodland? I believe there was and that the *léah* term, at least in its earliest usage, is most likely to signify such a meaning. It is derived from an Indo-European root meaning 'light', but the nearest equivalent is the Old High German *lòh*, supposedly 'grove, bush-grown clearing' coming down in Old English as 'a woodland with glades' (Johansson 1975, 2-3). This seems to be the type of open woodland Vera (2000) credits to woodland that is intensively used as wood-pasture for livestock, the derivative of the old open 'wildwood' (Hooke 2008).

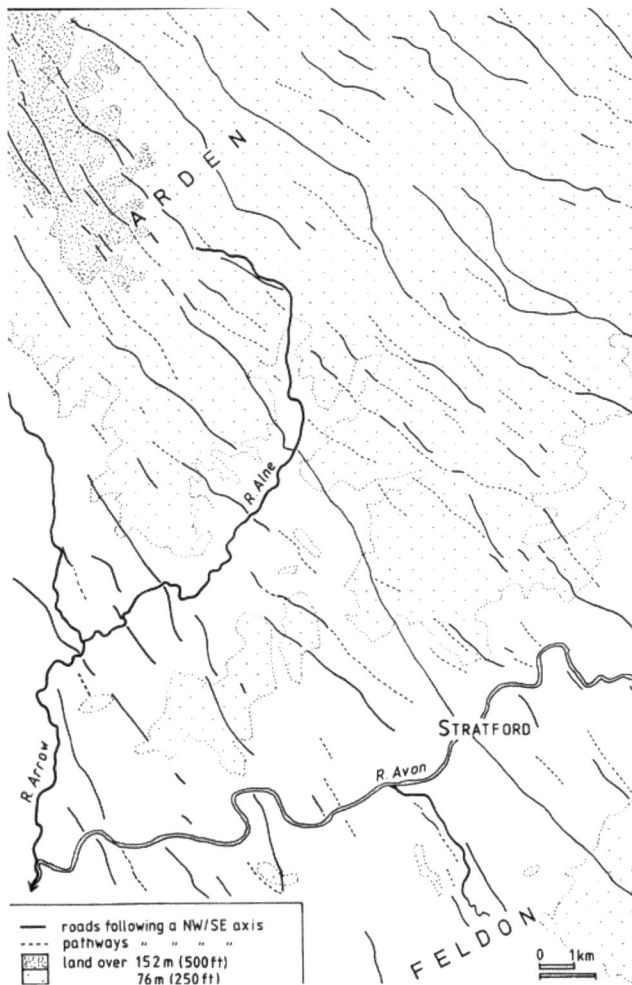

Figure 1b Possible drove routes in the Warwickshire Arden linking the intensively cultivated Feldon with the more heavily wooded Arden to the north-west (Hooke 1998a, 161, fig. 55).

That *léah* could suggest more extensive open woodland seems to be suggested from its regular use in regions of seasonal wood-pasture: an alternative name for the Weald was Andredesleah (Swanton 1996, 14, ASC 477). *Léah* place-names were, however, attached to both large and small areas: a string of settlements bearing *léah* names,

for instance, are found around and within *Weogorena leah* (Fig. 3), the wood-pasture region of the *Weogoran* tribe, whose territory was focused upon Worcester. The name also seems to be perpetuated in that of the Forest of Wyre, now remnant woodland found further to the north. The settlements took their names from the nature of the surrounding region, and several charters state specifically that some woods bore *léah* names: Mockley Wood in Arden was 'the old *léah*'; and both *ac wudu* and *pulle lea*, described in a boundary clause of Salwarpe, Worcestershire (Sawyer 1968, S 1596; Hooke 1990, 399), were stated to be woods. Wager's (1998) interpretation of *léah* as indicative of secondary woodland is not inconsistent with woodland used as wood-pasture, but only addresses a limited part of the evidence. In Domesday Book, the Latin terms *saltus*, *silva* or *silva pastilis* also appear to indicate wood-pasture.

Early medieval trees in the contemporary record

Largely as a diversion, I started some years ago to note every reference to specific species of trees in charters, place-names and early medieval literature, plotting them wherever they could be located; the results are interesting and this article only offers scope to gloss over them (for full discussion see Hooke forthcoming). Translation and interpretation are not always straightforward, for there are problems with the identification of some species and the apparent absence of others from the documentary record. Some species are poorly represented or have not been clearly identified, such as the sweet chestnut, known on Roman sites in southern England, the black poplar (*Populus nigra*), and the hornbeam (*Carpinus betulus*), although an unidentified *elebéam* is found in the charter-bounds of southern England and is unlikely to be the elder, as suggested by Rackham (1986, 211). Detailed study suggests that the *cwicbéam* was usually a reference to the rowan (*Sorbus aucuparia*).

Some species have restricted distributions: the box (*Buxus semervirens*), is virtually confined to the calcareous soils of southern England, and the beech (*Fagus sylvatica*), initially omitted from Rackham's lists because he had failed to recognise its Old English name, is commonest in Hampshire charters. The lime or linden (*Tilia cordata*), shows concentrations in its regional distribution: in Worcestershire, it occurs in wood-pasture regions like the north-east of the county, the Malvern area and on the margins of Wyre; in the Weald it is found in areas of seasonal pasture (as at Lindridge, Linhurst and Lindfield) and also in the New Forest of Hampshire (Lyndhurst and Linford, in Ringwood). Although Rackham (1990, 150, 174) has shown how, in Cambridgeshire, limes declined in wood-pasture regions, here the opposite seems to have been the case, for the species is still found in many of these regions today.

It is, however, the distribution of the oak and the ash which correlates most closely with the well-wooded regions of early medieval England and with the place-name term *léah*, and also with the hunting areas of Anglo-Saxon England and the area of Norman forest (Fig.

4). These were the characteristic trees of wood-pasture, the oak, especially, able to withstand the pressures of grazing and able to colonise grassland (Rackham 1980; Peterken 1993, 15-7). They were also often the dominant trees of the subsequent forests, and the concentration in the place-names and charters of Worcestershire and Hampshire fits well with the former having been some

40% wooded at the time of the Domesday survey (Rackham 1986, 50-1) and subsequently almost entirely designated as Norman forest, while almost all of Hampshire was also forested in medieval times. We can imagine a landscape with, in certain regions, much open grassland liberally scattered with woodland trees interspersed with patches of ancient woodland. The ash occurs in similar regions to the oak but is more frequent in a band across Somerset, west Berkshire and south Gloucestershire, regions where woodland was being actively assarted in the early medieval period (Hooke 1988, 141-6; 2003a; 2003b).

In charters, the oak, as the most economically useful tree, is of frequent occurrence, described as fair, elegant, tall, slender, broad, great or forked, or, alternatively, as crooked, bent-down or diseased; one as rough-barked, another smooth; one is described as green, another as red-leaved; some were named as 'boundary' oaks. The ash appears to have attracted fewer descriptive adjectives but could be described as old, ivy-covered, tall or broad. Both on occasion were referred to as 'holy', whatever that might signify. Whereas most of the oaks referred to were isolated specimens, more of the ashes were associated with topographical locations such as valleys, woods, springs, streams and rivers, as if frequent in such locations. Charter distribution is not ubiquitous and place-names help to extend the distribution further, beyond the range of the charters – into Herefordshire, for instance, for both the oak and ash as significant trees.

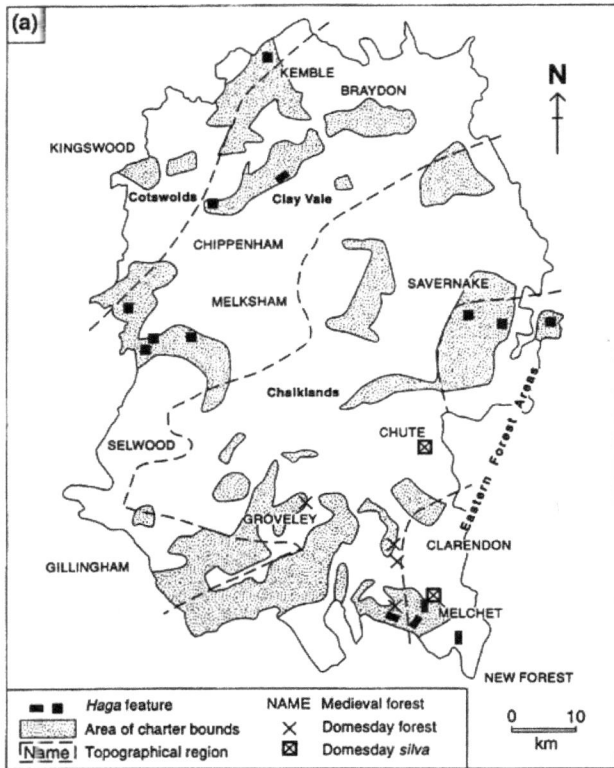

Figure 2a   Early medieval hunting areas and Norman forests: the incidence of the haga term shown against the location of medieval forests in Wiltshire (Hooke 1998b, 22, fig. 2.1a).

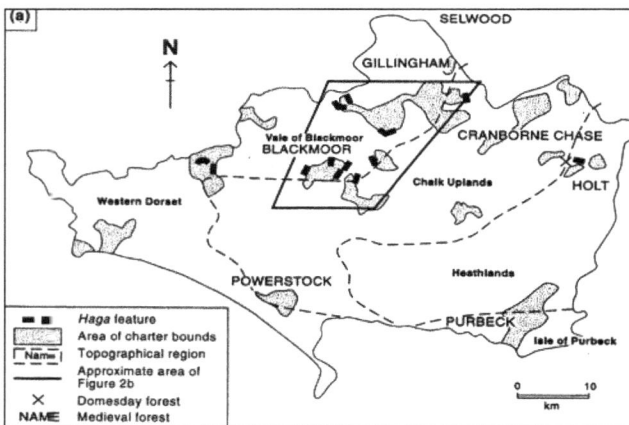

Figure 2b   The incidence of the 'haga' term shown against the location of medieval forests in Dorset (Hooke 1998b, 24, fig. 2.2a).

Many of the veteran oaks and ashes also survive in the same regions, occasionally on forest boundaries (the sad-fated Mawley Oak stands on the margins of Wyre) (Fig. 5). More often, they have survived as managed timber trees within medieval deer parks. Here they were often pollarded, which perpetuated their lives for hundreds of years. Some bear witness to former parks not found in the documentary record or hint at emparkment preceding that of a later designed parkland landscape, as at Cothelstone in Somerset. Parklands in effect perpetuated the wood-pasture landscape into medieval times when the more extensive marginal regions, including the Norman forests, were being assarted for expanding settlement. Some of the finest wood-pasture habitats can be found at Moccas in Herefordshire, where a designed parkland may have incorporated part of an earlier forest (Fig. 6), or in the unique landscape of Staverton Park in Suffolk, a park enclosed by the Earl of Norfolk in 1306 AD. Here the wood was established afresh in medieval times and the poor sandy soil kept the pollarded trees strangely small. Sutton Park near Birmingham partially preserves the open landscape of a once private chase; there are no ancient trees apart from some holly plantations, as all else was felled in the sixteenth century AD, the holly retained as a valuable fodder crop and now surviving as enormous trees. At the northern end of the Stiperstones in Shropshire, the old twisted hollies are also the remnants of an old wood-pasture 'forest'.

Close regional studies may have much to offer our understanding of landscape evolution. In the more remote areas to the west of the River Severn, along the western frontiers of the Hwiccan kingdom, an area within *Weogorena leah,* noted above, was granted to the church of Worcester in the eighth century AD as the estate of *Wican.* Hunting areas are recorded on the royal estates close to the western boundary but the area was also a known area of wood-pasture, used extensively for the seasonal pasturing of swine and other domestic stock. Several disputes occurred between the Crown and the Church in lands to the west of the River Severn over rights to swine pasture, but land at Bentley in *Weogorena leah* belonging to the Church was freed from pasturing the king's swine (a duty known as *fearnleswe* 'fernpasture') in AD 855 charters of this area, and today the area is particularly rich in oak and ash pollards that have survived not only in areas of former medieval parkland, but along field boundaries and trackways (Sawyer 1968, S 206; Hooke 1990). This may be a form of management inherited from medieval times but this, in turn, owes much to earlier usage. It is hoped that pollen samples may soon disclose greater evidence of early medieval land use in the area.

The iconography of trees
Very few trees standing today are likely to have been alive in the early medieval period. Limes may reproduce themselves almost indefinitely from an ancient root stock, and it has been suggested that those growing over Welshbury hill-fort in the Forest of Dean are growing from a root older than the hill-fort itself. Claims have been made for the antiquity of some oaks, and ancient oak pollards are a distinctive characteristic of old parkland and forest, but few, if any, are likely to go back to early medieval times: those found in Windsor Great Park, some of the oldest known today, may be at least 700 years old (ex. inf. T. Green), although a recent study of methods of aging oaks has concluded that '(l)arge, apparently old, trees...are often not as old as is frequently claimed for them' (Harris *et al.* 2003, 149). The yew is, however, a tree that can live for a very long time. It can also put out new growth after being severely pruned or even cut down – one of only a very few conifers with this ability. Perhaps because of this, this tree has been associated in ancient lore with notions of rebirth and regeneration, and seems to have been adopted into early Christianity from pre-Christian belief. Many may be of great age, like the ancient yew standing beside the church at Much Marcle in Herefordshire (Hooke forthcoming). Few other British trees are known to live for over a thousand years.

The traditional role of trees in a religious context is of particular interest, for they played an important role in much pre-Christian belief. In this country, this may be reflected in a number of *nemet-nemeton* place-names which appear to refer to a former 'sacred grove'. Some of these may derive from Roman usage: North Tawton in Devon may have been the site of the Roman fort known as *Nemeto Satio,* possibly 'sacred grove of Teutatis'; *Aquae Arnemetiae,* 'waters of Arnemetia', was the Roman name for Buxton in Derbyshire; *Vernemetum,*

'very sacred grove', was the name of the Roman settlement near Willoughby on the Wolds in Nottinghamshire. In Ireland, churches were established near the sites of sacred trees on several occasions: St. Patrick founded a church near the *Bile Tortan,* recorded in the eighth-century AD Book of Armagh (although at Armagh itself the sacred wood was burned). More often, churches and monasteries replaced sacred trees and groves, thus grafting Christianity onto an earlier faith. The name of Kildare, for instance, where St. Brigid established her monastery in the sixth century AD, means 'the church of the oak tree'. Springs were similarly to become associated with a Christian saint on numerous occasions: as symbols of purity they could not be ignored and could certainly not be destroyed. It is interesting to see how the early Christian church in Ireland was able to absorb pre-Christian beliefs in a much gentler manner than the Roman church that came to dominate in England. After the union of the Church in England, continuous edicts banning the worship of trees, springs, stones, etc., were issued right into the eleventh century AD and beyond.

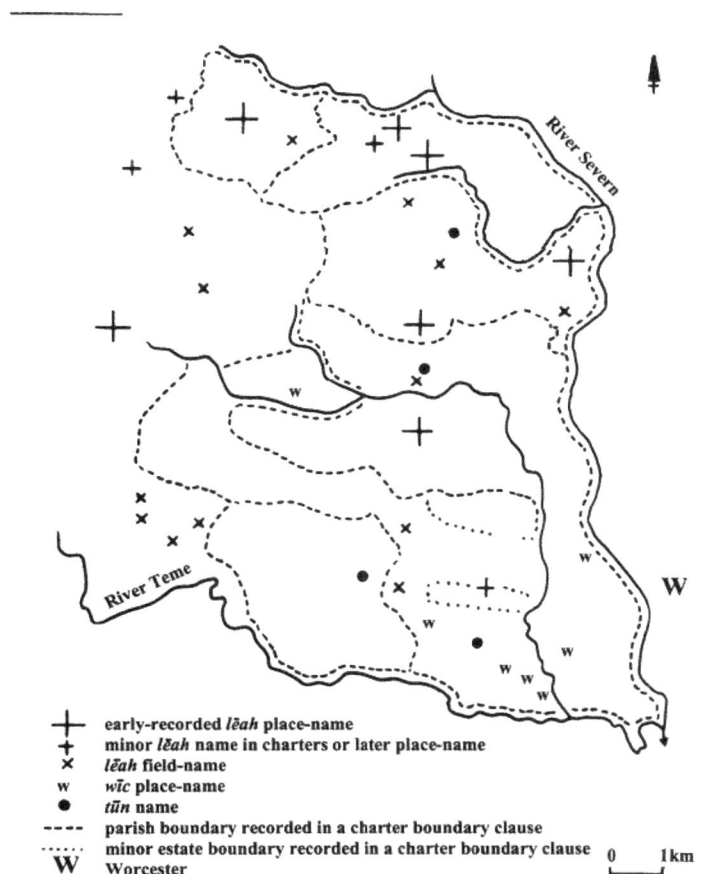

Figure 3 *'Léah' names in Weogorena leah (Worcs.). For clarity, the many topographical-type names have been omitted although 'wic' place-names, probably indicative of dairying centres, are shown. The number of 'tún' names, often indicative of new settlement and farming centres, are relatively few in number.*

There is a hint of earlier tree worship in a Somerset charter. A landmark on the boundary of Taunton estates was 'the holy ash', in a charter allegedly dating to AD 854 (Sawyer 1968, S 311). Although this occurs in a spurious charter that only survives in a twelfth-century AD manuscript, a second copy also refers to the 'ash-tree which the ignorant call holy'. The site seems to be Cat's Ash in Fitzhead parish close to the Quantock Hills. There are further charter references to 'holy oaks'. Although many of these bore crucifixes, probably carved into the trunk, they were not habitual features even on the boundaries of church estates. At Tardebigge in north Worcestershire there was one on each side of the parish and here the church was dedicated to St Bartholomew, the 'caster-out of devils' in Norman times.

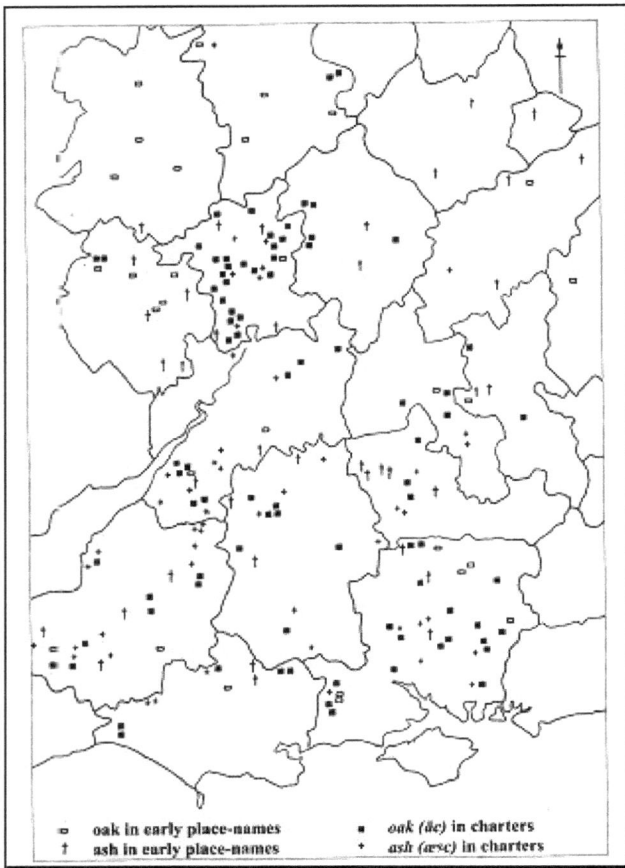

Figure 4   The distribution of oak and ash in the pre-Conquest place-names and charters of south-central England.

Trees were frequently used as boundary landmarks in the boundary clauses that accompanied many pre-Conquest charters, intended to act as markers defining the extent of an estate. The references are often to a tree associated with a particular named individual and these often stood beside roads, presumably referring to a local landowner. Other trees often stood at points along a boundary where they would have been particularly obvious. The ubiquitous thorn is the commonest kind of tree noted, but thorns grew readily on abandoned or neglected corners of land and may have been particularly obvious in open cultivated areas close to estate boundaries. In Worcestershire many were associated with headlands and corners of arable fields in the more intensively cultivated parts of the county, such as the Vale of Evesham.

In a similar way, trees often marked important central points, such as the meeting places of hundreds. Langtree Hundred in Gloucestershire is likely to have taken its name from a tall tree that grew on the high ground of the Chavenage Downs near the road between Avening and Tetbury. Other hundreds named after trees include *Cuferdestroua* (Cullifordtree) in Dorset and *Winburgetrowe* (Wimburntree) in Worcestershire, but it was the thorn tree that was most often singled out for such a purpose, giving its name to the hundreds of *Celfledetorn*, 'Céolflæds' thorn-tree' (Gloucestershire), *Goderonestona*, Godderthorn (Dorset), *Cicimethorn*, 'the thorn-tree of the dwellers at Chedglow' (Wiltshire), *Blakethorna*, 'the black thorn' (lost, in Somerset) and *Nachededorn*, 'the bare thorn-tree' (Berkshire). Near Burton upon Trent, in Staffordshire, a thorn tree marked another significant site where justice was meted out: *þan þorne þer ða þeofes licga*, 'the thorn where the thieves lie', or the point *þær þa ðeofes hangað on middan bere fordes holme*, 'where the thieves hang in the middle of barley ford island' (Sawyer 1968, S 920, S 930; Hooke 1983, 93-101); this stood beside a major route-way running eastwards from Burton. The iconography of the thorn tree obviously merits further enquiry (Hooke forthcoming).

Trees in early medieval literature and legend
Early Irish poetry reveals a love of nature that was never stifled: we hear how the hermit Marban loved his 'bothy in the wood', shaded by an ash, a hazel, yew, oak, apple etc. (Lehmann 1982, 43-44). There is no Germanic fear of woods in early Irish verse: 'The woodland thicket overtops me, the blackbird sings me a lay ...Well do I write under the forest wood'. In Old English literature, however, much of which is dominated by the hand of the Roman church, nature finds little expression. An interest in nature in 'this middle-earth' was deliberately stifled by the Christian church, with an insistence that it was the afterlife that mattered most (Neville 1999). At this stage, anyway, untamed nature represented a fearful wilderness, a place of insecurity and danger, more the place to test hermits and saints. Those references to trees that do occur are usually embodied within the scriptures: Cedars of Lebanon, for instance, thorns signifying travail, and the 'life tree' that destroyed Adam and Eve. The real sacred living tree is replaced by the dead cross, although to the early Christians this was the greatest honour that could befall any tree, a concept that is expressed in The Dream of the Rood.

Figure 5   The end of the Mawley Oak, Shropshire. Located on the western edge of the Wyre Forest, this old tree was damaged by a storm a few years ago.

Figure 6   Pollard oaks in parkland: Moccas Park, Herefordshire.

Trees and woodland in later iconography

In later periods, forests and woodlands continued to play a significant role in the iconography of landscape. Forests, established by the time of the Domesday survey but extended greatly by the early Norman kings, were not only involved in the complicated ritual of the hunt but were the training ground for those knightly pursuits essential for the protection of the realm. They were, on the other hand, the abode of those who rebelled against the rules of society, of outlaws and poachers. Individual trees continued to play a role as boundary markers (estates, forests, etc.), but were also to remain features of legend and ritual. Yews continued to be both preserved and planted in churchyards while other trees remained associated with the occult or with healing and fertility. Ash and rowan were thought to offer protection against witchcraft and the Devil, while the elder was believed to be the favourite tree of witches, and sometimes to be the transformed witch herself. The healing properties of willow were known, if misunderstood (salicin, an extract of willow bark, can be used to treat rheumatic fever, but it was the tendency for willows to grown in damp places

that linked them to the 'shivering disease' of rheumatism) (Wilks 1972, 125). The various 'marriage oaks', visited after wedding, may betray an association of trees with fertility, but the antiquity of such lore cannot be guaranteed, given the fashion of invoking so-called 'ancient traditions' that has recurred throughout history. Many trees, too, became associated with famous or royal personages, while others gained fame as 'hanging trees', a use to which some were undoubtedly put – the dool, or grief trees of Scotland were used as gibbets by the barons to hang their enemies. Henry VIII is said to have hung various church leaders on trees for failing to acknowledge his supremacy; other rebels were hung during the Bloody Assizes in the seventeenth century AD, and highwaymen frequently suffered a similar fate (*ibid.* 73-86).

Today, trees and woodland enjoy a renewed interest in the eyes of conservationists, preserved not only for their cultural associations but also their ecological benefits, which include helping to absorb pollution and providing habitats for wildlife. It is a professed government aim to extend the acreage under woodland enormously over the next few decades in Britain. A new 'national forest' now links what is left of the old woodlands of Needwood in Staffordshire with those of Charnwood in Leicestershire, incorporating areas degraded by coal mining and industry; new 'Community Forests' are being planted around urban conurbations; agricultural schemes encourage additional tree planting on farmland. 'Veteran' trees are recognised as being of special interest, both culturally and ecologically, and registers of these are being compiled by such bodies as The Woodland Trust; hopefully these trees will soon enjoy the status of monuments and buildings in being worthy of special protection. Public taste has also moved on: far from seeing woods as dark and dangerous places, inhabited in the mind's eye by threatening supernatural creatures or dangerous folk, woods are now increasingly seen as places of mental relaxation and healing, and few would dispute the beauty of a growing, living tree.

Endnotes
[1] Such links are recorded, however, in early charters: although a charter linking Shottery, an estate in the central Avon valley of Warwickshire (Sawyer 1968: S 64), with woodland in Arden may be spurious rather than an authentic charter of AD 699x709, Kelly (1994: 47) believes that this was forged, probably in the eighth century, upon the basis of a genuine early Mercian charter.

Bibliography
Attenborough, F.L. 1922. *The Laws of the Earliest English Kings*. Cambridge: Cambridge University Press.

Beckett, S.C. and Hibbert, F.A. 1979. Vegetational change and the influence of prehistoric man in the Somerset Levels. *New Phytologist* 83, 577-600.

Chambers, F.M., Mauquoy, D. and Todd, P.A. 1999. Recent rise to dominance of *Molinia caerulea* in environmentally sensitive areas: new perspectives from palaeoecological data. *Journal of Applied Ecology* 36, 719-33.

Columella, L.J.M. *Res rustica.* On Agriculture. Ed. and trans by H.B. Ash 1941. London: Loeb Classical Library.

Dark, P. 2000. *The Environment of Britain in the First Millennium A.D.* London: Duckworth.

Evans, J.G. 1999. *Land and Archaeology. Histories of Human Environment in the British Isles.* Stroud: Tempus.

Everitt, A. 1986. *Continuity and Colonization: the Evolution of Kentish Settlement.* Leicester: Leicester University Press.

Ford. W.J. 1976. Settlement patterns in the central region of the Warwickshire Avon. In Sawyer, P.H. (ed.) *Medieval Settlement: Continuity and Change*, 274-94. London: Edward Arnold.

Fox, C. 1932. *The Personality of Britain.* Cardiff: National Museum of Wales.

Fox, H. 1989. The people of the Wolds in English settlement history. In Aston, M. Austin D. and Dyer C. (eds.) *The Rural Settlements of Medieval England*, 77-101. Oxford: Blackwell.

Gelling, M. 1984. *Place-names in the Landscape.* London: Dent.

Greig, J. 2005. Pollen and waterlogged seeds. In Jones, A. 'Roman Birmingham 2 Excavations at Metchley Roman Forts 1998-2000 and 2002'. *Transactions of the Birmingham and Warwickshire Archaeological Society* 108, 76-81.

Harris, E., Harris, J. and James, N.D.G. 2003. *Oak. A British History.* Macclesfield: Windgather Press.

Higham, N. 1992. *Rome, Britain and the Anglo-Saxons.* London: Seaby.

Hodder, K.H., Buckland, P.C., Kirby, K.J. and Bullock, J.M. 2009. Can the pre-Neolithic provide suitable models for re-wilding the landscape in Britain? *British Wildlife* (supp. edn, June), 4-15.

Hodder, M. 2004. *Birmingham. The Hidden History.* Stroud: Tempus.

Hooke, D. 1978. Early Cotswold woodland. *Journal of Historical Geography* 4, 333-41.

Hooke, D. 1983. *The Landscape of Anglo-Saxon Staffordshire: The Charter Evidence.* Keele: University of Keele Department of Adult Education.

Hooke, D. 1985. *The Anglo-Saxon Landscape: The Kingdom of the Hwicce.* Manchester: Manchester University Press.

Hooke, D. 1988. Regional variation in southern and central England in the Anglo-Saxon period and its relationship to land units and settlement. In Hooke, D., (ed.) *Anglo-Saxon Settlements*, 123-52. Oxford: Blackwell.

Hooke, D. 1989. Pre-Conquest woodland: its distribution and usage. *Agricultural History Review* 37, 113-29.

Hooke, D. 1990. *Worcestershire Anglo-Saxon Charterbounds.* Woodbridge: Boydell Press.

Hooke, D. 1998a. *The Landscape of Anglo-Saxon England.* London: Leicester University Press.

Hooke, D. 1998b. Medieval forests and parks in southern and central England. In Watkins, C. (ed.) *European Woods and Forests: Studies in Cultural History*, 19-32. Wallingford: CABI.

Hooke, D. 2003a. Trees in the Anglo-Saxon landscape: the charter evidence. In Biggam C.P. (ed.) *From Earth to Art: 1739.* Amsterdam: Rodopi.

Hooke, D. 2003b. The distribution of the oak and the ash in early medieval England. In *Wood-Pasture and Parkland Habitat Action Plan*, 24-30. English Nature Research Report No. 539. Peterborough: English Nature.

Hooke, D. 2008. Early medieval woodland and the place-name term *lēah*. In Padel, O.J. and Parsons, D.N. (eds.) *A Commodity of Good Names. Essays in Honour of Margaret Gelling*, 365-76. Donington: Shaun Tyas.

Hooke, D. Forthcoming. *Trees in Anglo-Saxon England: Literature, Lore and Landscape.* Woodbridge: Boydell Press.

Johansson, C. 1975. *Old English Place-names and Field-names Containing Lēah.* Stockholm: Almqvist and Wiksell International.

Kirby, K. 2004. A model of a natural wooded landscape in Britain driven by large herbivore activity. *Forestry* 77, 405-20.

Klingelhöfer, E. 1992. *Manor, Vill and Hundred. The Development of Rural Institutions in Early Medieval Hampshire.* Studies & Texts 112. Toronto: Pontifical Institute of Mediaeval Studies.

Lehmann, R.P. (trans. and ed.) 1982. *Early Irish Verse.* Austin: University of Texas Press.

Miles, D. (ed.) 1986. *Archaeology at Barton Court Farm, Abingdon, Oxon.* London: Oxford Archaeological Unit and Council for British Archaeology.

Neville, J. 1999. *Representations of the Natural World in Old English Poetry.* Cambridge: Cambridge University Press.

Peterken. G.F. 1993. *Woodland Conservation and Management.* London: Chapman and Hall.

Rackham, O. 1980. *Ancient Woodland: Its History, Vegetation and Uses in England.* London: Edward Arnold.

Rackham, O. 1986. *The History of the Countryside.* London: Dent.

Rackham, O. 1990. *Trees and Woodland in the British Landscape.* Revised edition. London: Phoenix.

Rackham, O. 1998. Savanna in Europe. In Kirby, K.J. and Watkins, C. (eds.) *The Ecological History of European Forests*, 124. Wallingford: CABI.
Sawyer, P.H. 1968. *Anglo-Saxon Charters: An Annotated List and Bibliography.* London: Royal Historical Society.

Swanton, M. (Trans. and ed.). 1996. *The Anglo-Saxon Chronicle.* London: Dent.

Thomas, J.A. and Elms, G.W. 1998. Higher productivity at the cost of increased host-specificity when Maculinea butterfly larvae exploit ant colonies through trophallaxis rather than by predation. *Ecological Entomology* 23, 457-64.

Thorpe, H. 1971. Historical geography, the evolution of settlement and land use. In Cadbury, D.A., Hawkes, J.G. and Readett, R.C. *A Computer-mapped Flora: A Study of the County of Warwickshire*, 20-44. London: Academic Press.

Trier, J. 1963. *Venus: Etymologien um das Futterlaub.* Münstersche Forschungen 15. Münster/Koln: Böhlau Verlag.

Vera, F.W.M. 2000. *Grazing Ecology and Forest History.* Wallingford: CABI.

Wager, S.J. 1998. *Woods, Wolds and Groves: The Woodland of Medieval Warwickshire.* British Archaeological Reports British Series 269. Oxford: British Archaeological Reports.

Walker, M.F. and Taylor, J.A 1976. Post-Neolithic vegetation changes in the western Rhinogau, Gwynedd, northwest Wales. *Transactions of the Institute of British Geographers (new series)* 1, 323-45.

Waton, P.V. 1982. Man's impact on the chalklands: some new pollen evidence. In Bell, M. and Limbrey, S. (eds.) *Archaeological Aspects of Woodland Ecology*, 75-91. British Archaeological Reports International Series 146. Oxford: British Archaeological Reports.

Waton, P.V. 1983. *A Palynological Study of the Impact of Man on the Landscape of Central Southern England, with Special Reference to the Chalklands.* Unpublished PhD thesis, University of Southampton.

Wilks, J.H. 1972. *Trees of the British Isles in History and Legend.* London: Frederick Muller.

Wetting the fringe of your habit: medieval monasticism and coastal lifescapes

Joe Flatman

Introduction
This paper is ostensibly concerned with questions of environment and landscape: specifically, the coastal environment, and its exploitation by monastic communities, including monastic familiarity with the sea and the maritime world, and exploitation of marine resources in light of recent archaeological fieldwork around the coastline of Britain. However, what is also considered is how the art, archaeology and literature of one specific sector of medieval society (monastic communities, especially the Cistercians) in one particular sector of the medieval landscape, the coast, reflect deeper and more widely-rooted medieval views of water, including its types, uses and meaning in Christian allegory, and the conceptual differences between fresh vs. salt water. This is a search through our physical explorations for an understanding of how people perceived the maritime 'landscape' of the Middle Ages, travelled around the coastline, used and 'felt' about this zone.

Monasticism and coastal communities
A concern with the emotional characteristics of the medieval coastline is unashamedly influenced by developments in prehistoric archaeology over the past decade, which have profoundly changed our understanding of how ancient societies viewed the coast and the sea. The concept of the phenomenology of land-, life- and sea-scape is central to this (Tilley 1991; 1994; Ingold 1993; 2000), how people perceived of and moved through specific environments, and also how they went about situating major monuments, particularly coastal rock and monumental 'art' (Bradley 1997; Henderson 2000; Housley and Coles 2003). Within the specialised community of maritime archaeology, such concerns are best encapsulated in the term 'maritime cultural landscape', those distinctive characteristics that mark out a maritime sphere of influence both near and far from the sea, real and imagined (Helskog 1985; Westerdahl 1992; Jasinski 1993; Crumlin-Pedersen and Munch-Thye 1995; Hingley 1996; Kaul 1998; Helskog 1999; Parker 2001).

The closest that studies of the medieval world have come to such considerations of 'marine spiritual locale' are through the works of scholars such as Roberta Gilchrist (1994 1995), who has explored the issue of monastic involvement in marginal wetland environments. The clear evidence of such marshland areas being liminal zones of one kind or another in prehistory (Van de Noort and O'Sullivan 2006, 55-59), together with archaeological and documentary evidence from the Middle Ages, has been taken to imply a similarly marginal, liminal role at this time. Wetlands appear to have been particularly associated with the topographic seclusion of nunneries and female recluses in this period (such as Crabhouse in Norfolk, Denney in Cambridgeshire, and Minster in Sheppey in Kent), a result of the perceived similarities between such locations and the innate characteristics of women. Gilchrist also notes that many nunneries placed their churches to the south end of the cloister, linked to a view of women as phlegmatic, watery and fluid in nature (from Galenic medicine), and in need of an invigorating north wind (Gilchrist 1994, 64-9; 1995, 115-18, 157-62; see also Ballantyne 2004).

There has also been considerable discussion of the phenomenon of island and promontory hermitages within early Christian 'Celtic' monasticism, ever since E.G. Bowen and O.G.S. Crawford first raised such issues (e.g. Bowen 1934; 1944; 1954; 1968; 1968-69; 1969; 1970; 1972a; 1972b; Crawford 1936, recently the subject of reassessment by Cunliffe 2001; Charles-Edwards 1976; 1984; Cramp 1973; 1981). These discussions include the consideration of sea journeys and island settlement as forms of desert community, both real and spiritual. Being on an island, it is argued, allows one both to separate one's spiritual life from the sins of the world, and also to combat evil within the world. To this can be added considerable historical discussion about the major 'Celtic' saints, brethren and their lives, such as Brendan, Patrick, Cuthbert, Samson and Columba (Chadwick 1961; Bullough 1965; Thomas 1978; Bourgeault 1983; MacDonald 1984; Bonner et al. 1995; McCarthy and Breen 1997; O'Sullivan 2001).

Islands occupied by monastic communities in this sense encapsulate the spiritual and ideological battle against evil, an important focus of early Christian doctrine (Hughes 1960; Burn 1969; Herity 1977; Thomas 1978; Cramp 1981). Most of the coastal locations in north-western Europe settled by monastic groups are both remote and exposed, and the ability to reach, settle and 'control' such harsh landscapes became a way of 'winning' the battle against evil at an elemental level, as expressed most dramatically at sites such as the island hermitage of Skellig Michael off southwest Ireland. However, on a more practical level, an understanding of and familiarity with the marine environment is crucial to survival in such conditions. Life under such circumstances requires an intimate knowledge of the marine environment and also maritime technology, and sources such as Adamnan's *Vita Columbae* present an image of a well-adapted maritime community attuned to both the sea and land environment and the island's resources (Anderson and Anderson 1991). Similar technical information, together with a wonderful amount of environmental detail and geographical knowledge, comes from both the ninth century AD *Vita sancti Brendani* as well as the tenth century *Navigatio sancti Brendani* (Marcus 1951; 1953-54; 1954; McGrail 1989; Schnall 1989; Sneddon 2001; Wooding 2001).

The shift from 'Celtic' to 'Roman' monasticism witnessed a marked change in critical debate on the subject of monastic spiritual engagement with the coastal environment. The considerations of, for instance, O'Loughlin (1996; 1997) on monastic perception of the coasts in relation to their spiritual identity are simply absent for this later period. Partly this lack of attention is undoubtedly a response to altered monastic priorities in the period; maintaining and adopting Classical models of water management known from sources such as Vitruvius and Frontius, the origins of High Medieval monasticism arguably led to an institutional preoccupation with the supply of fresh water to the new range of inland monasteries, as stressed in the Benedictine rule. This turn away from the analysis of coastal monastic settlement is also undoubtedly influenced by the types of archaeological and iconographic materials available, both of which favour inland sites; no major coastal monastery has been subjected to the sorts of sustained investigation witnessed by countless inland houses, and for many coastal houses scanty records exist, or such records have simply not been subjected to modern inquiry – although one notable exception is arguably Tintern Abbey, Co. Wexford, southern Ireland, where excavation took place throughout the 1980s and early 1990s (see Lynch 2003; Bennett 2005).

It is only really D.H. Williams' analyses of the impact of the Cistercians in Wales that provide a full appreciation of the overall range of maritime activities in which High Medieval monasteries could become involved (Williams 1976; 1990; 2001). Taking Williams' work alongside the sporadic evidence within general syntheses such as Aston (1993), Gilchrist and Mytum (1989; 1993), Greene (1995), Aston *et al.* (2001) and Bond (2000; 2003), as well as the distribution data available from the Ordnance Survey (1954; 1955), Easson's (1957), Knowles and Hadcock's (1971) and Gwynn's (1970) surveys of High Medieval monastic houses, and documentary records, especially of finances (Snape 1926), what becomes clear is the number of monastic houses either on or near the coast or maintaining coastal properties, their breadth of distribution around the British coast, and above all the sheer range of maritime activities in which these houses were involved. On broad-based consideration, if one looks at where people were working and living, what they were doing and how they believed and perceived in the High, compared to the Early Middle Ages, then it is clear that as regards the coastline, things had changed very little: there may have been more people on and around the coast, but their behaviour had not altered radically. Modern scholarship has chosen to sideline such activities, rather than such activities being absent.

The medieval Church and water

If monastic communities were hard at work exploiting the resources of the rivers and coasts of Britain, then a survey of a series of very different sources brings up an interesting contradiction: monastic houses appear to have been operating in the coastal zone under strict theological constraints, driven as much by spiritual motives as economic impetuses. *Fresh* water, and by default springs, streams, rivers and lakes, in medieval Christian literature and the arts is entirely associated with positive connotations, including life, birth and baptism, sustenance and redemption (Foot 1992; Collins 1995; Rattue 1995). In comparison, *salt* water, and by default the seas and oceans, is usually associated with, or directly analogous to, some of the most negative of connotations and/or marginality in the available sources (Flint 1984; Borsje 1994; 1996; 1997; 1999; Wright 2001). The seas and oceans are at best akin to deserts, at worst, the realm of Satan, and are thus at the forefront of the battle between Christianity and the devil. This places zones like the coastline, the literal boundary between 'good' (land, fresh water) and 'evil' (sea, salt water), at the spiritual battlefront (O'Loughlin 1997, 13). Examples of the positive connotations of fresh water abound in the Bible and biblical commentaries[1]. Examples of the negative connotations of salt/sea water are similarly legion (Thimmes 1992)[2], and this ambiguity is reflected extensively in surviving iconography. Illuminated manuscripts, for example, tend to depict only ambiguous situations and events in relation to biblical imagery[3]. There is also allied evidence from other sources of the ambiguity of the seas and oceans, such as various attempts by religious communities in this period to 'control' an otherwise marginal and unconstrained environment, including the Church focus on laws of the sea, and the provision of coastal lights, chantries and chapels (Wright 1967; Hague and Christie 1975, 14-20).

There is an extremely ambiguous relationship within the whole of Judaeo-Christian cosmology towards salt water and the seas; this is quite simply a philosophy which does not understand, nor fully trust, the seas and oceans. Such ambiguity is consistently represented in textual and iconographic sources, but so far has been virtually ignored within archaeological analyses. There is also a tendency to downplay this negativity because of the growing exploitation and manipulation of the maritime zone in the High Middle Ages, but exploitation and familiarity do not necessarily imply positive emotion. If one considers Christian maritime iconography in comparison to the maritime iconography of the pre-Christian era of northwest Europe and Scandinavia (Crumlin-Pedersen and Munch-Thye 1995; Kaul 1998), this deep-seated ambiguity becomes extremely clear. Prehistoric and immediately pre-Christian pagan society is full of strong, pro-sea/ocean messages and imagery relating the seas and oceans to evocations of loyalty, competence and trust, power (both figurative and literal power), status and membership, movement/transference, altered states and rites-of-passage, especially birth and death, and more ephemerally, broad-based cultural definition through, for instance, ostentatious display of 'maritime' attributes. Christian imagery does none of these things, and instead sends a consistent message of a desire to control, channel and conquer the seas as an unrelenting, unremitting and cunning enemy, both literally and figuratively, to gain redemption, salvation or rescue from the sea, or else the corollary of this, the inevitable destiny of sinners being to fall prey to the temptations and depths of the sea as a version of hell. All of these negative messages come in comparison to the life-giving properties of fresh, inland waters and are made clear through a startlingly broad array of textual and iconographic sources.

The High Middle Ages also witnessed a serious concern with 'purposeless' travel, exemplified in the medieval monastic mind as the life of the *gyrovagi*, tempted by *curiositas*. From the earliest times, the temptation of *curiositas*, any morally excessive and suspect interest in observing the world, seeking novel experiences or acquiring knowledge for its own sake, was warned against. For medieval monastics in particular, individuals known as *gyrovagi* were symbolic of this instability of mind and body, 'slaves to their own wills and to the enticements of gluttony'. The world outside that of the *gyrovagi* offered temptations, but threats also of disorder and waywardness (Constable 1976; 1979; 1988; Caner 2002 Dietz 2004; 2005). Aquinas, Bernard and Augustine, among many others, habitually describe *curiositas* as a kind of wandering, manifesting a deep-set inability to observe an established spiritual and social order. *Gyrovagi* exemplify this sort of restless instability, exhibited in travelling, gossiping and tale-telling. Curiosity in this sense is seen as a morally useless exercise, contributing nothing to human progress toward heavenly wisdom.

However, as early as the twelfth century AD it is clear that the amassed responsibilities of large-scale monasticism were felt to be seriously weakening monastic adherence to the root principle of *stabilitas*, promoting renewed anxiety about the dangers of *curiositas*. In his *Steps of Humility and Pride* (*c.* 1125), Bernard repeats Benedictine Rule in the twelve steps a monk must climb to reach the Knowledge of Truth: *curiositas* is the first critical step down in the descent towards pride, and Bernard devotes more space and polemic to it than to any of the other eleven stages. The expanding opportunities offered by 'purposeful', sanctioned travel such as pilgrimage, the scores of 'travel' books, logs, guides and accounts, itineraries, pilgrim songs and narrative poems of the High Middle Ages, all reflect an increasingly contradictory interplay between the impulses of life and literature, the itch to explore (the vice of *curiositas*) versus the sanctioned practice of pilgrimage. By the late Middle Ages, despite the Church's warnings, the older set of assumptions about the fearful seductiveness of the visible world was undoubtedly giving way before strong new feelings, a new 'search for a common world', the world of physical nature, a naturalistic, scientific attitude emerging out of the twelfth century, resurrected since the early Church Fathers separated wisdom and human knowledge.

Building on the work of earlier monastic observers such as Aldhelm and Bede (Cameron 1985; Stevens 1986; Low 2002), this growth in 'landscape knowledge' and 'landscape learning' is reflected by authors such as Gerald of Wales' theories on location of *Ultima Thule* (Holmes 1936), observers of local flora and fauna, winds and tides, routes and ways (also seen in Robert Grosseteste's *Optics* and his fascination with natural phenomena in *De Natura Locorum*) (Eastwood 1968), and Geoffrey of Monmouth's and Walter Map's explorations of the countryside, observing flora and marvels. Adelard of Bath, Daniel of Morley (Silverstein 1948) and Alfred of Shareshill also join this group, a unique, and uniquely English, group of 'scientists' of the twelfth century, concerned in particular with natural observation, the nature of earthly things and astronomy (Wright 1923; Grinell 1946; Gransden 1972; Burnett 1995). Religious communities of this period also demonstrate a marked proclivity towards, for want of a better term, 'map'-making and the 'iconography of landscape', maps as cultural representations coloured by ideological discourse, and influenced by multiple levels of meaning through medieval hermeneutical ideals, and analogies in texts to the visual structure of maps. Numerous visual exegetical schemes in written forms of *mappae mundi* were produced in this period, with implicit references to a '*sensus spiritualis*' and geographical elements in visually mapped *mappae mundi* (Hooglviet 2000).

Such concepts are most elegantly reflected in the illustrated chronicles of Matthew Paris (*c.* 1236-59), a piece of 'performance art' giving the dynamic setting of an 'imagined pilgrimage' to Jerusalem (Connolly 1999). Paris' views show a profound understanding of the relative perspective of space, as in Ingold's (2000) models of taskscape: Paris' are very specific views of space, place and locus from 'within' the world, a 'dwelling perspective' of the landscape as a record of and testimony to the lives and works of past generations. Paris' and others' views have, in turn, major implications for our understanding of medieval coastal resource use and travel through, across and along the coastal zone. In travelling, and particularly in thinking about travelling, medieval society made an important cognitive leap with profound implications for the understanding and exploitation of the coastline. This apparently inconsequential step impacted upon not only the concept of 'cultural landscapes' and the phenomenology of landscape, but the depiction of landscapes and movement in the medieval arts, and the 'art' of wayfinding and *real* movement (Woodward 1985; Kupfer 1994; Hoogvliet 2000; Lozovsky 2000; Klein 2003).

Reassessing the monastic coast of Britain
Archaeological evidence indisputably demonstrates sustained monastic intervention in the coastal zone of northwest Europe from the early medieval period onwards. This is not contested here. What is contested is the motivation behind such intervention: why monasteries were on the coast in the first place. What is suggested is

that the archaeological evidence for settlement location can be juxtaposed with contemporaneous documentary and iconographic evidence for an involvement in the coastal zone borne not from a purely positive if utilitarian economic impetus as usually assumed, but rather from a far more ambiguous and negative impetus, part of a long-running spiritual battle in which the coastline was the 'front line' in the battle between good and evil. It is suggested that the economic benefit of coastal locations, while recognised, was not the primary motivation of monastic involvement in the coastal zone. The desire to place monasteries in a marginal, liminal coastal zone was, rather, a product of an emphasis in both existing biblical texts and interpretations, and also new theological works, that perceived of the coastal zone as the literal boundary on earth between good and evil, God and the Devil, reflected in perceptions of fresh-water as good, positive, and sea-water as bad, negative. Exploitation of this zone, both through reactive industries such as fishing and mining, and proactive industries such as farming, milling and land-reclamation, may have made good economic sense, but it also made good spiritual sense as well. What this amounts to is a challenge to reassess our entire understanding of how medieval society felt about the coastline, perceived it, and went about operating within and along the coast, a *cognition* of the medieval coastline. It is argued here that monasteries were consciously placed on the high ground immediately adjacent to or even alongside intertidal coastal zones to offer both offence and defence against the forces of evil. This idea places a totally different understanding upon all monastic activities along the coast, particularly along the immediate foreshore, literally the front line of the battle. The entire nature of medieval coastal exploitation has to be reassessed under such circumstances, including:

1. Type of activities/exploitation of the foreshore: are activities proactive or reactive? (including land reclamation, drainage, fish-traps, lighthouses, sea-defences and dykes, etc.

2. Localised location of activities: are activities in sight of the sea or hidden away? On the foreshore, just inland, or at 'transference locations' such as watersheds, tidal limits, river mouths, etc.?

3. Relative locations of major coastal features such as monastic precincts (including regional gaps).

4. Relationship of coastal monasteries to hinterlands, routes and connections, including connected river routes like the Severn, Thames and Humber, in relation to inland properties with coastal estates, granges and rights, etc.

5. Precinct placement: where is the precinct placed in coastal monasteries – within sight of the sea on a natural rise in the land or a cliff, etc., or hidden from sight of the sea? Does the precinct look out towards the sea, or inwards to the land? How does this layout relate to sources of fresh-water such as wells, streams or springs?

6. Environment and topography: what types of coastline are activities taking place on: low-energy coasts like estuaries, marshes, etc. with large expanses of inter-tidal foreshore, or high-energy coasts like rocky or cliff-fronted areas with a limited foreshore?

7. Dates, phasing and sequence of monastic coastal settlement.

8. Comparison to lay estates on the coast.

9. Variation between different monastic groups such as the Cistercians and Benedictines.

A range of examples exists of monastic precincts that fit the broad pattern proposed here, and four case studies can be chosen that combine both archaeological and documentary evidence with variations on the theme of a tidal locale as a spiritual conflict zone: Beaulieu in Hampshire, Quarr on the Isle of Wight, Abbotsbury in Dorset, and Greyabbey in Northern Ireland. Considering the immediate environment of the precincts of each of these houses, what is notable is that, while their locations all meet the standard monastic preoccupation with a well-drained site and plentiful fresh water, these sites also meet a series of spiritual objectives along the foreshore:

- all are within immediate sight of the foreshore;
- the foreshore is low-lying with a high tidal range – at low tide are expanses of mudflats;
- there is a tidal (brackish) river or creek nearby; and
- there is fresh water, which is manipulated or otherwise managed.

Beaulieu, Hampshire
At Beaulieu (Cistercian, founded *c.* 1203 AD), Hockey (1975) provides details of the annual account for 1269-70 that includes the year's income and expenditure for each grange, manor, department and workshop, interspersed with rules and tables for checking each account at audit. This includes records of the abbey's ship *La Stelle*, the house's flock of over five thousand sheep, and its involvement in the international wool trade, as well as the forester's accounts for the production of vine stakes, which further implies involvement in the international wine trade. There are also substantial details of the numerous fishing rights along the Beaulieu River, as well as operations at its fishing bases established in the thirteenth century at Northtown, Yarmouth on the Isle of Wight, and at Porthoustock, St. Keverne in Cornwall.

The monastic precinct lay at the head of the tidal Beaulieu River (Fig. 1), which reveals wide mudflats and reed beds at low tide. The abbey precinct sits alongside a sluice at the head of the tidal portion off the river, the sluice controlling the damned Palace Lake, assumed to have originally been one or more fishponds servicing the abbey. Archaeological investigations by the University of Southampton over the 1990s revealed a wealth of materials in and along the river from both the High Middle Ages and the early and post-medieval periods, including substantial inter-tidal and underwater remains associated with the management and exploitation of the river and its hinterland (Adams 1994).

Figure 1   Map of the immediate modern surroundings of Beaulieu Abbey.

Quarr, Isle of Wight

At Quarr (Cistercian, founded *c.* 1131-32), Hockey (1970) provides documentary evidence for the Cistercian role on the foreshore after the arrival of the founding community from Savigny. This includes details of the abbey's ownership as well as leasing of ships, its significant imports of wine, and its fisheries, including both those immediately adjacent to the precinct on Wooton Creek as well as further afield, such as off Hayling Island in Langstone harbour. Before 1300 AD the abbey acquired a 'salt pit in a marsh' in Lymington, and Quarr is also known to have owned a warehouse in Portsmouth, a merchant's house in Southampton, property in Honfleur and wharves at Great Yarmouth, together with mills at Christchurch and Holdenhurst, as well as a tide mill adjacent to the precinct at the mouth of Wooton Creek on the Isle of Wight, and an undershot fulling mill at Heasley on the Isle of Wight, built shortly before the end of the twelfth century.

As can be seen in Fig. 2, the monastic precinct lay adjacent to the tidal Wooton Creek, and within sight of the foreshore of the Solent, both of which reveal a substantial muddy foreshore at low tide. Archaeological investigations by the University of Southampton over the 1990s revealed a wealth of material in both Wotton Creek and along the foreshore, from not only the High Middle Ages, but also from the early and post-medieval periods and also prehistory, including substantial inter-tidal and underwater remains associated with the management and exploitation of both the creek and foreshore and their hinterland, including at least one fish-trap (Sly and Clark 1997; see also Stone 1891).

Abbotsbury, Dorset

At Abbotsbury (Benedictine, founded *c.* 1024-26 AD? Re-founded *c.* 1044 AD?), portions of various pre-Conquest documents survive. Following the dissolution of the abbey in 1539 AD, its estates and muniments were acquired by Sir Giles Strangways, of Melbury Sampford, Dorset, whose descendants still own substantial portions of the estate. The muniments included a number of pre-Conquest charters in single-sheet form, and a cartulary (Davis 1). The cartulary was lost during the Civil War, probably when the Strangways' house at Melbury was ransacked in 1644 AD, but its contents can be reconstructed to some extent from the writings of antiquaries active in the first half of the seventeenth century (Keynes 1989). The house's foundation is attributed to one Orc, Orcy or Orcus ('servant' of either King Canute or King Edward the Confessor) and his wife Thola, who somewhere between 1024-26 AD founded the house through the gift of the manors of Portisham, Hilton, 'Anstic' and Abbotsbury, including the right to any wrecks and control of the shore in these manors. Moule (1886 39) suggests that this may have been a re-foundation of an older Celtic monastery or monastic cell dedicated to St. Peter. William the Conqueror, Henry I, Stephen, Henry II and Henry III all confirmed and extended such rights, and Edward I gave the monks leave to hold a market at Abbotsbury. In 1315 AD, Edward II confirmed anew their right to wreck of the sea in connection with a whale (*crassus piscis*) cast up on the coast (see also Anon 1908; Keen 1983). However, neither the precinct nor any of its surroundings have ever been subject to sustained archaeological investigation.

70

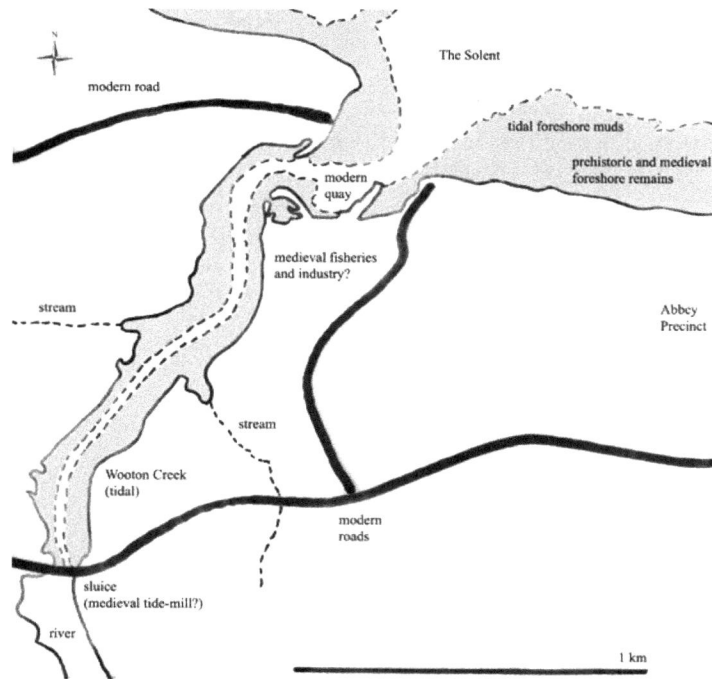

Figure 2 Map of the immediate modern surroundings of Quarr Abbey.

The monastic precinct lay within a small valley less than a kilometre from the brackish lagoon known as the Fleet, created by the shingle bank of Chesil Beach (Fig. 3). The abbey maintained control over the swannery still in existence on the Fleet, as well as over the fisheries of the lagoon and foreshore of Chesil, together with the above-mentioned rights to wreck and whale. In addition, the abbey maintained substantial fish-ponds and a mill, the remains of which survive adjacent to the site of the former precinct, together with the partially surviving remains of the original monastic tithe barn. There is also a chapel dedicated to St. Catherine on a nearby hill, the masonry dating to the fourteenth century AD, but possibly a replacement for an earlier structure, and reputed to have been used as both a sea-mark and a lighted beacon (Fig. 4; Hague and Christie 1975, 18).

Greyabbey, Strangford Lough
At Greyabbey (Cistercian, founded mid-twelfth century AD), McErlean *et al.* (2002) have analysed a wealth of archaeological and documentary analyses for the functioning of the abbey. A daughter house of Holm Cultram in Cumbria, which has substantial interests in Irish Sea commerce (especially the grain trade), Greyabbey rapidly became involved in its mother-house's concern, shipping, for example, two hundred crannocks of wheat 'to sell for profit' in 1223 AD (*ibid.* 184). It seems possible that Greyabbey rapidly developed into a commercial base or 'out-port' for Holm Cultram: stone structures close to the monastery on shore of Ballydorn Sounds are thought to constitute an early harbour, with thirteenth century green-glazed pottery. The commercial export of fish from Greyabbey is also a real possibility. In

1298 AD, Edward I made Holm Cultram the base of his campaign against the Scots, and made Skinburness, the port of the abbey, his naval base: he ordered twenty thousand dried fish among other victuals to be delivered from Ireland; it is possible, indeed likely, that Greyabbey played a role in this (*ibid.* 185). The abbey was particularly strong in respect of foreshore fisheries: there are fishtraps on the eastern shore of Strangford Lough in the immediate vicinity of the abbey at Greyabbey Bay, as well as on the foreshore to the northern side of Mahee Island beside Nendrum monastery that belonged to Greyabbey (*ibid.* 144-85). Over fifty percent of all the fishtraps in the whole of Strangford Lough are grouped in the small area of Greyabbey Bay, representing the most significant cluster both in the lough and the whole of Ireland, and implying a systematic organisation of exploitation management.

As can be seen in Fig. 5, the monastic precinct lay adjacent to an extremely extensive muddy tidal foreshore covered in numerous fish-traps.

Conclusion
If salt water and the ocean represent uncontrollable chaos, evil and the realm of the devil, then sites such as Beaulieu, Quarr, Abbotsbury and Greyabbey are at the front line of a spiritual battle in the High Middle Ages. This is not to downplay the very real and tangible economic exploitation of such locations; rather, it is to suggest that economic exploitation came within a broader spiritual agenda that was the primary motivation for choosing such locales. These types of site, low-lying, adjacent to and immediately accessible from the intertidal zone, often associated with tidal creeks, are deeply

symbolic places, as most famously reflected in St. Cuthbert's hermitage on the Farne Islands, for which a key series of illuminations of the religious coastal landscape survives in the British Library Yates Thompson MS 26, folios 10v-11r, 26r and 45v, a copy of Bede's *Life and Miracles of St. Cuthbert* produced in Durham in c. 1200 (see Flatman 2009, 28-9, 51, 65, figs. 15, 38, 56). Witnessing the daily rise and fall of the tides in such a location against the rhythm of the monastic daily cycle of prayer and meditation, exposing and then covering the foreshore, was, it is argued, a deeply spiritual event for medieval Christianity. So too would have been the physical hardships of exploiting such a zone: the discomfort, cold and dirt, as best expressed in the numerous monks and saints (most famously St. Cuthbert) reputed to have stood praying for hours at end while fully or partially immersed in lakes, rivers or the sea (Ward 1995, 72; O'Donovan 1864, 249; Plummer 1922, 106).

Foreshores and tidal rivers such as those of the four houses discussed here, with a high tidal range, are extremely powerful, liminal places, and monasteries placed in such locations are not there either through accident or purely economic motive. It was important to such monasteries that they were present both to witness and to meditate this natural conflict between good and evil, land and sea, fresh and salt-water, and to find ways of becoming actively involved in this conflict through use of the foreshore, reclaiming this liminal 'half-land' both figuratively and literally. Such activities fit into a long chronology of monastic preoccupation with such types of conflict with the sea and coast ever since the advent of monasticism in north-western Europe. In the earlier, Celtic period the challenge was to travel across the sea and inhabit rocky, dynamic coastal zones (e.g. O'Loughlin 1997; Sneddon 2001; Wright 2001); by the later Benedictine period the challenge had shifted subtly to conflict-through-labour (often in association with formalized travel, be this real or imagined) in low-energy, intertidal zones (Connolly 1999; Bond 2003: 73-84, 183-210, 296, 307-9, 319-20), but the preoccupation and the spiritual motivation remained the same.

What we witness here is merely a new manifestation of a long-term monastic preoccupation with the coast as a living example of the battle of good versus evil, a shift of battleground but the same war, the core concept remaining the same. While the locations may have been different, the impetuses behind monastic settlement of these different coastal zones were the same: a conscious placement at the forefront of the physical and spiritual battleground between good and evil, land and sea, fresh and salt-water. The challenge to modern scholarship is to accept that a coastal monastic locale does not have to be rocky and dramatic to be a place of spiritual conflict; this new conflict type and zone reflects the new preoccupations of High Medieval monasticism. Such a preoccupation also readdresses much older conflicts running since prehistory with such liminal, boggy, wetland zones. Time and again, prehistory has demonstrated the complex, layered meanings of such

environments to ancient peoples (Champion 2004; Clark2004). Medieval scholarship now needs to undertake similar analyses. If we can accept, entirely on the archaeological evidence, that prehistoric coastal environments were liminal, marginal, 'other' in the past, then to deny such a condition given the rich archaeological, documentary and iconographic sources for the medieval world would be very wrong indeed.

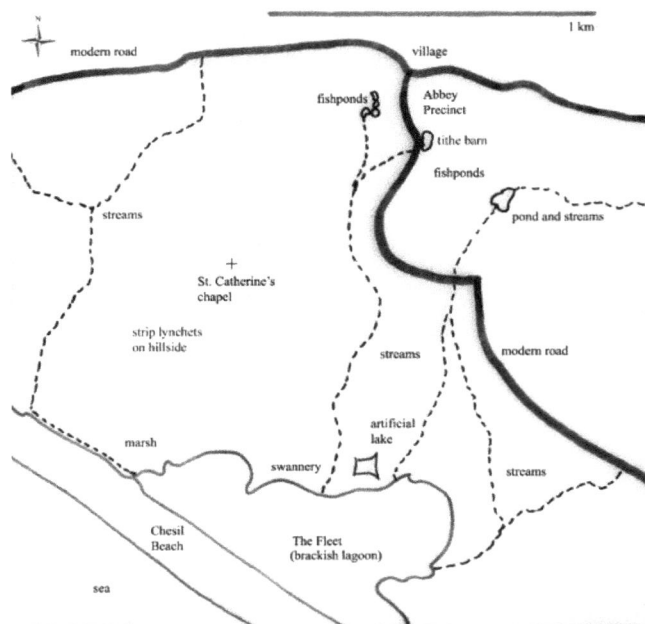

Figure 3 Map of the immediate modern surroundings of Abbotsbury Abbey.

Figure 4 Abbotsbury from the west, with St. Catherine's Chapel in the centre, the Fleet and Chesil Beach to the right, and Portland Bill in the background. The village and former abbey of Abbotsbury lie just beyond the crest of St. Catherine's Hill to the left of the photo.

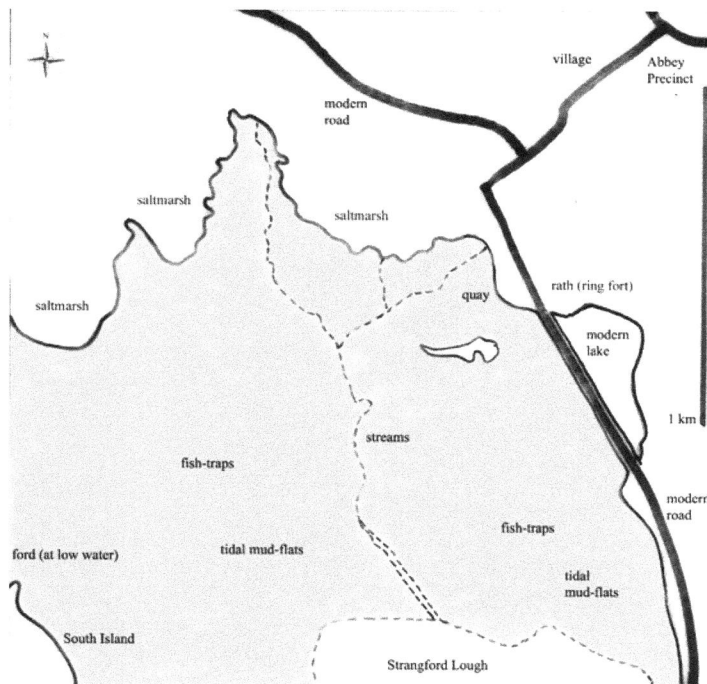

Figure 5 Map of the immediate modern surroundings of Greyabbey.

Endnotes

[1] Examples of the positive connotations of fresh water include: [a] fresh water as a symbol of life as well as a means of cleansing (Genesis 1:2, 6-8); [b] fresh water as the element closest to God (Psalms 17; 28:3; 76:17, 20; 103:3; 148:4); (Hosea 6:3); (Exodus 15:23-35; 17:2-7; Psalms 1:3; 22:2; 41:2; 64:10; 77:20; Isaiah 35:6-7; 58:11); (Psalm 45:5); [c] fresh water as used in baptism (Matthew 28:19-20); (Matthew 3:16; Mark 1:10; Colossians 2: 10-12); [d] 'living water' (John 4: 1-42); [e] how the scarceness of fresh water is very serious, and drought often a result of the wrath of God (1 Kings 17:1, Jeremiah 14: 1-6 and Haggai 1: 10-11 respectively) – conversely, rainfall is regularly seen as a sign of God's favour and goodness; [f] polluted and undrinkable water is also very serious (Exodus 7:14-24) – conversely, God allowed Moses to perform the miracle of making the water sweet, thus restoring the Israelites faith in him (Exodus 15:22-27); [g] fresh water as important for cleansing (Exodus 29:4); (Leviticus 16:4, 24, 26); (Leviticus 11:40, 15:15, Deuteronomy 23:11 etc); (Leviticus 11:32; 13:58; 14:8, 9; 15-17; 22:6; cf. Isaiah 1:16); [h] fresh water as a powerful purifying element that can destroy evil and enemies (Genesis 3:1-15; Exodus 14:1-15:21); [i] fresh water as used in healing (2 Kings 5:1-14); (John 5:1-4); (Matthew 3:1-6; Mark 1:4-5; Luke 3:2-16; John 1:26-33); [j] fresh water as symbolic of God's blessing and spiritual refreshment (Isaiah 41:17-18); [k] the longing for fresh water indicates spiritual need (Psalm 42:1 – *as the heart pants after the water brooks, so pants my soul after thee oh God*; [l] Ezekiel's vision of God's house, in which the waters that poured from under the threshold represent the unrestricted flow

of God's blessings upon his people (Ezekiel 47:1-12); [m] Jeremiah describes God as *the fountain of living waters* (Jeremiah 2:13, 17:13); [n] fresh water as connected with the gift of eternal life (John 4:14; Revelation 21:6).

[2] Examples of the negative connotations of salt/sea include: [i] the particular combination of the sea serpent and powerful rider/ruler from psalm 51, an analogy made by both Cassiodorus and Augustine. The latter went on to make the visual synecdoche of a man and a sea-monster as a symbol of the Antichrist aping Christ enthroned in Psalm 29 (*the Lord enthroned upon the flood, the sea*): by riding on a sea dragon, the antichrist figure presents a distinct challenge to God, as the antichrist is demonstrably enthroned on the sea waters which he literally sets below his feet; [ii] the seas and oceans as '*the habitat of serpents whose heads God crushed*' (Psalm 73:13-14) and of the dragon (Job 41:25; Psalm 103:26); [iii] in Genesis 1:2 the analogy is made that '*the Spirit of God was hovering over the face of the waters*', linked to the imagery that the earth was founded upon the sea, order created from uncontrolled and uncontrollable chaos (Genesis 1:6-7, 9-10); [iv] in a different thread, authors such as Gregory the Great drew parallels between the darkness of the ocean and the ignorance of man in his *Homilies on Ezekiel*: '*dark waters were, and thickest clouds of the air, because the wisdom of prophets is obscured*' (Psalm 18:11). Gregory expands this with quotations from Gospels – '*what I tell you in darkness, that ye speak in light*' (Matthew 10:27). Gregory's *Homilies* also make frequent references to the apocalypse; [v] the 'ocean' as an expanse of water is also depicted as being quantifiably different from other waters

(like the Mediterranean Sea) in that it is at the very limit of habitable reality: the '*primeval abyss*' (Genesis 1:2) its' shore marking the point of separation between the waters and dry land (Genesis 1:9), and its role as the home of the Leviathan (cf. Job 41:23 for example), connected with the abode of demons (cf. Luke 8:31) and Satan (cf. Revelations 20:1-3); [vi] from the oceans, at the end of time, the apocalyptic beast will arise to destroy humankind (Apocalypse 11:7; 17:8).

[3] Depictions of ambiguous situations and events in relation to biblical imagery in illuminated manuscripts include: [a] *Old Testament*: [a i] Noah and the ark (Genesis 6-9); [a ii] Jonah and the whale (Jonah 1-2); [a iii] Moses in the reed basket (Exodus 2:2-6); [b] *New Testament*: [b i] Peter and the miraculous draught of fishes (John 21:1-14; Luke 5:1-11; Mark 6:45-51); [b ii] the calling of Peter and Andrew (Mark 1:16-20); [b iii] the storm on the lake of Genneserath (Luke 8:22-25; Mark 4:35-41); [b iv] Christ preaching from a boat (Mark 13:1-52); [b v] Christ walking on the water (Matthew 15:25; John 6:17); [b vi] Christ going by ship to a lonely place (Matthew 15:13), also [b vii] St. Paul sailing to various places including Rome in the Acts. Many of these themes are only 'positive' in that they demonstrate victory over the uncontrolled element of the seas and oceans, a pacification of a hostile environment

Bibliography

Adams, J. (ed.) 1994. *Buckler's Hard: A Report on Work Carried Out During 1993 and 1994 at the 18ᵗʰ Century Shipbuilding Village of Buckler's Hard and Related Areas* Southampton: University of Southampton.

Anderson, A.O. and Anderson, M.O. (eds.) 1991. *Adomnan's Life of Columba*. Edinburgh: Thomas Nelson.
Anon. 1908. Houses of Benedictine monks: the Abbey of Abbotsbury. *A History of the County of Dorset, Volume 2,* 48-53. Downloaded from: http://www.british-history.ac.uk/report.asp?compid=40138 on 15ᵗʰ August 2006.

Aston, M. 1993. *Monasteries*. London: Batsford.

Aston, M., Keevill, G. and Hall, T. (eds.) 2001. *Monastic Archaeology*. Oxford: British Archaeological Reports.

Ballantyne, R. 2004. Islands in wilderness: the changing medieval use of the East Anglian peat fens, England. *Environmental Archaeology* 9, 189-98.

Bennett, I. 2005. Archaeological excavations in Co. Wexford: a review of the last 35 years. *Journal of the Wexford Historical Society* 20, 184-96.

Bond, J. 2000. Landscapes of monasticism. In Hooke, D. (ed.) *Landscapes: the Richest Historical Record*, 63-74. Oxford: Oxbow.

Bond, C.J. 2003. *Monastic Landscapes*. Stroud: Tempus.

Bonner, G., Rollason, D. and Stancliffe, C. (eds.) 1995. *St. Cuthbert, His Cult and His Community to AD 1200*. Woodbridge: Boydell.

Borsje, J. 1994. The monster in the River Ness in *Vita Sancti Columbae*: a study of a miracle. *Peritia* 8, 27-34.

Borsje, J. 1996. *From Chaos to Enemy: Encounters With Monsters in Early Irish Texts*. Bruges: Turnhout.

Borsje, J. 1997. The movement of water as symbolised by monsters in Early Irish texts. *Peritia* 11, 153-70.

Borsje, J. 1999. Omens, ordeals and oracles: on demons and weapons in Early Irish texts. *Peritia* 13, 224-48.

Bourgeault, C. 1983. The monastic archetype in the *Navigatio* of St. Brendan. *Monastic Studies* 14, 109-22.

Bowen, E.G. 1934. The travels of St. Sampson of Dol. *Aberystwyth Studies* 13, 61-7.

Bowen, E.G. 1944. The travels of the Celtic saints. *Antiquity* 18, 16-28.

Bowen, E.G. 1954. *The Settlements of the Celtic Saints in Wales*. Cardiff: University of Wales Press.

Bowen, E.G. 1968. The seas of western Britain: studies in historical geography. In Bowen, E.G., Carter, H. and Taylor, J.A. (eds.) *Geography at Aberystwyth*, 150-66. Cardiff: University of Wales Press.

Bowen, E.G. 1968-69. The Irish Sea in the Age of Saints. *Studia Celtica* 3-4, 56-71.

Bowen, E.G. 1969. *Saints, Seaways and Settlement in the Celtic Lands*. Cardiff: University of Wales Press.

Bowen, E.G. 1970. Britain and the British seas. In Moore, D. (ed.) *The Irish Sea Province in Archaeology and History*, 11-28. Cardiff: Cambrian Archaeological Association.

Bowen, E.G. 1972a. *Britain and the Western Seaways*. London: Thames and Hudson.

Bowen, E.G. 1972b. The geography of early monasticism in Ireland. *Studia Celtica* 7, 30-44.

Bradley, R. 1997. *Rock Art and the Prehistory of Atlantic Europe*. London: Routledge.

Bullough, D.A. 1964-1965. Columba, Adomnán and the achievement of Iona, parts 1 and 2. *Scottish Historical Review* 43-44, 111-30 and 17-33.
Burn, A.R. 1969. Holy men on islands in pre-Christian Britain. *Glasgow Archaeological Journal* 1, 2-6.

Burnett, C. 1995. Mathematics and astronomy in Hereford and its region in the twelfth century. In Whitehead, D. (ed.) *Medieval Art, Architecture and*

Archaeology at Hereford, 50–59. Leeds: British Archaeological Association.

Cameron, M.L. 1985. Aldhelm as naturalist: a re-examination of some of his *Enigmata*. *Peritia* 4, 117-33.

Caner, D. 2002. *Wandering, Begging Monks: Spiritual Authority and the Promotion of Monasticism in Late Antiquity*. Berkeley: University of California at Berkeley Press.

Chadwick, N.K. 1961. *The Age of the Saints in the Early Celtic Church*. Oxford: Oxford University Press.

Champion, T. 2004. The deposition of the boat. In Clark, P. (ed.) *The Dover Boat*, 276-81. London: English Heritage.

Charles-Edwards, T. 1976. The social background to Irish *Peregrinatio*. *Celtica* 11, 43-59.

Charles-Edwards, T. 1984. The Church and settlement. In Chatháin, P. Ni and Richter, M. (eds.) *Ireland and Europe*, 167-75. Dublin: Four Courts Press.

Clark, P. 2004. Discussion. In Clark, P. (ed.) *The Dover Boat*, 319-22. London: English Heritage.

Collins, A.Y. 1995. The origin of Christian baptism. In Johnson, M.E., Kavanagh, A. and Kretschmar, G. (eds.) *Living Water, Sealing Spirit*, 35-57. Collegeville: Liturgical Press.

Connolly, D.K. 1999. Imagined pilgrimage in the itinerary maps of Matthew Paris. *Art Bulletin* LXXXI(4), 598-622.

Constable, G. 1976. Opposition to pilgrimage in the Middle Ages. *Studia Gratia* 19, 123-46.

Constable, G. 1979. Opposition to pilgrimage in the Middle Ages. In Constable, C. (ed.) *Religious Life and Thought*, 125-46. Cambridge: Cambridge University Press.

Constable, G. 1988. *Monks, Hermits and Crusaders in Medieval Europe*. London: Variorum.

Cramp, R. 1973. Anglo-Saxon monasteries of the North. *Scottish Archaeological Forum* 5, 104-24.

Cramp, R. 1981. *The Hermitage and the Offshore Island*. London: National Maritime Museum.

Crawford, O.G.S. 1936. Western seaways. In Dudley-Buxton, L.H. (ed.) *Custom is King*. London: Hutchinson. Crumlin-Pedersen, O. and Munch-Thye, B. (eds.) 1995. *The Ship as Symbol in Prehistoric and Medieval Scandinavia*. Copenhagen: Danish National Museum.

Cunliffe, B. 2001. *Facing the Ocean: the Atlantic and Its Peoples*. Oxford: Oxford University Press.

Dietz, M. 2004. Itinerant spirituality and the late antique origins of Christian pilgrimage. In Ellis, L. and Kinder, F.L. (eds.) *Travel, Communication and Geography in Late Antiquity*. Aldershot: Ashgate.

Dietz, M. 2005. *Wandering Monks, Virgins and Pilgrims*. University Park: Pennsylvania State University Press.

Easson, D.E. 1957. *Medieval Religious Houses: Scotland*. London: Longman.

Eastwood, B.S. 1968. Medieval empiricism: the case of Grosseteste's *Optics*. *Speculum* 43(2), 306-21.

Flatman, J. 2009. *Ships and Shipping in Medieval Manuscripts*. London and Chicago: British Library and University of Chicago Press.

Flint, V.I.J. 1984. Monsters and the Antipodes in the early Middle Ages and the Enlightenment. *Viator* 15, 65-80.

Foot, S. 1992. 'By water in the spirit': the administration of baptism in early Anglo-Saxon England. In Blair, J. and Sharpe, R. (eds.) *Pastoral Care Before the Parish*, 171-92. London: Leicester University Press.

Gilchrist, R. 1994. *Gender and Material Culture: the Archaeology of Religious Women*. London: Routledge.

Gilchrist, R. 1995. *Contemplation and Action: the Other Monasticism*. London: Leicester University Press.

Gilchrist, R. and Mytum, H. (eds.) 1989. *The Archaeology of Rural Monasteries*. Oxford: British Archaeological Reports.

Gilchrist, R. and Mytum, H. (eds.) 1993. *Advances in Monastic Archaeology*. Oxford: British Archaeological Reports.

Gransden, A. 1972. Realistic observation in twelfth-century England. *Speculum* 47(1), 29-51.

Greene, J.P. 1995. *Medieval Monasteries*. London: Leicester University Press.

Grinell, R. 1946. The theoretical attitude towards space in the Middle Ages. *Speculum* 21(2), 141-57.

Gwynn, A.O. 1970. *Medieval Religious Houses: Ireland*. London: Longman.

Hague, D.B. and Christie, R. 1975. *Lighthouses: Their Architecture, History and Archaeology*. Llandysul: Gomer.

Helskog, K. 1985. Boats and meaning: a study of change and continuity in the Alta Fjord, Arctic Norway, from 4200 to 500 years BC. *Journal of Anthropological Archaeology* 4, 177-205.

Helskog, K. 1999. The shore connection: cognitive landscape and communication with rock carvings in northernmost Europe. *Norwegian Archaeological Review* 32(2), 73-94.

Henderson, J. (ed.) 2000. *The Prehistory and Early History of Atlantic Europe*. Oxford: British Archaeological Reports.

Herity, M. 1977. The High Island hermitage. *Irish University Review* 7(1), 52-69.

Hingley, R. 1996. Ancestors and identity in the later prehistory of Atlantic Scotland: the reuse and reinvention of Neolithic monuments and material culture. *World Archaeology* 28(2), 231-43.

Hockey, S.F. (ed.) 1970. *Quarr Abbey and Its Lands, 1132-1631*. London: Leicester University Press.

Hockey, S.F. (ed.) 1975. *The Account-Book of Beaulieu Abbey*. London: Royal Historical Society.

Holmes, U.T. 1936. Gerald the naturalist. *Speculum* 11(1), 110-21.

Hooglviet, M. 2000. *Mappae Mundi* and the medieval hermeneutics of cartographical space. In Ainsworth, P. and Scott, T. (eds.) *Regions and Landscapes: Reality and Imagination in Late Medieval and Early Modern Europe*, 25-46. Bern: Peter Lang.

Housley, R.A. and Coles, G. (eds.) 2003. *Atlantic Connections and Adaptations*. Oxford: Oxbow.

Hughes, K. 1960. The changing theory and practice of Irish pilgrimage. *Journal of Ecclesiastical History* 11, 143-51.

Ingold, T. 1993. The temporality of landscape. *World Archaeology* 25(2), 152-74.

Ingold, T. 2000. *The Perception of the Environment*. London: Routledge.

Jasinski, M. 1993. The maritime cultural landscape: an archaeological perspective. *Archaeologia Polski* 38, 7–21.

Kaul, F. 1998. *Ships on Bronzes: A Study in Bronze Age Religion and Iconography*. Copenhagen: National Museum of Denmark.

Keen, L. 1983. Abbotsbury Abbey. *Archaeological Journal* 140, 21-4.

Keynes, S. 1989. The lost cartulary of Abbotsbury. *Anglo-Saxon England* 18, 207-43.

Klein, N.R. 2003. *Maps of Medieval Thought*. Woodbridge: Boydell.

Knowles, D. and Hadcock, R.N. (eds.) 1971. *Medieval Religious Houses: Volume 1 - England and Wales*. London: Longman.

Kupfer, M. 1994. Medieval world maps: embedded images, interpretative frames. *Word and Image* 10(3), 262-88.

Low, M. 2002. The natural world in early Irish Christianity: an ecological footnote. In Atherton, M. (ed.) *Celts and Christians*, 169-203. Cardiff: University of Wales Press.

Lozovsky, N. 2000. *'The Earth is Our Book': Geographical Knowledge in the Latin West, c. 400-1000*. Michigan: Michigan University Press.

Lynch, A. 2003. Summary of archaeological excavations, 1982-1994. In Finn, A. (ed.) *Tintern Abbey, Co. Wexford: Cistercians and Colcloughs, Eight Centuries of Occupation*, 2nd edition. Saltmills: Friends of Tintern.

MacDonald, A. 1984. Aspects of the monastery and monastic life in Adomnán's life of Columba. *Peritia* 3, 271-302.

Marcus, G.J. 1951. Irish pioneers in ocean navigation of the Middle Ages, parts 1 and 2. *Irish Ecclesiastical Review* 76, 353-63 and 469-79.

Marcus, G.J. 1953-54. Factors in early Celtic navigation. *Studies Celtiques* 6, 12-27.

Marcus, G.J. 1954. Further light on early Irish navigation. *Irish Ecclesiastical Review* 82, 93-100.

McCarthy, D. and Breen, A. 1997. Astronomical observation in the Irish annals and their motivation. *Peritia* 11, 1-43.

McErlean, T., McConkey, R. and Forsythe, W. (eds.) 2002. *Strangford Lough: An Archaeological Survey of the Maritime Cultural Landscape*. Belfast: Backstaff.

McGrail, S. 1989. Pilotage and navigation in the time of St. Brendan. In de Courcy-Ireland, J. and Sheehy, D.C. (eds.) *Atlantic Visions*, 25-35. Dun Laoghaire: Boole.

Moule, H.J. 1886. Abbotsbury Abbey. *Proceedings of the Dorset Natural History and Antiquarian Field Club* 8, 38-48.

O'Donovan, A. 1864. *Calendar of the Saints of Ireland*. Dublin.

O'Loughlin, T. 1996. The view from Iona: Adomnán's mental maps. *Peritia* 10, 98-122.

O'Loughlin, T. 1997. Living in the ocean. In Bourke, C. (ed.) *Studies of the Cult of St. Columba*, 11-23. Dublin: Four Courts Press.

Ordnance Survey 1954. *Map of Monastic Britain: South Sheet*. Chessington: Ordnance Survey.

Ordnance Survey 1955. *Map of Monastic Britain: North Sheet*. Chessington: Ordnance Survey.

O'Sullivan, D. 2001. Space, silence and shortage on Lindesfarne: the archaeology of asceticism. In Hamerow, H. and MacGregor, A. (eds.) *Image and Power in the Archaeology of Early Medieval Britain*, 33-52. Oxford: Oxbow.

Parker, A.J. 2001. Maritime landscapes. *Landscapes* 2(1), 22-41.

Plummer, C. 1922. *Lives of the Irish Saints*. Oxford: Clarendon.

Rattue, J. 1995. *The Living Stream: Holy Wells in Historical Context*. Woodbridge: Boydell.

Schnall, U. 1989. Practical navigation in the late Middle Ages. In Villain-Gandossi, C., Busittil, S. and Adam, P. (eds.) *Medieval Ships and the Birth of Technological Societies. Volume 1: Northern Europe*, 272-79. Malta: Foundation for International Studies.

Silverstein, T. 1948. Daniel of Morley, English cosmologist and student of Arabic science. *Medieval Studies* 10, 179-96.

Sly, T.J. and Clark, K.M. 1997. *Survey at Quarr Abbey, IOW, 1997*. Unpublished report downloaded from http://www.arch.soton.ac.uk/Research/IOW/Quarr.pdf on 17th August 2006.

Snape, R.H. 1926. *English Monastic Finances in the Later Middle Ages*. Cambridge: Cambridge University Press.

Sneddon, C.R. 2001. Brendan the Navigator, a 12th century view. In Liszka, T.R. and Walker L.E.M. (eds.) *The North Sea World in the Middle Ages*, 211-29. Dublin: Four Courts Press.

Stevens, W.M. 1986. Bede's scientific achievement. In Lapidge, M. (ed.) *Bede and His World*, 3-44. Aldershot: Variorum.

Thimmes, P. 1992. *Studies in the Biblical Sea-Storm Type Scene*. San Francisco: Mellon Research University Press.

Thomas, C. 1978. Hermits on islands or priests in a landscape? *Cornish Studies* 6, 28-44.

Tilley, C. 1991. *Material Culture and Text*. London: Routledge.

Tilley, C. 1994. *A Phenomenology of Landscape*. Oxford: Berg.

Van de Noort, R. and O'Sullivan, A. 2006. *Rethinking Wetland Archaeology*. London: Duckworth.

Ward, B. 1995. The spirituality of St. Cuthbert. In Bonner, G., Rollason, D. and Stancliffe, C. (eds.) *St Cuthbert, His Cult and His Community to AD 1200*, 65-76. Woodbridge: Boydell.

Westerdahl, C. 1992. The maritime cultural landscape. *International Journal of Nautical Archaeology* 21(1), 5-14.

Williams, D.H. 1976. *White Monks in Gwent and the Border*. Pontypool: Hughes and Son.

Williams, D.H. 1990. Mapping Cistercian lands with special reference to Wales. In Loades, J. (ed.) *Monastic Studies: the Continuity of Tradition*, 58-63. Bangor: Headstart.

Williams, D.H. 2001. *The Welsh Cistercians*. Pontypool: Hughes and Son.

Wooding, J.M. 2001. St. Brendan's boat: dead hides and the living sea in Columban and related hagiography. In Carey, J., Herbert, M. and Ó Riain, P. (eds.) *Studies in Irish Hagiography*, 77-92. Dublin: Four Courts Press.

Woodward, D. 1985. Reality, symbolism, time and space in medieval world maps. *Annals of the Association of American Geographers* 75(4), 510-21

Wright, J.K. 1923. Notes on the knowledge of latitudes and longitudes in the Middle Ages. *Isis* 5(1), 75-98.

Wright, R.F. 1967. The high seas and the Church in the Middle Ages, parts 1 and 2. *Mariner's Mirror* 53, 3-10 and 115-27.

Wright, R.M. 2001. The rider on the sea-monster. In Liszka, T.R. and Walker L.E.M. (eds.) *The North Sea World in the Middle Ages*, 70-87. Dublin: Four Courts Press.

Still living with the Dobunni

Steven Yeates

Introduction

Despite the perception of cultural breaks in British history in the first century AD, and again in the fifth and sixth centuries AD, studies of landscape archaeology, history and onomastics can be used to suggest continuity of local community identity through both of these periods. A study of the Gloucestershire region, the home of the Dobunni and later Hwicce, suggests that we should consider cultural change on a landscape level in order to better understand how local communities developed through these periods.

The Dobunni were a late Iron Age tribe, who became integrated into the *civitas* structure of Roman Britain. Their name is recorded in a number of cases (Rivet and Smith 1979, 339-40), and their territory is defined generally by the distribution of their coinage (van Arsdell and de Jersey 1994). The Dobunni occupied a similar territory to that of the Hwicce, the latter people being first documented in AD 603 (Colgrave and Mynors 1969, EH.I..2). The Hwicce territory is defined generally by the analysis of ecclesiastical texts (Bassett 1989b, 6; Hooke 1985, 12).

In a study of religious systems from the Iron Age to the early medieval period it is essential to consider the development of communal groupings within the Dobunni, which recent study of the Roman period religion in this area suggests are closely identified with rivers (Yeates 2005, chapter 4; Yeates 2008). This differs from the approach of Roymans (1990, 49-94), who in his ethnographic approach to Gallic religion, hypothesised that local Roman divinities represented Iron Age tribal groups. In Gaul there are a number of inscriptions which agree with this suggestion. In the town of Naix an altar was dedicated to the *Genio Leuc(orum)*, the presiding spirit of the *Leuci* tribe (Espérandieu 1915, no. 4650). From Altrip there is a dedication to the *Geni(o) G(ermaniae) S(uperioris)* and a *Genio Loci* (Espérandieu 1922, no. 5993). In Britain, this connection can be recognised in the form of the tribal goddess *Brigantia* from Greetland, Castleford, Adel and Slack (RIB(I) 1995, nos. 623, 627-628, 630), and on an inscription from Winchester to the Matres of Italy, Germany, Gaul and Britain (RIB(I) 1995, no. 88). The Genio Leucorum and the goddess Brigantia use names of pre-Roman conquest tribes, while the *Genio Germaniae* and the matres of Italy, Germany, Gaul and Britain use the names of Roman provinces. From these examples Roymans would seem correct in recognising an association between deity and tribe, but the framework and process through which this relationship arose have never been demonstrated satisfactorily. To understand these complex associations, especially the relationships between a divinity and a tribe, and the longevity of some of these associations, it is

necessary to conduct an analysis of underlying tribal social structures, and the degree to which 'folk-groups' continued to exist despite the widespread changes seen at the national level. There has been much investigation and debate on this subject, for example by Cunliffe (1991, 170-5, 354, 363-4) on the Iron Age, and by Millett (1990, 65-9) on the Roman period. Both of these fit their discussions into a national context.

Many discussions have conceived of tribal territorial arrangements, and have relied largely on schematic themes; they have used central-place theory and catchment analysis, along with Thiessen polygons, as exemplified by Hodder (Hodder and Orton 1976, 58-60) in his spatial analysis of Roman small towns. Another way to consider tribal divisions is to use a dichronological approach as pioneered by Braudel (1972, 20, 1244); this uses not only archaeological data and theory but also considers aspects such as place-names and religious iconography. If there was a link between a local 'folk' and a Roman deity, then the surviving corpus of sculpture and votive literature may help highlight this (see below). Regarding place-names, the survival of certain place-names with pre-Roman roots, for example *Weogorna* (Gelling 1969, 26), and *Salenses* (Smith 1964b, 15-16), both group names of British peoples who lived in the Severn Valley, challenges the myth that there was no continuity between the Iron Age and the Roman period or the early medieval period. The survival of such names is important and needs to be explained, and this can only be achieved within a structured historical framework. If a group name did survive, then a community that identified itself with that name probably also survived. There should also have been a survival of known territorial patterns, and these should relate to recognisable archaeological site-type distribution patterns for both the Roman period and the Iron Age. This type of approach may be compared to that expressed by Giddens (1984, 110-62) in his *structuration*, and Ingold (2000, 194-200) in his idea of *taskscapes*. In both of these there is a systematic zoning of specific types of human activity, and hence archaeological monuments, over time and space. Giddens' approach has already been applied in part of the area under consideration by Lucas (2001, 51-72) but, although the theoretical approach was good, there were problems with application and the collection of data, coupled with a lack of discussion of religion, and little apparent understanding of how folk-names survive.

Three types of archaeological monuments have been used consistently to determine the way in which territories and communities interacted during the periods discussed here, but the important consideration that these sites were constructed for and by communities, rather than individuals or families, is rarely explored in depth. These site-types are: minsters in the early medieval period, nucleated settlements in the Roman period, and hill-forts in the Iron Age.

The minster and the folk-group

Minsters were some of the most important monuments of the early medieval period; they have been the focus of much debate by Blair (1988, 1-19; 1992, 226-66), Bassett (1992, 13-40; 1996, 147-73) and Hadley (2000), amongst others. The underlying hypothesis, which will be expanded upon later here, is that the central church was established over a territory; it was served by a team of priests and, in turn, had control or influence over lesser churches established in its territory. This minster hypothesis has become an orthodoxy of early medieval historical and archaeological analysis; only rarely has it been questioned (Taylor 1995, 259-79).

During the high to late medieval period (from the eleventh to fifteenth centuries AD) there was a flowering of monastic culture, producing an abundance of textual sources. Among these are manuscripts discussing the payment systems that had developed between various churches, for example regarding pensions, portions and rents. Fosbrooke (1821, 116) recognised that these payments were established in the early medieval period (the seventh to tenth centuries AD), and that they could be used to identify the status of daughter churches or chapels relative to their mother church or minster. The pensions and portions recorded were either one-off payments or, more likely, annual payments to the mother church to compensate it for the loss of revenue in tithe and soul-scot (burial dues), which had come about through the daughter churches' independence. The longevity of such practices and the ability of church organisation to reform itself has been discussed by Sims-Williams (1990) with respect to the West Country; this was developed further by Hadley (2000) in the East Midlands. These two discussions are important critiques of early medieval church organisation and how it was portrayed in later texts, and they demonstrate that the estates around which a parish was based changed constantly. In the region discussed here, transfer of estates appears to have occurred in the early medieval period in the centre of the Hwicce territory. There is a charter concerning the grant of Elmstone Hardwick, Gloucestershire, dated AD 889 (Finberg 1972, no. 84), which states that the tithes of that manor belonged to the church of Bishop's Cleeve. However, in the thirteenth century AD the independence of the church at Elmstone Hardwick was disputed by the church of Deerhurst (VCH(Gl8) 1968, 58; Willis-Bund 1899, 195, 197). This is a case of a sub-manor which once belonged to one minster becoming attached to another. What should perhaps be considered is that a minster or major church presided over a territory which, despite shifting boundaries, had a stable and cohesive core.

During the early medieval period a number of important legislative texts were produced. One of these was the *Law code of Ine* (AD 668-684), which declared that church-scot (tithes) should be paid to the Church at Martinmass (Whitelock 1979, 399, 406). This and other rights, for example soul-scot, were detailed in the later laws of II, III, IV Edgar (*ibid.* 431-2, 434-7) and V Æthelred (*ibid.* 444). Core ideas developed by Willis-Bund (1906, 2-3) and Houghton (1919, 23-114) on the role of the mother church in the early twentieth century were derived from an interpretation of this legislation. They hypothesised that the central churches, or minsters, were established within a system of *parochia*, and that each church had a team of priests to serve its land-unit.

Finberg (1955) suggested that the underlying structure of these estates had developed in the Roman period. This was a reaction to the work of Myres (Collingwood and Myres 1937) in which the 'British' were perceived as being removed from the landscape. Finberg attempted to demonstrate that this was not so by using the manors of Withington and Blockley, both locations of minster churches in Gloucestershire, as examples. He argued that there had been a continuity of both settlement and administration from the Roman period into early medieval times. For Withington, Finberg realised there were major problems with the previous assessment of the boundary clauses (Grundy 1936, 262-71). He then debated the location of the present church, and its relationship to Withington Roman villa, seeing this spatial relationship as a demonstration of continuity. In many ways, Finberg was the first to notice that Roman sites were reused in the early medieval period; however, the assertion that this type of activity represented only reuse, not continuity, was put forward by Bradley (1987, 1-17).

Reece (1976, 61-79; 1984, 186-7) considered Finberg's hypothesis to be consistent with the existing evidence, and indeed it is one of the most important local studies carried out in Gloucestershire. The problem with the model, however, is that it focuses primarily on the few existing texts dating from the seventh and eighth centuries AD and uses little data derived from excavation. Finberg's hypothesis has, nevertheless, served as an important stimulus for further research in the West Midlands, most notably that carried out by Bassett (1989a, 225-56) at Worcester. Bassett argued for the continuation of Roman Church organisation into the 'sub'-Roman period, and went on to suggest that the associated land-unit formed the basis of the later parish of Worcester Cathedral. Although the large early medieval multiple estates and the larger *parochiae* coincided with each other in many cases, the survival of the Roman church has not yet been established archaeologically.

Hooke (1981, 58-68) has also considered the origin of the parochial and the associated multiple estate. She perceived an Iron Age origin to these territories, claiming a single central hill-fort as a key factor in respect to Bredon, Fladbury and Hanbury, all in Worcestershire. This, however, was more implied than proven.

From certain surviving texts, for example that concerning the establishment of a church at Wootton Wawen,

Warwickshire, in AD 716-737, it is clear that churches were established for specific communities in the Hwicce. In the case of Wootton Wawen this was for the *Stoppingas* (Hart 1975, no. 46; Hooke 1999, 21-2; Sawyer 1968, no. 94). Studies of similar mother churches in Wales have suggested that each church was established over a *cantref* or commote (Pryce 1992, 49), and in Ireland over a *túath* or people (Charles-Edwards 1992, 64-5; Sharpe 1992, 101). If mother churches were usually established for distinct communities, then the *parochiae* of the Hwicce, to some extent at least, must have reflected local folk-groups. It can also be shown that the *parochiae* occupied well-defined topographical locations. For instance, when the wood of the *Weogorna* is referred to in AD 816 (Gelling 1969, 26), this is a folk-group with a 'British' name, for which the church at Worcester was established to minister the pastoral care of their souls. The church at Worcester was also a cathedral established for the larger Hwicce folk-group, for which the *Weogorna* must have been an integral part. Another example is that of Hailes, believed to be derived from the British folk-name *Salenses* (Smith 1964b, 15-16), a place-name which is found as an integral part of the *parochia* of Winchcombe. These two centres, at Worcester and Winchcombe, were the ecclesiastical and royal centres of the Hwicce; at a more local level, however, they retained individual 'British' identities. This ties in with Bassett's (2000, 107-18) assertion that when the Hwicce were first mentioned by Bede, they were placed in a wholly British context; the only thing that does not fit this is the Old English tribal-name Hwicce; however, the name was only used initially in an 'Old English' text and not in a 'Welsh' one.

That there was an association between tribe and minster at least on some occasions is evident in the textual sources; a landscape study of these sources could establish territorial units of folk-groups. These areas can be referred to as land-units, the term used by Bassett (1989b, 18). If it is true that minster catchment areas reflect the survival of defined tribal areas, then the early church *parochiae* were probably not continuations of the villa estates, as implied by Finberg in 1955, or the survival of Roman period British-church parishes as suggested by Bassett in 1989b; rather the early medieval church was forming a more permanent record on the landscape of the folk-groups that existed in the sixth to eighth centuries AD. That some of these groups still retained British names may mean that these groups represent communities established at a far earlier date.

Finberg and Bassett both implied that continuity of social organisation took place; the history of the place-names *Weogorna* and *Salenses* also implies continuity. The mechanisms which caused or allowed this have, however, not yet been demonstrated. *Weogorna* was the name of a wood to the west of a small Roman town at Worcester, while *Salenses* was the name of a medieval village next to the site of a large Roman settlement, covering 34 hectares (Wills 2001, 206-7). Perhaps Finberg and Bassett, because they were concentrating on the villa and

the church, had been looking at the wrong archaeological features.

Religion and the development of nucleated settlement
During the Roman period a large number of nucleated settlements, small towns and road-side settlements developed throughout Britain. These settlements had names constructed from a series of components; two examples are *Colonia Nerv(iana) Glevum*, and *Civitas Corinium Dobunnorum*. Of their name components *Nerv(iana)* is a Roman imperial name, and *Corinium* and *Glevum* are proper names, a river-name in the case of *Corinium* (Smith 1964a, 5), and a probable river-name in the case of *Glevum* (Ekwall 1928, 173). This is part of a common northwest European phenomenon. *Dobunnorum* is a name derived from a tribe, the Dobunni. The last components *Colonia* and *Civitas* are designations of status. The use of these names informs us of the way in which territory was structured in the Roman period. First, there is a range of names designating a town's status; in the area under consideration there are four names which could fall into this category: *colonia*, *civitas*, *vicus* and *castellum*. These designations indicate that there was a structured settlement pattern. The use of the term *Dobunnorum* indicates that this organised and structured system was sometimes linked to the late Iron Age tribal system.

The word *vicus* was used in Roman times to describe a settlement that had attained a designated status (Rivet and Smith 1979, xviii). Another low-level designated status used at that time was *castellum*, sometimes interpreted as 'a fort' (*ibid.*), although originating as a title for a settlement ranging in size from a village to a city (Purcell 1986, 164). Gelling (1967, 87-104) has written a key article on the use of the Latin word *vicus*, 'a town', in English place-names as '*wic*-'. She showed that the compound names *wic-ham*, *wic-ton* and *wic-stow* were associated with Roman archaeological remains. Spatial analysis of this, however, was not followed through and there was no attempt to integrate this within the socio-political framework. A subsequent study was carried out by Coates (1999), who perceived the interpretation of the place-name *wic-ham* as one of the most important in English place-name studies. The *vici*, he noted, along with the *regions* were classed by Suetonius as divisions of the Roman *urbs*, or territories of cities.

Gloucester and Cirencester have had much archaeological investigation, and in both cities a central forum and basilica can be identified. Basilicas were large aisled buildings from which a *civitas* and *colonia* were run. In such structures it was common for there to be an *aedes* or shrine associated with the local tribal divinity. These features conformed to accepted norms around the Roman Empire. In considering Cirencester more closely, it is possible to start to understand how religion in the Roman period was linked to aspects of identity and territoriality. Previously, deities and *genius* of provinces and tribes, and even sub-groups, were recognised in Gaul and Britain. These traditions can be expanded into the lower status towns and their respective groups. The remains of city *tyche* (female presiding spirits) can be recognised in Gaul, for example at Paris (Espérandieu 1911, no. 3136) and Lyon (Espérandieu 1910, no. 1744). The view that only city *tyche* could preside over cities is incorrect, as in Gaul at Hyères, originally *Olbia*, a dedication was found to the *Genio Viciniae Castellanae Olbiensium* (Espérandieu 1925, no. 6688), while in Britain the presiding spirit of Colchester, originally *Camulodunum*, must be *Camulos*. Masculine and feminine spirits were very much interchangeable.

Following Roman norms, in the basilica at Cirencester there would have been a cult statue of the deity of the local Dobunni tribe. Rudder (1779, 343-9), an antiquary of Gloucestershire, stated that sculptural pieces had been taken out of the town to build and repair roads, including the head of the divinity of the city, which had a spiky crown. Fosbrooke (1807, 479-82) also mentions this sculpture and considers it to have been part of an arch. The head, if referring to the same sculptural piece, is later described as that of Jupiter for unknown reasons (Henig 1993, no. 47), but the interpretation of this as a local deity may be supported by the later find of an altar in Sheep Street. This altar (*ibid.* no. 33) shows a genius with a spiked priestly head-dress or mural crown, tightly bunched curls, a bare torso, and a mantle or loin cloth, which is draped over an altar by his side. The altar contains the inscription G(enio).S(ancto).HVI[V]S. LOC[I], which refers to the *genius* of *this place*, the presiding or guardian spirit. The altar, although it does not contain the name of the divinity, with its use of the mural crown implies that this is the deity of the *civitas* town. Mural crowns occur on *genii* across the empire, but the use of this feature is restricted. In Saalburg, Feldberg, Zugmantel and Mayence they occur on *Genius Centuria* (Espérandieu 1918, no. 5762; Mattern 2001, nos. 8-14, 18-19, 36, 38), at Altrip on the *Genius Germaniae Superioris* (Espérandieu 1922, no. 5993). In other cases the genius with the crown occurs alongside Minerva at *Carnutum* (Krüger 1967, no. 59), or Fortuna at Changé (Espérandieu 1910, no. 2023), where the *genius* occurs as part of a divine couple being treated as a god in its own right.

The *genius locus* may thus be a symbol of the civic identity of Cirencester, and of the community that created the city. The spirit of Cirencester would, in a very local way, have had parallels with the way in which Roma was used in Rome: a goddess of a place of a city, but also a symbol of a designated group.

How this related to the presiding spirit of the river Churn, on which *Corinium* lay, is not known. In the early medieval period the name Churn can be recognised as the name of two estates to the north and south of Cirencester (Smith 1964a, 58, 148), indicating that there was a territory including Cirencester which also used the name of the river and the city, and was the territory of the city. Hence Cirencester developed from *Corinium*, the city on the *Corin* or later Churn, which is also the recognised root for Cerney.

The designs of the two Roman settlements, Cirencester and Gloucester, are different in a number of ways. Cirencester is enclosed in its entirety by a wall, with cemeteries lying outside. Gloucester had a smaller enclosed space in which the main civic buildings were located, and an external or extramural settlement. Other settlements in the Dobunni tribal area had a similar design to Gloucester, with a small defended area around which an extramural area developed, for example Bath. In some of the sites there is circumstantial evidence that religion may have been associated with group identity and important in determining town layout, such that towns were all similar to each other. It has been suggested by Dark (1993, 254-5) that the large pentagonal enclosure at Bath was an extension of the sacred site of the local goddess Sulis Minerva. The name Sulis was applied to the goddess, the springs, and the town of *Aquae Sulis*; that some of this territory was associated with Bath prior to the medieval period is possible. It can not be confirmed that *Sulis* was used as a territorial name, but Bath, the name which replaced *Sulis*, was later used as the name of a hundred. In Gloucester a relief was recovered from the Bon Marché site which showed three figures (Henig 1993, no. 80). The central of these figures is a female in a long pleated dress, wearing what has been described as a possible coiffure. An alternative possibility is that this is a type of mural crown. Gloucester would have had a presiding spirit and an associated folk-name, that of *Glevensis*, which in the early medieval period became *Glywysinga*. The Bon Marché panel is similar to a partial relief from Wellow, Somerset (Cunliffe and Fulford 1982, no. 116). This is either a representation of the *colonia* presiding spirit, which due to distance seems unlikely, or of a more localised group.

The layout of Gloucester and Bath, of an enclosed intramural central space with evidence for sanctuaries, and an area of extramural settlement around this, is reflected in other towns in the area, including Droitwich and Kenchester. The development of this arrangement may be rooted deeply within the display of group identity. In another example, the third century AD Bays Meadow enclosure had a villa and two long buildings constructed around three sides of what appears to have been a temple. The site has been associated with administrative activities (Freezer 1979, 4-8), supported by the find of an intaglio depicting the Roman emperor Lucius Verus (Henig 1978, no. App 45), which was presumably worn by an official. Outside of this enclosed area was a settlement extending into the valley to the south (Woodiwiss 1992). At Weston-under-Penyard there is again evidence for an enclosed intramural area at Bury Hill, which was levelled in 1785 (Fosbrooke 1821, 36; Jack 1922, A 1-44; RCHME 1932, 209). It is evident from the statuary recovered from the site that there was a temple in the centrally enclosed space, and the ram-horned head of a cult statue was recovered. A settlement estimated to have covered 50 hectares lay outside of this area. This layout is also evident at Dorn, where two altars were recovered *c.* 1875 (Henig 1993, nos. 38, 39). These altars depicted the same distinctive image, of Dorn's genius wearing a mural crown, a mantle, a short tunic, and boots. In his left hand is a cornucopia, and in his right a large *patera* over an altar.

An assessment of the archaeology of these small towns indicates that they were settlements with an intramural area and an extramural settlement. In the enclosures there is some evidence, although not on the scale of the *civitas* and *colonia*, that these sites had some type of civic attribute and that a local spirit formed part of this. There is increasing evidence that a nucleated Roman period settlement may have existed in every parochia. Of the fifty seven land-units identified in the part of Gloucestershire discussed, 50.8% of them have been confirmed as having a nucleated settlement pattern and, including these confirmed cases, in 73.6% there is some evidence for one (Figs. 1 and 2).

The Roman invasion of Britain is often seen as an event which brought about radical change; in many respects this is correct, while in others this is less obvious. Part of the problem is perhaps the way in which the passage of history is viewed as a single linear progression. Society has many different attributes, and it is quite clear that, in the wake of the Roman invasion, major changes did take place. In the case of the development of nucleated settlements there was significant technological change; this was driven by the introduction of new architectural techniques such as the construction of rectangular structures of stone. This is the type of change that archaeological investigation is good at determining. There may also have been major changes in surveying techniques, leading to a more regimented way of laying out settlements, with organised rows of building plots. Regarding the social use of space within the settlement, however, there appears to be less change. Roman period Dobunnic nucleated settlements were composed primarily of two different components: an intramural settlement and an extramural settlement. From the intramural area there is evidence of religious activity related to the identity of the place as well as to the identity of the local people. In some of the remains of middle Iron Age settlements this same division, of intramural and extramural spaces, exists. The prime example of this is the large settlement at Beckford (Britnell 1975, 1-12; Wills 1978, 43-5), a settlement of 6.5 hectares. At the middle of this complex is a defended enclosure in which, it has been hypothesised, some form of religious activity took place. It can be said that, on a very simplistic level, pre-Roman settlements, such as Beckford, had the same basic settlement design which in the Roman period saw a technological transformation.

There was also continuity of settlement from the Roman period. Heighway (2003, 3-12) has discussed the continuation of occupation in the area around Westgate in Gloucester. This pattern is also evident at other locations. Due to the size of the cemetery at Cassington (Harman *et al.* 1981, 145-88), there was possibly a Roman period nucleated settlement there, which seems to have been the focus for a fifth to seventh century AD semi-dispersed settlement (Clayton 1973, 382-4), and where use of the surrounding space for cemeteries continued as in the Roman period. Similar developments at Roman roadside settlements in the neighbouring area, with vast quantities of post-Roman finds, can be discerned at the complexes at Bidford-on-Avon/Tower Hill (Booth 1996, 39; Wise and Seaby 1995, 57-64), and Staple Hill/Marlcliffe (Booth 1996, 42; Dinn and Hughes 1987, 40). At Bidford the fifth to seventh century settlement has been interpreted from the distribution of finds as having covered an area of 13 hectares.

One aspect which may help to throw light on this transformation process, and the importance of pre-Christian religion, is the use of such sites for burials from the third century through into the sixth and seventh centuries AD. This is evident at Henley Wood, Somerset (Watts and Leach 1996), and also at Wasperton, Warwickshire (Frere 1984, 295-300; Geake 1997, 186), where the base of a Roman altar was recovered along with a fifth to sixth century AD cemetery.

Hill-forts and the Iron Age
Hill-forts are the defining feature of the British Iron Age. They were interpreted as central fortified towns in a discussion developed by Cunliffe (1991, 353-356; Cunliffe and Miles 1984, 12-45) in regard to Danebury. This argument was followed by Stanford (1980, 79-116) in his study of Herefordshire, and also by Burrow (1981, 23) for Somerset, although the latter recognised that there were problems with the application of the model. Increasingly, this interpretation has become less convincing. The debate has now moved on to identify diversity within this group of monuments and recognise that not all of them would have operated in the same way.

Excavations by Sharples (1991, 260) at Maiden Castle indicated that the banks of that hill-fort were not simple constructions of a single period, but that the banks and ditches were constructed through phases of re-dumping over 300 years. This interpretation has implications for every hill-fort or enclosure, as ditch cleaning and re-dumping means that construction dates can no longer be ascertained from the initial silt fill of the ditches. This ties in with important research carried out at Uffington by Gosden and Lock (1998, 2-12), and their belief that people were visiting the site seasonally. This interpretation may indicate that people were coming together at a specific time of the year and that part of that process was to clean the rampart ditch and to raise the height of the rampart, or construct another length of it. The excavation report for the Breddin hill-fort (Musson *et al.* 1991), on the Welsh border, followed the traditional view of it being a centre of occupation. Buckland *et al.* (2001, 51-76), however, noted that the insect fauna indicated that there had been no permanent occupation. These accounts would seem to suggest that hill-forts were used for a central ceremonial function (possibly seasonal), with the bank being a symbolic boundary (Bowden and McOmish 1987, 476-84).

Table 1 All the mother church or minster sites in Gloucestershire and some of the adjacent areas. '(?)' indicates that there are possibilities that a site exists but one has not been proven categorically.

Mother church	Roman town	Enclosure 1	Enclosure 2	Enclosure 3	Enclosure 4
Almondsbury		Bury Hill	Winterbourne (?)	Wallscourt (?)	
Ampney Crucis (?)	Ampney (?)	Ransbury Ring	Calmsdown		
Great Barrington (?)		Norbury	Nosebury (?)		
Bath	Bath	Bathampton	Solsbury	Berewick Camp	
Beckford		Treddinton Camp	Conderton Camp	Oxenton Camp	Dixton (?)
Bedminster	Rosebury	Stokeleigh	Burroughwalls	Clifton Camp	
Berkeley	Hill Flats	Bloody Acre	Berkeley	Blisbury (?)	
Beverstone	Kingscote	Beverstone (?)	nr. Kingscote	Ykeburg (?)	
Bibury	White Walls (?)	Ablington	Castle Ditches	Winters Well	Hasenbury (?)
Bishop's Cleeve	Tredington Rise	Nottingham Hill	Cleeve Hill	Hewlett's (?)	Woolstone (?)
Bisley	The City (?)	Bisley (?)	Bury (?)	Rodborough (?)	
Bitton	Hanham	Hinton Camp	Doynton Camp	Wick Camp	Burmead
Blockley	Dorn	Campden (?)	Ebrington Hill (?)		
Bourton-on-the-Water	Bourton-on-the-Water	Salmonsbury	Lower Slaughter Knave's Hill	Whiteshoots Hill (?)	Stanborough (?)
Bredon		Bredon Hill	Nafford (?)	Bredon village (?)	
Brimpsfield	Birdlip-Nettleton	Norbury		Oldbury (?)	
Cadaminster		Codsbury	Hinchwick Camp (?)		
Cam/Dursley	Wickster (?)	Uley Bury	Nympsfield (?)	Dursley	
Cheltenham	Stanborough (?)	Dowdeswell	Leckhampton	Whistley Hill	Battledown (?)
Churcham (?)	Morwent (?)	Long Brook			
Churchill		Icombe Camp	Kingham (?)	Westcote (?)	
Cirencester	Cirencester	The Ditches	Watercombe	Duntisbourne Grove	North Cerney Camp
Coln Saint Aldwyns	Coln Saint Aldwyns	Lea Wood	Castle Ho	Homeleaze	
Daglingworth	Frampton Mansell (?)	Pinbury	Green Ditches	Brimpsfield Castle (?)	Edgeworth (?)
Daylesford	Fossborough (?)	Stow Camp	Chastleton Barrow	Bourton-on-the-Hill (?)	
Deerhurst		Deerhurst (?)	Wainload (?)		
Evesham	Black Banks	Willersey Camp	Cleeve Hill	Tunnel Hill	Saintbury (?)
Frocester	Eastington (?)				
Gloucester	Gloucester	High Brotheridge	Churchdown	Crickley Hill	Painswick Beacon
Guiting Power		Guiting Power	Cutsdean		
Hawkesbury		Horton Camp			
Kemble	(?)	Trewsbury	Coates	Hullasey (?)	
Kempsford	Kempsford	Blunsdon Castle	Black Burr		
Longdon	(?)	Kilbury	Hasfield Bank	Howler's Heath (?)	Gadbury
Lydney/Awre	Blakeney	Lydney Camp	Willsbury		
Minchenhampton	Hazlewood-Avening (?)	Hazlecote Farm (?)	Minchinhampton (?)	Limbury	Chernbury (?)
Monmouth	Monmouth	Buckholt Wood			
Much Markle	Dymock	Oldbury			
Newent	Newent				
Northleach	Aldsworth	Windrush Camp	Camp Wall (?)	Dean Camp	
Olveston		Knowle Hill	Almondsbury (?)	Elburton	Burhill
Pucklechurch		Ashbury (?)	Hyddes burgh (?)	Howmore	
Quenton		Knaveshill (?)	Fox Hill	(?)	
Ripple	Upton-upon-Severn (?)	Midsummer Hill	Ripple (?)	Bushley	
Ross	Weston-under-	Chase Camp	Wall Hill (?)	Hill-of-Eaton	

	Penyard				
Sodbury (Old)	Brutton Wood	Little Sodbury Camp	Barn Hill (Sodbury)	Doddington (?)	Springfield Farm
Sherston	White Walls	Sherton	Oldbury (?)	Chilbury (?)	Bury Hill (?)
Standish	Quedgeley	Haresfield Beacon	Harescombe Camp	Randwick Wood	
Stanway	Hinton-on-the-Green	Burhill	Shenberrow		
Tetbury		Tetbury	Hazleton Covert	Hocberry	
Tewkesbury	Oldbury	Tewkesbury (?)	Holm Castle (?)		
Thornbury	Oldbury-on-Severn	Oldbury-on-Severn	Camp Hill	Thornbury	
Tiderham	Oldbury (?)	Spital Meand	Yewbury	Combesbury Camp	Ashbury (?)
Weford-upon-Avon	Marlcliffe-Staple Hill	Meon Hill	Long Marston (?)		
Westbury-on-Trym	Sea Mills	King's Weston	Blaise Castle	Combe Hill	Sea Mills (?)
Westbury-on-Severn	Chester Field (?)	Welshbury	Welchbury-Westbury	Dry Wood	
Whitchurch (Her)	Whitchurch	Doward	Symond's Yat	(?)	
Wincncombe	Millhampost	Roel Camp	Langley Hill	Winchcombe	Beckbury (?)
Withington	Wycomb	Old Ditch Prestbury Hill (?)	Arle Grove (?)	Old Ditch Puckham (?)	
		Brackenbury	Elbury (?)		
Wotton-under-Edge					
Yate	Rangeworthy	Little Abbey	Tytherington	Grovesend	(?)

Figure 1 The location of the study area and Figs. 2 (Map A) and 3 (Map B)

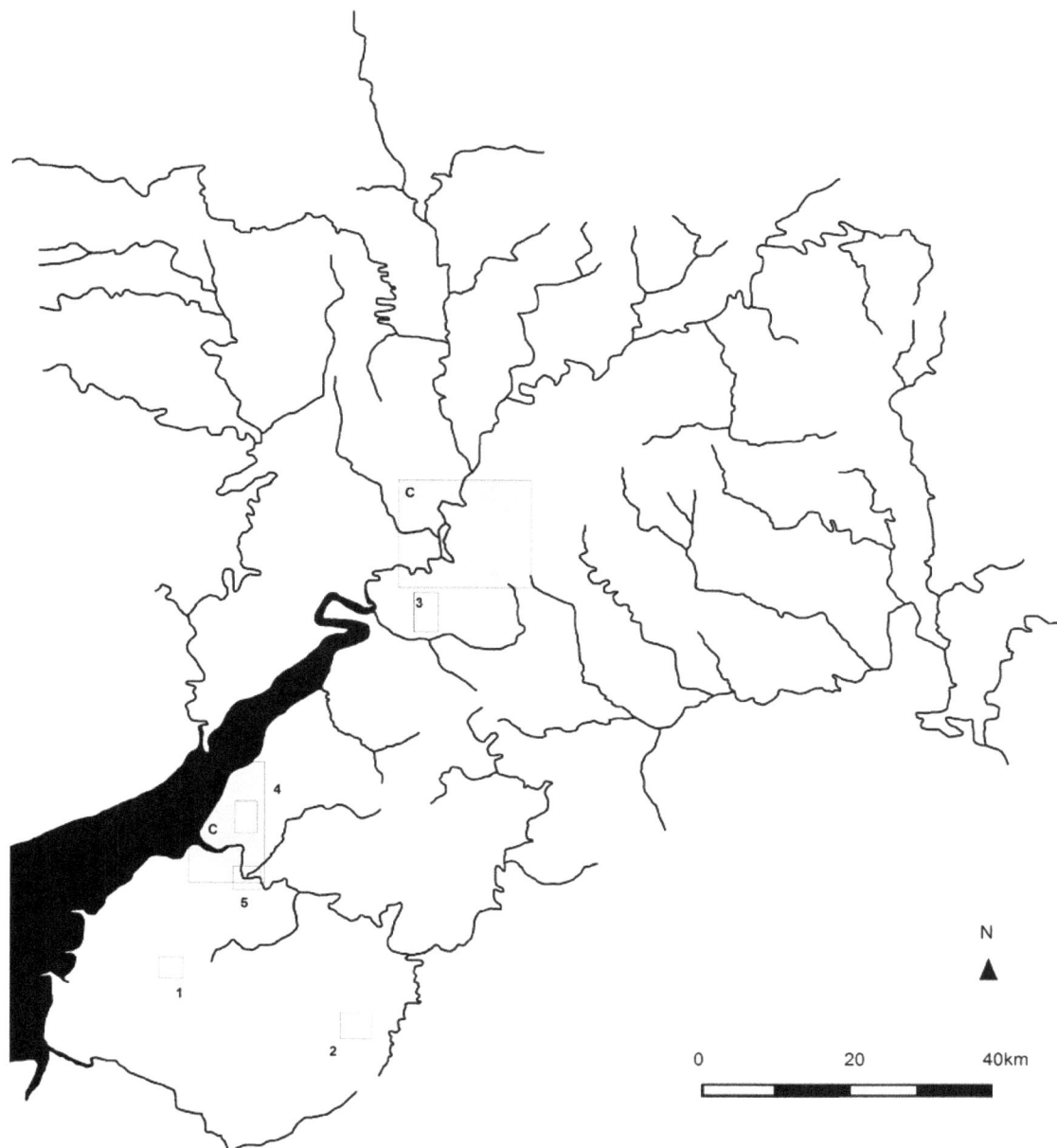

Figure 2 Map A: certain and possible nucleated and road-side settlements in the area in and around Gloucestershire.

These counter-arguments present a view of the hill-fort as a site which took generations to build, in a process in which there was not permanent hill-fort occupation, but where people turned up at certain times for specific seasonal activities. These sites obviously need to be reassessed, along with the assumption that enclosure banks with no ditch, or an internal ditch, were not hill-fort locations. It has also been assumed that sites without evidence of occupation were not hill-forts. In addition to these doubts regarding date and type of occupation, further questions can be asked regarding the landscape interpretation of the hill-fort as a central place. The Thiessen polygon diagram for Somerset produced by Burrow (1981, fig. 5) used specific sites, but discounted other sites with the same size and type of ramparts (see also Cunliffe's (1991, 353-6) argument regarding the Wessex and Sussex downlands).

Kymesbury on Painswick Beacon is a developed hill-fort in Gloucestershire, yet it has produced no evidence of occupation; the only significant feature seems to be a votive well, or pit, in the middle of the camp (Darvill 1987, 135-6). This hill-fort, therefore, stands in opposition to Danebury (Cunliffe 1993), which does show occupation. A study of Somerset reveals that hill-fort sites were grouped spatially in specific ways (Fig. 3). The sites of Tedbury, Wadbury and Newbury by Mells, for example, form a coherent group of three large enclosures which could be classed as hill-forts or hill-top enclosures. They all overlook a coomb which lies to the north of the Mells River (Burrow 1981, 205-6, 224; Pevsner 1958, 227). The grouping obviously has some significance and they could have functioned together as a cohesive group. It is possible to recognise the occurrence of such a group of three hilltop enclosure sites elsewhere in the region. Dolebury, Somerset, forms part of a group of three along with two damaged sites at Rowburrow and Dinghurst (Burrow 1981, 207-8, 265-6). On the Gloucestershire-Somerset border is another group of three camps above the Avon Gorge: Burwells, Clifton Camp and Stokesleigh Camp (*ibid.* 221-2, 224-5, 235-6). All of these have similar occupation and construction evidence, and lie on the three nearest cliff tops to the point along the Avon where a warm spring called Hotwells comes to the surface. In Gloucestershire, at Henbury, there is again a group of three hill-forts around the confluence of the Westbury Trym with the Henbury Trym (*ibid.* 232-3, 239-240, 252). Near Standish is another group of three hill-forts: the camp on Haresfield Beacon (RCHME 1976, 62-4), the camp at Harescombe (*ibid.* 62), and the cross-ridge dyke on Maiden Hill (*ibid.* 97), which closes off a promontory. There thus appear to be clusters of hill-forts and some sort of structured siting of them in the landscape. If there is a structure behind these locations, does this relate to folk-groups and their territories, and if so how does this relate to the Roman period and early medieval period characteristics discussed?

Hill-forts and nucleated Roman settlements in each *parochiae*

The arrangement discussed above could in theory provide an underlying basis for the formation of Iron Age land-units. There are problems, and these concern primarily the nature of archaeological survival, the interpretation of aerial photographs, and the obtaining of secure dates. Even so, it is worth hypothesising that there is some type of physical pattern of structure which underlies the long term development of what became the *parochiae*.

Table 1 shows a list of hill-forts, Roman period nucleated settlements, and early medieval mother church sites. Sixty-six percent of the *parochia* appear to contain three large enclosures or hill-forts, and 25.4% contain four. There are also parallels in the presence of the later sites. For instance, in the *parochia* of Westbury-on-Trym, there is the well-documented minster at Westbury, the Roman settlement at Sea Mills, and the three hill-forts at the major confluence of the two branches of the river Trym (Fig. 4). In addition there is a further larger undated enclosure which surrounded the town at Sea Mills. Standish shows the same basic archaeological features.

The church at Standish, although not recognised as a minster, was a significant mother church, while just to the north of the *parochia* there is some evidence of a Roman roadside settlement at Quedgeley (Atkin and Garrod 1988, 209-18; Frere 1988, 469; Garrod 1988, 28). The large Iron Age enclosures around the Standish coomb have already been discussed above.

The same type of arrangement can be seen at Gloucester and Cirencester. At Gloucester a minster is known to have been founded in AD 671 (Finberg 1972, no. 1). East of Gloucester there is good evidence for four hill-forts (Fig. 4). These are Crickley Hill, where excavations revealed an enclosure constructed in the fifth century BC (Dixon 1994), the hill-fort on Churchdown Hill (Hurst 1977, 5-10), the surviving bank on the east side of the camp on Cooper's Hill/High Brotheridge (RCHME 1976, 21-2, 40-1) (the rest of the site has been quarried away), and a camp at Painswick Beacon. The same pattern of archaeological sites can be seen at Cirencester, where the minster was founded in the old Roman *civitas*. There are a number of large Iron Age enclosures in the Perrott's Brook valley to the north of Cirencester, including the Ditches (Trow 1988, 19-85), a large undated enclosure at Watercombe (RCHME 1976, 54), and a large enclosure at Duntisbourne Grove (Allen *et al.* 1999, 86-97). The Ditches and Duntisbourne Grove have no absolute dating evidence but are dated to the late Iron Age from artefacts recovered from their ditches. The site of a possible fourth enclosure has not been determined, but there is an antiquarian account of a camp at North Cerney (RCHME 1976, 85), and there are medieval references to Oldbury, the old fort, at the head of the Perrott's Brook valley (Smith 1964a, 160).

Finberg's study covered the minster of Withington, Gloucestershire, previously cited, and the same basic structure can be found in this *parochia*. There is a major Roman period town at Wycomb (Timby 1998, 347-51), which may have been called Onna. Atkyns (1712, 650) claims that there was a large camp on Prestbury Hill, and the 'camp' at Puckham (RCHME 1976, xxx) (long disputed) shows a linear boundary on aerial photographs, which may be part of a triangular enclosure (Gloucestershire SMR 4274). At both of these sites, Finberg relates a place-name, the 'old ditches', of the Withington charter (Finberg 1955, 7-8). There are antiquarian accounts of a camp at Arle Grove (Cardew 1988, 68-9), where part of an uninvestigated bank (RCHME 1976, 23-4), has been identified. On a spur to the south of this valley there is evidence of a prehistoric enclosure with a deep ditch; it is of an unknown size (Gloucestershire SMR 6695) and has now been quarried away.

Previously, the idea that hill-forts were central places, and had similar functions as primary settlements has been considered. If one accepts that it is not an individual hill-fort, but the small local region that functions as the focus of a community (e.g. Giddens 1984; Ingold 2000), then these patterns can be interpreted as showing long-lasting continuity and the importance of location. Further work on whether there is a structural patterning relating these areas needs to be done. Can the place-name evidence support the suggestion that these areas represent community groups in distinctive social landscapes?

Folk and estate names

The construction of a 'diachronic' (in the sense of 'through time'), stable historical framework is the only way in which the survival of folk-names of a British origin can be explained. Names which have survived the change to the English language, including *Woegorna* and *Salenses* are derived from river-names, from the Celtic

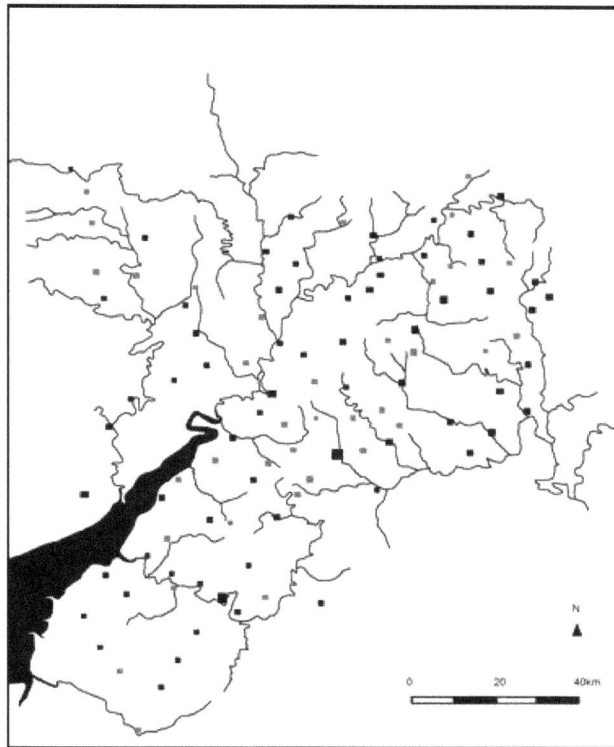

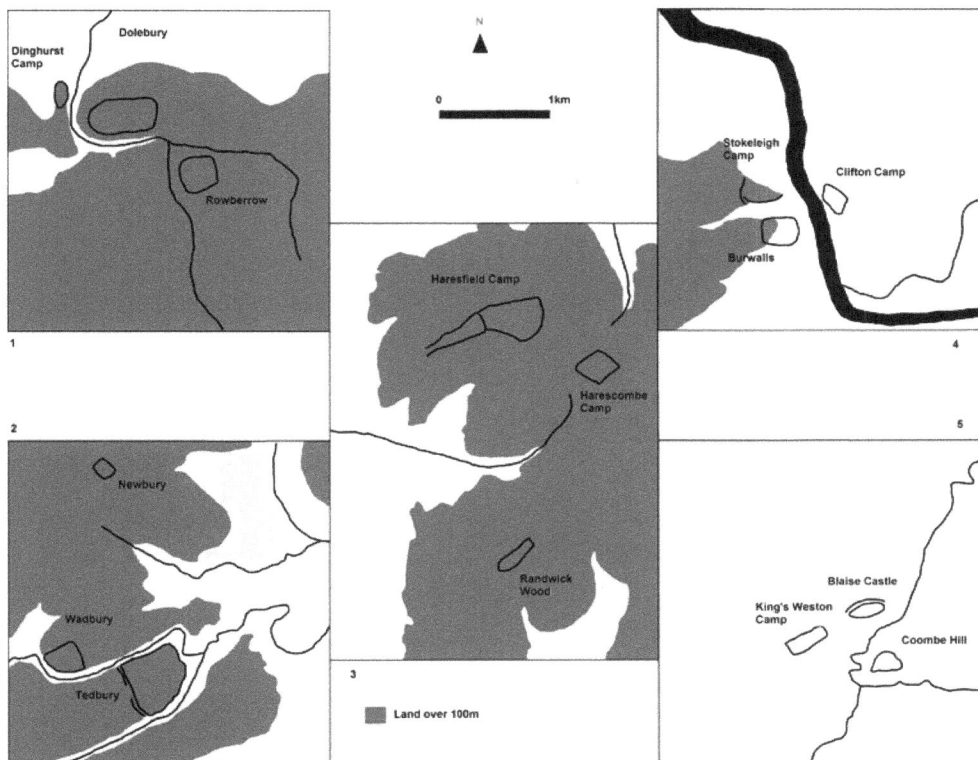

Figure 3 Map B (upper), and the remaining insets (lower – see Fig. 1 for national grid positions). The black squares in Map B are known nucleated Roman towns; the grey squares are probable Roman towns. The lower part of the figure shows examples of the clusters of fortified enclosures.

N

0 1 2 3km

G L E V E N S E S

late Iron Age

GLEV-

Llyn Loyw
or Llwan?

CHURCHDOWN
or SPELLWALL

100m

Middle
Iron Age

Early
Iron Age

Shurdington Hill
IA burials

pos.
Sub-
Roman

Colonia
Nerviana
Glevum

CRICKLEY HILL

Portway
(Cunomaglos)

Late
Bronze Age

Great Witcombe
(Glev- shrine)

Barrow
Wake
LIA burials

HIGH
BROTHERIDGE

KYMESBURY

BLAIZE
CASTLE

COOMBE HILL

KING'S
WESTON

WESTBURY-UPON-TRYM

SEA MILLS

80m

N

0   2km

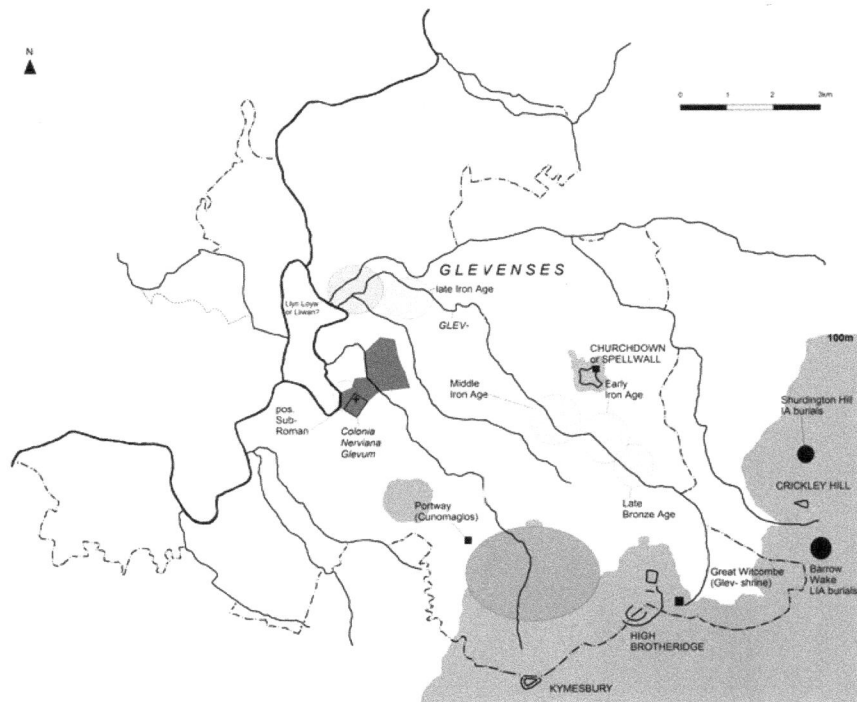

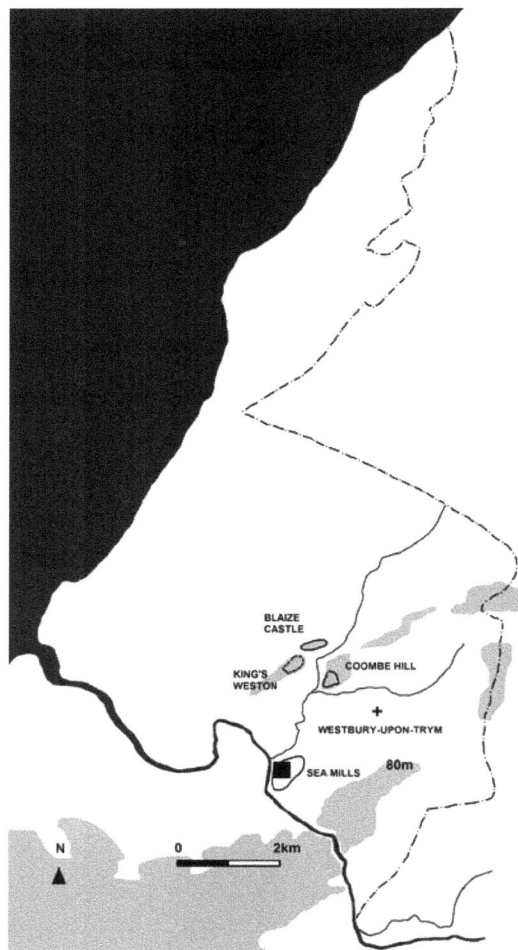

*Figure 4 The parochiae or land-units of Gloucester (above) and Westbury-on-Trym (below), both of which show the
remains of four certain or probable Iron Age enclosures, a major nucleated Roman period settlement and also the
remains of a minster church.*

Vigora and *Salia*. In the Gloucestershire part of the Severn basin there are also surviving folk-names, for example *Glevensis* from which *Glywysinga* developed, also derived from a river-name.

There are numerous surviving folk-names associated with river names. The way in which place-name studies have attempted to deal with these names is problematic in that they have created an Old English personal name to explain their origin. For instance, in Somerset there are the folk-names *Lockinga* and *Glastinga*. Locking lies in the centre of the *parochia* of Banwell. Ekwall (1960, 302) interpreted the name as *Locc's* People, especially with the form *Lokkinges* of AD 1249. Watts (2004, 378), however, interpreted the name as a river name and not a personal name. The Locking Rind, a drainage channel on the levels, cannot be where the name originated from; instead it must have derived from the Lox Yeo. It is probable, therefore, that the name is associated with Loxton, the settlement on the Lox, a river-name derived from the British name *Losca*, the winding one (Ekwall 1928, 267; Watts 2004, 385). The name Locking probably derived from the word *Loscaingas*, the etymology of which would be 'the dwellers on the river Losca'. This could relate to the early Iron Age settlement and significant cemetery excavated on the slopes above the banks of the river Lox during the construction of the M5 motorway at Dibble's Farm (Morris 1988, 23-81). The name Glastonbury, in its earliest form *Glastingaea* in AD 704 'the island of the *Glastingas* people' (Ekwall 1960, 198; Watts 2004, 251-2), is derived from the Celtic *glast-*, or Gallic *glastum*, 'woad'. Glas is a recognised British lake or river-name, the etymology of which means blue-green (Ekwall 1960, 198; Smith 1964b, 175), and probably applied to the large lake at Meare. The earliest known occupation on or near this lake is also Iron Age in date (Coles and Minnitt 1995). There are many *-ingas*, or *saeta* names throughout the other counties of the Dobunnic area which are also associated with river names.

The folk-name *Glevensis*, originating at Gloucester, is derived from a river which is now a lost name. Late Bronze Age and early Iron Age settlement has been identified along the length of the Horsebere brook (Thomas *et al.* 2003). The folk-name *Salenses* applied to the people of the *parochia* of Winchcombe, where the large nucleated settlement of Millhampost has been located along the Hailes Brook, and where there is evidence for four large enclosures, the hill-forts at Roal Camp (RCHME 1976, 112) and Beckbury (*ibid.* 116-7), and the disputed large undated enclosure at Langley Mount (*ibid. xxxiv*), and there is also evidence for a defended enclosure under Winchcombe (Wills 2002, 255). In Gloucestershire, then, some folk-names seem to relate to this 'diachronic' landscape pattern, showing a local Iron Age group identity focused on a local geographical feature (a river), within a territory defined, and retained over time, through continued settlement focus.

Conclusion

In the period from the Iron Age to the early medieval period a number of events occurred which provide important points for discussion: the two most contentious issues are the nature of change at the time of the Roman invasion, and ethnic changes after the departure of the Roman legions. A number of the old folk-names that have survived in place-names defy general interpretations based on the discontinuity hypothesis. These folk-names were derived from pre-medieval and sometimes demonstrably pre-Roman river names. The major settlement evidence from along these rivers seems to be mainly Iron Age, and is extensively lowland. It seems that the group of folk-names that arose derived from the names of the dwellers on the river, and incorporated the name of the river, or, in some cases, another natural feature, for example the *Wreocensætan*, dwellers on the Wrekin (Watts 2004, 704), a hill outside the region. There are other indications of continuity. The interpretation of hill-forts has been a problem, but there is evidence to indicate that these sites were constructed over a long period of time, for seasonal uses and with only limited evidence for long-term occupation. Their relatively isolated locations on upland sites may also hint at a more limited and seasonal use. From looking at the spatial arrangement of these sites in the landscape, it seems that groups of three occur quite regularly, although the clusters may have contained more, with possible religious or ceremonial activities taking place in them. (Four would be an appropriate number as it would fit into the pattern of seasonal cycles and festivals).

In the Roman period nucleated settlements become more evident. Although apparently a disjunction of settlement patterns, at the hearts of these settlements were large enclosed areas apparently reflecting Iron Age organisation patterns, and some in which evidence can be found for the worship of *genii loci*, the presiding spirits of the local landscape and of the peoples who dwelt there. These spirits were the images of the communities, around which a continuity of identity was apparently maintained from pre-Roman times. The Romans manipulated this process through their diverse concept of spirit of place, and their ideas of local affiliation and ethnicity. These communities were stable; people could move in and out of them, but the *genius* of the river and their common origin and perception of originating from a shared landscape bound them together. The religious images may have been destroyed, but these deities were not lost, becoming folk-lore. When Christianity came to dominate, it also used the folk structure as the initial basis for religious manipulation; hence minsters were founded for groups of people, some of whom still retained their British names. The minsters operated as central places and were a core component which enables these areas to be recognised in later times.

These different types of evidence show examples of changing settlement patterns from the Iron Age, Roman period and early medieval period which can be seen to overlap spatially. Although they cannot be linked together in a clean overall picture of continued meaning, they do demonstrate the importance of local community and its religion, the significance of place and association, and also possible settlement pattern. Over time, despite the huge changes brought about by the Roman invasion and the migration period, the spatial arrangement of these key sites points towards stable communities identified through group and landscape relations.

Bibliography

Allen, T., Lupton, A. and Mudd, A. 1999. The later prehistoric period. In Lupton, A. (ed.) *Excavations Alongside Roman Ermin Street, Gloucestershire and Wiltshire: The Archaeology of the A419/A417 Swindon to Gloucester Road Scheme, Part 1*, 35-97. Oxford: Oxford Archaeology Unit.

Atkin, M., and Garrod, A.P. 1988. Archaeology in Gloucester, 1987. *Transactions of the Bristol and Gloucester Archaeological Society* 106, 209-18.

Atkyns, R. 1712. *The Ancient and Present State of Gloucestershire*. Reprinted 1974. Gloucestershire County Histories. London: W. Bowyer.

Bassett, S. 1989a. Churches in Worcester before and after the conversion of the Anglo-Saxons. *Antiquaries Journal* 69, 225-56.

Bassett, S. 1989b. In search of the origins of Anglo-Saxon kingdoms. In Bassett, S. (ed.) *The Origins of Anglo-Saxon Kingdoms*, 3-27. Leicester: Leicester University Press.

Bassett, S. 1992. Church and diocese in the West Midlands: the transition from British to Anglo-Saxon control. In Blair, J. and Sharpe, R. (eds.) *Pastoral Care Before the Parish*, 13-40. Leicester: Leicester University Press

Bassett, S. 1996. The administrative landscape of the diocese of Worcester in the tenth century. In Brooks, N. and Cubitt, C. (eds.) *Saint Oswald of Worcester: Life and Influence*, 147-73. Leicester: Leicester University Press.

Bassett, S. 2000. How the west was won: the Anglo-Saxon takeover of the West Midlands. *Anglo-Saxon Studies in Archaeology and History* 11, 107-18.

Blair J. 1988. Introduction: from minster to parish church. In Blair, J. (ed.) *Minsters and Parish Churches: The Local Church in Transition 950-1200*, 1-19. Oxford: Oxford University Committee for Archaeology.

Blair J. 1992. Anglo-Saxon minsters: a topographical review. In Blair, J. and Sharpe, R. (eds.) *Pastoral Care Before the Parish*, 226-66. Leicester: Leicester University Press.

Booth, P. 1996. Warwickshire in the Roman period: a review of recent work. *Transactions of the Birmingham and Warwickshire Archaeological Society* 100, 25-57.

Bowden, M. and McOmish, D. 1987. The required barrier. *Scottish Archaeological Review* 4, 476-84.

Bradley, R. 1987. Time regained: the creation of continuity. *Journal of the British Archaeological Association* 140, 1-17.

Braudel, F. 1972. *The Mediterranean and the Mediterranean World in the Age of Philip II, Volume I*. New York: Harper and Row.

Britnell, W.J. 1975. An interim report upon excavations at Beckford, 1972-4. *Vale of Evesham Historical Society Research Papers* 5, 1-12.

Buckland, P.C., Parker Pearson, M., Wigley, A. and Girling, M. 2001. Is there anybody out there? A reconsideration of the enviromental evidence from the Breiddin Hillfort, Powys, Wales. *Antiquaries Journal* 81, 51-76.

Burrow, I. 1981. *Hillfort and Hill-top Settlement in the First to Eighth Centuries AD*. British Archaeological Reports British Series 91. Oxford: British Archaeological Reports.

Cardew, A. 1988. The moats or waterforts of the vale of the Severn. *Transactions of the Bristol and Gloucestershire Archaeological Society* 21, 58-69.

Charles-Edwards, T. 1992. The pastoral role of the church in the early Irish laws. In Blair, J. and Sharpe, R. (eds.) *Pastoral Care Before the Parish*, 63-77. Leicester: Leicester University Press.

Clayton, N. B. 1973. New Wintels, Eynsham, Oxfordshire. *Oxoniensia* 38, 382-4.

Coates, R. 1999. New Light from Old Wicks: the progeny of Latin vicus. *Nomina* 22, 75-116.

Coles, J., and Minnitt, S. 1995. *Industrious and Fairly Civilized: The Glastonbury Lake Village*. Taunton: Somerset County Council Museum Services.

Colgrave, B. and Mynors, R.A.B. 1969. *Bede: Ecclesiastical History of the English People*. Oxford: Clarendon Press.

Collingwood, R.G. and Myres, J.N.L. 1937. *Roman Britain and the English Settlement*. Oxford: Oxford University Press.

Cunliffe, B. 1991. *Iron Age Communities in Britain*. Third edition. London: Routledge.

Cunliffe, B. 1993. *English Heritage Book of Danebury*. London: B.T. Batsford.

Cunliffe, B.W. and Fulford, M.G. 1982. *Corpus of Sculpture of the Roman World. Volume I, Fascicule 2:*

Great Britain, Bath and the Rest of Wessex. Corpus Signorum Imperii Romani. Oxford: British Academy.

Cunliffe, B. and Miles, D. 1984. *Iron-Age Wessex: Continuity and Change*. Oxford University Committee for Archaeology Monograph 2. Oxford: Oxford University Commitee for Archaeology.

Dark, K.R. 1993. Town or temenos? A reinterpretation of the walled area of Aquae Sulis. *Britannia* 24, 254-55.

Darvill, T. 1987. *Prehistoric Gloucestershire*. Gloucester: Alan Sutton Publishing.

Dinn, J., and Hughes, J. 1987. West Midlands archaeology in 1987. *West Midlands Archaeology* 30, 1-76.

Dixon, P. 1994. *Crickley Hill. Volume 1: The Hill-fort Defences*. Nottingham: Crickley Hill Trust and University of Nottingham.

Ekwall, E. 1928. *English River-names*. Oxford: Oxford University Press.

Ekwall, E. 1960. *The Oxford Dictionary of English Place-names*. Fourth edition. Oxford: Oxford University Press.

Espérandieu, É. 1910. *Recueil Général des Bas-reliefs, Statues, et Bustes de la Gaule Romaine. Tome Troisième: Lyonnaise. Première Partie*. Paris: Imprimerie Nationale.

Espérandieu, É. 1911. *Recueil Général des Bas-reliefs, Statues, et Bustes de la Gaule Romaine. Tome Quatrième: Lyonnaise. Deuxième Partie*. Paris: Imprimerie Nationale.

Espérandieu, É. 1915. *Recueil Général des Bas-reliefs, Statues, et Bustes de la Gaule Romaine. Tome Sixième: Belgique. Deuxième Partie*. Paris: Imprimerie Nationale.

Espérandieu, É. 1918. *Recueil Général des Bas-reliefs, Statues, et Bustes de la Gaule Romaine. Tome Huitième: Germanie Supérieure*. Paris: Imprimerie Nationale.

Espérandieu, É. 1922. *Recueil Général des Bas-reliefs, Statues, et Bustes de la Gaule Romaine. Tome Huitième: Gaule Germanique. Deuxième Partie*. Paris: Imprimerie Nationale.

Espérandieu, É. 1925. *Recueil Général des Bas-reliefs, Statues, et Bustes de la Gaule Romaine. Tome Neuvième: Gaule Germanique. Troisième Partie*. Paris: Imprimerie Nationale.

Finberg, H.P.R. 1955. *Roman and Saxon Withington: A Study in Continuity*. Leicester: Leicester University Press.

Finberg, H.P.R. 1972. *The Early Charters of the West Midlands. Vol. II. Studies in Early English History*. Second edition. Leicester: Leicester University Press.

Fosbrooke, T.D. 1807. *Abstracts of Records and Manuscripts Respecting the County of Gloucester; Formed into a History Correcting the Very Erroneous Accounts, and Supplying Numerous Deficiencies in Sir Rob. Atkyns, and Subsequent Writers. Volume 2.* Gloucester: Jos. Harris.

Fosbrooke, T.D. 1821. *Ariconensia or Archæological Sketches of Ross and Archenfield Illustrative of the Campaigns of Caractacus: The Station of Ariconium, and with Other Matters*. Ross: W. Farror.

Freezer, D.F. 1979. *From Salting to Spa Town: The Archaeology of Droitwich*. Worcester: Hereford and Worcester County Museum.

Frere, S.S. 1984. Roman Britain in 1983: 1, sites explored. *Britannia* 15, 265-332.

Frere, S.S. 1988. Roman Britain in 1987: 1, sites explored. *Britannia* 19, 416-84.

Garrod, A.P. 1988. Annual review of minor development sites in Gloucester. *Glevensis* 22, 25-8.

Geake, H. 1997. *The Use of Grave-goods in Conversion Period England c. 600-c. 850*. British Archaeological Reports British Series 261. Oxford: British Archaeological Reports.

Gelling, M. 1967. English place-names derived from the compound wicham. *Medieval Archaeology* 11, 87-104.

Gelling, M. 1969. A note on the name Worcester. *Transactions of the Worcestershire Archaeological Society (Third Series)* 2, 26.

Giddens, A. 1984. *The Construction of Society*. Oxford: Polity Press.

Gosden, C. and Lock, G. 1998. Prehistoric histories. *World Archaeology* 30 (1), 2-12.

Grundy, G.B. 1936. *Saxon Charters and Field Names of Gloucestershire*. Gloucester: Bristol and Gloucester Archaeological Society.

Hadley, D.M. 2000. *The Northern Danelaw: Its Social Structure c. 800-1100*. Leicester: Leicester University Press.

Harman, M., Molleson, T.I. and Price, J.L. 1981. Burials, bodies and beheadings in Romano-British and Anglo-Saxon cemeteries. *Bulletin of the British Museum Natural History (Geology)* 35(3), 145-88.

Hart, C.R. (ed.) 1975. *The Early Charters of Northern England and the North Midlands*. Leicester: Leicester University Press.

Heighway, C.M. 2003. Christian continuity and the early medieval topography of Gloucester. *Glevensis* 36, 3-12.

Henig, M. 1978. *A Corpus of Roman Engraved Gemstones from British Sites*. Second edition. British Archaeological Reports British Series 8. Oxford: British Archaeological Reports.

Henig, M. 1993. *Corpus of Sculpture of the Roman World, Great Britain Volume I Fascicule 7: Roman Sculpture from the Cotswold Region with Devon and Cornwall. Corpus Signorum Imperii Romanii*. Oxford: British Academy and Oxford University Press.

Hodder, I. and Orton, C. 1976. *Spatial Analysis in Archaeology*. Cambridge: Cambridge University Press.

Hooke, D. 1981. *Anglo-Saxon Landscape of the West Midlands the Charter Evidence*. British Archaeological Reports British Series 95. Oxford: British Archaeological Reports.

Hooke, D. 1985. *The Anglo-Saxon Landscape: The Kingdom of the Hwicce*. Manchester: Manchester University Press.

Hooke, D. 1999. *Warwickshire Anglo-Saxon Charter-bounds. Studies in Anglo-Saxon History X*. Woodbridge: Boydell Press.

Houghton, F.T.S. 1919. The parochial and other chapels of the County of Worcester. *Transactions of the Birmingham Archaeological Society* 45, 23-114.

Hurst, H. 1977. The prehistoric occupation on Churchdown Hill. *Transactions of the Bristol and Gloucestershire Archaeological Society* 95, 5-10.

Ingold, T. 2000. *The Perception of the Environment: Essays in Livelihood, Dwelling and Skill*. London: Routledge.

Jack, G.H. 1922. Excavations on the site of Ariconium: a Romano-British smelting town, situated in the parish of Weston-under-Penyard, South Herefordshire. *Transactions of the Woolhope Naturalists' Field Club* 23(2) Addition, 1-44.

Krüger, M.-L. 1967. *Corpus Signorum Imperii Roman: Corpus der Skulpturen der Römischen Welt, Österreich, Band II, Faszikel 2, Die Rindskulpturen des Stadtgebietes von Carnuntum*. Graz-Wien-Köln: Herman Böhlans Nachf.

Lucas, J. 2001. Material culture patterns and cultural change in South-West Britain In Carruthers, M., van Driel-Murray, C., Gardner, A., Lucas, J., Revell, L. and Swift, E. (eds.) *TRAC 2001: Proceedings of the Eleventh Annual Theoretical Roman Archaeological Conference Glasgow 2001*, 51-72. Oxford: Oxbow Books.

Mattern, M. 2001. *Corpus Signorum Imperii Roman: Corpus der Skulpturen der Römischen Welt, Deutschland, Band II, 12 Germania Superior*. Bonn: Rudolf Habelt GMBH.

Millett, M. 1990. *The Romanization of Britain: An Essay in Archaeological Interpretation*. Cambridge: Cambridge University Press.

Morris, E.L. 1988. The Iron-Age occupation at Dibble's Farm, Christon. *Proceedings of the Somersetshire Archaeological and Natural History Society* 132, 23-81.

Musson, C.R., Britnell, W.J. and Smith, A.G. 1991. *The Breiddin Hill-fort: A Later Prehistoric Settlement in the Welsh Marches*. Council for British Archaeology Research Report 76. York: Council for British Archaeology.

Pevsner, N. 1958. *The Buildings of England: North Somerset and Bristol*. Harmondsworth: Penguin.

Pryce, H. 1992. Pastoral care in early medieval Wales. In Blair, J. and Sharpe, R. (eds.) *Pastoral Care Before the Parish*, 41-62. Leicester: Leicester University Press.

Purcell, N. 1986. The arts of Government. In Boardman, J., Griffin, J. and Murray, O. *The Roman World*, 150-81. Oxford: Oxford University Press.

RCHME. 1932. *An Inventory of the Historical Monuments in Herefordshire II: East*. London: Her Majesty's Stationary Office.

RCHME. 1976. *Ancient and Historical Monuments in the County of Gloucester, Volume 1: Iron Age and Romano-British Monuments in the Gloucestershire Cotswolds*. London: Her Majesty's Stationary Office.

Reece, R. 1976. From Corinion to Cirencester: models and misconceptions. In McWhirr, A.D. (ed.) *Studies in Archaeology and History of Cirencester: Based on Papers Presented to a Research Seminar on the Post-Roman Development of Cirencester Held at the Corinium Museum, November 1975*, 61-79. British Archaeological Reports British Series 30. Oxford: British Archaeological Reports.

Reece, R. 1984. The Cotswolds: an essay on some aspects and problems of Roman rural settlement. In Saville, A. (ed.) *Archaeology in Gloucestershire: From the Earliest Hunters to the Industrial Age, Essays Dedicated to Helen O'Neil and the Late Elsie Clifford*, 181-90. Cheltenham: Cheltenham Art Gallery and Museums and the Bristol and Gloucestershire Archaeological Society.

RIB(I). 1995. *The Roman Inscriptions of Britain I: Inscriptions on Stone*. Stroud: Alan Sutton.

Rivet, A.L.F. and Smith, C. 1979. *The Place-names of Roman Britain*. London: B.T. Batsford.

Roymans, N. 1990. *Tribal Societies in Northern Gaul: An Anthropological Perspective*. Amsterdam: Albert Egges van Giffen Instituut voor Prae- en Protohistories.

Rudder, S. 1779. *A New History of Gloucestershire (Comprising the Topography, Antiquities, Curiosities, Produce, Trade, and Manufactures of That County)*. Cirencester: Samuel Rudder.

Sawyer, P.H. (ed.) 1968. *Anglo-Saxon Charters: An Annotated List and Bibliography*. London Historical Society Guide and Handbook 8. London: London Historical Society.

Sharpe, R. 1992. Churches and communities in earl medieval Ireland: towards a pastoral model. In Blair, J. and Sharpe, R. (eds.) *Pastoral Care Before the Parish*, 81-109. Leicester: Leicester University Press.

Sharples, N.M. 1991. *Maiden Castle: Excavations and Field Survey*. English Heritage Archaeological Report 19. London: English Heritage.

Sims-Williams, P. 1990. *Religion and Literature in Western England 600-800*. Cambridge: Cambridge University Press.

Smith, A.H. 1964a. *The Place-names of Gloucestershire: Part 1. The Rivers and Road Names, the East Cotswolds. Vol. XXXVIII*. Cambridge: Cambridge University Press.

Smith, A.H. 1964b. *The Place-names of Gloucestershire: Part 2. The North and West Cotswolds. Vol. XXXIX*. Cambridge: Cambridge University Press.

Stanford, S.C. 1980. *The Archaeology of the Welsh Marches*. London: Collins.

Taylor, P. 1995. Boundaries and margins: Barnet, Finchley, and Totteridge. In Franklin, M. J. and Harper-Bill, C. (eds.) *Medieval Ecclesiastical Studies in Honour of Dorothy M. Owen*, 259-79. Woodbridge: The Boydell Press.

Thomas, A., Holbrook, N. and Bateman, C. 2003. Late prehistoric and Romano-British burial and settlement at Hucclecote, Gloucestershire: excavations in advance of the Gloucester Business Park link road, 1998. *Bristol and Gloucestershire Archaeological Report 2*.

Timby, J. 1998. *Excavations at Kingscote and Wycomb, Gloucestershire: A Roman Estate Centre and Small Town in the Cotswolds with Notes on Related Settlement*. Cirencester: Cotswold Archaeological Trust.

Trow, S.D. 1988. Excavations at Ditches hillfort, North Cerney, Gloucestershire, 1982-3. *Transactions of the Bristol and Gloucester Archaeological Society* 106, 19-85.

van Arsdell, R. D. and de Jersey, P. 1994. *The Coinage of the Dobunni: Money Supply and Coin Circulation in Dobunnic Territory with a Gazetteer of Findspots*. Monograph 38. Studies in Celtic Coinage 1. Oxford: Oxford University Committe for Archaeology.

VCH(Gl8). 1968. *The Victoria History of the Counties of England: A history of the County of Gloucester 8*. London: Oxford University Press.

Watts, L. and Leach, P. 1996. *Henley Wood. Temples and Cemetery: Excavations 1962-69 by the Late Ernest Greenfield and Others*. Council for British Archaeology Research Report 99. York: Council for British Archaeology.

Watts, V. 2004. *The Cambridge Dictionary of English Place-names*. Cambridge: Cambridge University Press.

Whitelock, D. (ed.) 1979. *English Historical Documents 1: Circa 500-1042*. Second edition. London: Eyre Methuen.

Willis-Bund, J.W. 1899. Episcopal register diocese of Worcester: register of Bishop Godfrey Giffard, 1273-1284, II. *Worcestershire Historical Society* 14, 53-224.

Willis-Bund, J.W. 1906. Ecclesiastical history. In Willis-Bund, J.W. and Page, W. (eds.) *The Victoria History of the County of Worcester, 2*, 1-92. London: James Street Haymarket.

Wills, J. 1978. Beckford, 1978. *West Midlands Archaeological News Sheet* 21, 43-45.

Wills, J. 2001. Archaeological review no. 25, 2000. *Transactions of the Bristol and Gloucestershire Archaeological Society* 119, 185-210.

Wills, J 2002. Archaeological review no. 26, 2001. *Transactions of the Bristol and Gloucestershire Archaeological Society* 120, 233-56.

Wise, P.J., and Seaby, W.A. 1995. Finds from a new productive site at Bidford-on-Avon, Warwickshire. *Transactions of the Birmingham and Warwickshire Archaeological Society* 99, 57-64.

Woodiwiss, S. 1992. *Iron Age and Roman Salt Production and the Medieval Town of Droitwich: Excavations at the Old Bowling Green and Friar Street*. Council for British Archaeology Research Report 81. York: Council for British Archaeology.

Yeates, S.J. 2005. *Religion, Community, and Territory: Defining Religion in the Severn Valley and Adjacent Hills from the Iron Age to the Early Medieval Period*. Unpublished PhD, University of Oxford.

Yeates, S.J. 2008. *The Tribe of Witches: The Religion of the Dobunni and Hwicce*. Oxford: Oxbow Books.

The Gray Hill Landscape Archaeology Project, Llanfair Discoed, Monmouthshire, Wales

Adrian M. Chadwick, with contributions by Joshua Pollard

Introduction

Gray Hill or Mynydd Llwyd is a distinctive red sandstone hill in south-east Monmouthshire, Wales, approximately two kilometres north-east of Caerwent in a prominent position overlooking the Severn estuary (Fig. 1). A stone circle, several standing stones and prehistoric cairns are part of the known archaeology on the hill (Bagnall-Oakeley and Bagnall-Oakeley 1889), but only the stone circle and outlying stones had been surveyed in any detail, and are the only protected Scheduled Ancient Monuments. A large cairn on the highest, western end of the hill remains unprotected, and is being eroded by walkers and horse riders. In historic times the hill was used as unimproved upland grazing, with some limited quarrying, and while much of it is now in private ownership, there are still limited commoners' rights over it. Since the 1960s, however, no animals have been grazed there, and bracken, birch scrub and other trees have progressively invaded areas of the hill. Yet Gray Hill retains remnants of upland heath vegetation, a rare habitat in south-east Wales, and important for birds, reptiles and mammals. The hill is popular with walkers, but has also suffered from the depredations of motorcycle scrambling, mountain biking and horse riding, which have damaged some of the archaeology.

In light of this, and in discussion with landowners and commoners, Monmouthshire County Council proposed a Management Plan for the hill, and as part of this work they commissioned an archaeological assessment of the area. From November 1999-January 2000, using aerial photographs, maps and GPS-based survey, many new archaeological features were identified (Makepeace 1999; 2000). These include a large, D-shaped scarp-edge enclosure that appeared to be one of the earliest constructions on the hill, which Graham Makepeace (*ibid.*) believed shares some features with other upland enclosures in Britain, including Gardom's Edge in Derbyshire (Ainsworth and Barnatt 1988; Barnatt *et al.* 2002), perhaps indicating a Neolithic date. Further prehistoric cairns were also found, and a series of double orthostat, co-axial stone boundaries radiating out from the D-shaped enclosure, which were suggested to be Bronze Age. Several recumbent or turf-covered stones also indicated a possible stone row leading from the stone circle to the existing standing stone. Makepeace also found a possible medieval enclosed settlement with a longhouse, and a series of boundaries and enclosures relating to post-medieval and early modern intakes, fields and crofts.

I became interested in Gray Hill after commencing a joint lecturing/project officer post set up by the University of Wales, Newport and Wessex Archaeology. I was looking for an area suitable for a multi-period landscape archaeology project, and I happened to meet and talk to Graham Makepeace about his survey. Since 2002 Gray Hill has formed the focus of more detailed earthwork survey and targeted excavation, undertaken by staff (Adrian Chadwick, Joshua Pollard and Mike Hamilton) and students of the University of Wales, Newport, and the University of Bristol. Local and foreign volunteers, and students from other British universities have also taken part. This mix of people of all ages and experiences has given the project a very special atmosphere. We have also used recording methodologies and working practices which try to make the fieldwork as inclusive, interpretative and reflective as possible (Chadwick 2003; forthcoming). In this paper, I will summarise the results of our survey and excavation, although detailed post-excavation analyses have not taken place, and so as yet there are no absolute ^{14}C or OSL dates available. I feel that it is important to make the results available at this stage though, and to discuss them in light of the approaches we have adopted, which have aimed to explore issues of interpretation and field survey, reflexive fieldwork practices, and the complex histories of landscape. I will also be outlining how these approaches have enriched our knowledge and experiences of the landscape and archaeology of Gray Hill, and the implications this has for other landscape projects.

Survey practice and praxis

On-going survey work has added considerably to the known archaeology of Gray Hill, much of this undertaken as an undergraduate module where the principal objective was to ensure students learn more than simply how to use a Total Station. There is a *potential* danger, especially with recent digital recording techniques, that the methodology employed becomes the main focus of archaeological enquiry and discussion (Chadwick 2004, 21). In some publications, there has been a tendency to focus on survey data, viewsheds and predictive modelling at the expense of considerations of how people in the past inhabited their world. The people themselves disappear from the landscape. But we cannot blame the methodologies for this – they are merely techniques. There have been some welcome notable exceptions to this trend, where archaeologists have used these techniques in a much more interpretative manner to investigate past human movements and practices (e.g. Edmonds and

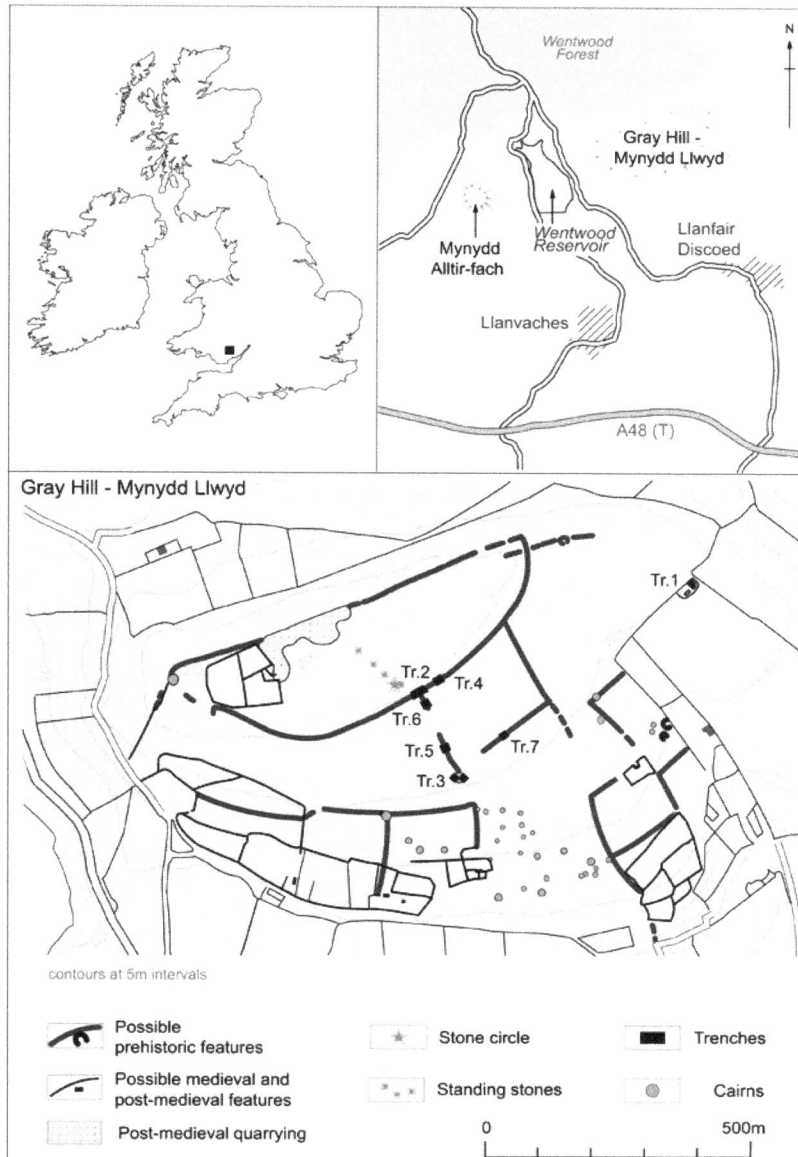

Figure 1 Location map of Gray Hill showing trench locations and known archaeological features, including some recently added by UWN survey (A. Leaver).

McElearney 1999; Llobera 1996; Pollard and Gillings 1998; Wickstead 2002; 2004).

The aim of the Gray Hill survey work has therefore been to inculcate students with the ability to recognise and interpret often quite subtle upstanding earthwork features, and to be able to establish the stratigraphic relationships between them. This 'analytical survey' to establish 'soft detail' is often best undertaken using fairly low-tech methods such as offset tape survey or plane tabling (Bowden 1999, 60-2), once control grids and some 'hard' detail have been established. These rather traditional methods continue to be used by the excellent archaeological surveyors of RCAHMW, Historic Scotland and English Heritage. I have also aimed to demonstrate how walkover survey or measured topographic and earthwork survey is always inherently interpretative. This

does not mean that we cannot record archaeological features, or try to make objective statements about them. Rather, survey work can be regarded as a wider form of praxis, a way of engaging with the landscape whereby our observations form part of 'a logic of inference' (Adams 1991).

For example, when looking at an area of upland landscape, the surveyor should attempt to map the archaeological features as objectively and accurately as possible, but this necessarily involves a first level of interpretation and inference, in deciding which features are archaeological, and which are parts of the 'natural' landscape, or in choosing where to mark the tops and bottoms of slopes. But during this process, they should also be interpreting these features from a classificatory perspective, such as whether a small, walled feature was

95

an enclosure for livestock, or possibly for human habitation. Was a cairn for clearance, or was it a funerary structure? There is then a third level of inference, which comes through thinking about the functional attributes of features. How did an enclosure gateway or a field boundary structure human and animal movements around the landscape, or how did a series of boundaries and trackways actually 'work' in terms of an agricultural regime? From which direction might a cairn have been approached from in the past? And finally, there is a fourth level of inference, which entails thinking about social practices such as land allotment, tenure and cosmology. Might constructional differences in surveyed boundaries reflect different phases of allotment, or different tenurial approaches? Why were a series of cairns sited (and sighted) in a particular place within the landscape? What might the experiential inhabitation of a particular landscape have been like for people in the past, on a daily, seasonal or longer-term basis?

Some archaeologists might argue that surveyors should, in the first instance and in the field, only restrict themselves to the first level of inference, to the supposedly objective recording of empirical information. Certainly within some commercial archaeology units there is a tendency to concentrate only on the recording side of the survey process, and not the interpretation. But as surveyors move about landscapes, many of them are already subconsciously or implicitly engaged in thinking about the other levels of inference too. All these different levels of inference should all be taking place at the same time. In addition to the actual survey plans or digital records therefore, surveyors should explicitly note their thoughts on these inferences, complementing the 'objective' recording. These can be in the form of notebooks, or in notations on the actual plans themselves. This does not alter the primary drawn or digitally mapped record, but instead substantially enhances it. This may seem self-evident to some, but I believe that it is important to get people to realise this when they are being trained, hence the focus on this at Gray Hill.

One important discovery at Gray Hill has been that the D-shaped enclosure bank does not simply end where it meets the scarp-edge on the north-eastern side of the hill, as originally proposed (Makepeace 1999, 72). More detailed survey by Daryl Williams and Jonathan Burton, aided by aerial photograph analysis, revealed a pronounced 'corner' in the bank, where it returns to run along the scarp edge (Fig. 1). Much was hidden in dense birch scrub, and early modern quarrying also destroyed a large section, but it emerges again on the western side of the disturbance. Here, a section of the bank was marked on the the tithe map of 1847, and as an 'old wall' on the 1882 first edition Ordnance Survey map, and was probably re-used as part of a post-medieval intake boundary. The enclosure bank meets the large cairn on the highest, westernmost point of Gray Hill, but the stratigraphic relationship between them is not clear from the earthwork evidence alone.

Unlike the excavated sections (see below), the scarp-edge bank is either of double orthostat construction, or takes the form of subrectangular sandstone blocks laid end to end, and survives as two courses in places, also making use of a line of naturally outcropping red sandstone. Towards the north-east corner of the D-shaped enclosure there are several gaps apparent in the bank, including one where a pronounced holloway cuts through the scarp-edge. There is a natural geological fault line here, and it is not clear whether the holloway cut through the enclosure, or if the enclosure bank respects it. Another holloway, parallel to a later boundary, runs towards the eastern side of the enclosure (see Fig. 1), but here relatively regular stonework on each side of a narrow gap suggests that this was an original entrance. On the south-western side of the hill, the D-shaped enclosure bank also appears to extend further west than previously proposed, with a newly identified section on the far side of a wide gap that may be an original entrance (Fig. 1).

Further linear banks, double orthostat boundaries, cairns and boulder-walled enclosures on the eastern and south-eastern slopes of the hill have also been identified (Fig. 1), in areas now covered by extremely dense vegetation. A more detailed survey of the cairn group by Dave Roberts and Samantha Williams established that although many were clearance cairns, some were probably funerary monuments, matching earlier descriptions of the Bagnall-Oakeleys (1889). Several were subject to antiquarian disturbance, including one example with a stone-lined cist, though the capstone was removed and the contents robbed. This cist contained a nineteenth century horseshoe. There has also been survey of parts of the Penhein estate on the eastern flank of Gray Hill, including post-medieval and early modern 'polite' features such as a ha-ha and a nuttery, in addition to remains of agricultural improvement, such as a series of limekilns. However, a possible later prehistoric or Romano-British enclosure, roundhouse ring gullies and ditched boundaries have also been identified through topographic and geophysical survey. The latter worked especially well as Penhein was built on an outcropping limestone shelf.

Reflective excavation, recording and practice
Archaeologists have realised that the recording techniques of the 1970s and 1980s, whilst innovative in their day, are no longer adequate to deal with the complexities of archaeological deposits and archaeologists' interactions with them. Key summaries of more recent approaches can be found elsewhere (Adams and Brooke 1995; Barber 1993; Chadwick 1998; 2003; Hodder 1998; Lucas 2001; Shepherd 1994; Steane 1992). As part of the Gray Hill project, we have incorporated a greater concern with recording and interpretation of formation processes with a more self-critical and interpretative approach to the excavation and recording process, to empower the individual excavator and encourage her or his subjective insights. Existing multi-purpose context recording sheets were too limiting, and so a number of separate cut, deposit/fill, and stone structure sheets have been designed, creating more possibilities for interpretation and commentary on both

the 'objective' and subjective aspects of excavation, and about the nature and contextual associations of the finds recovered (Blinkhorn and Cumberpatch 1998), and the *inference potential* of each context.

The latter refers to the potential information contexts might provide to the archaeologist (Adams 1991; 1992; Adams and Brooke 1995). For example, a floor layer full of worn pottery sherds and other artefacts, along with seeds and other carbonised plant remains, might relate to activities on or near that floor surface, or to formation processes after abandonment. Such a context could be said to have a good inference potential. In contrast, a floor makeup layer may contain little or no finds, and does not provide as much potential information about past human practice. On Gray Hill, a buried land surface or a post-removal episode might have greater inference potential than a root-reworked upper stone layer from a cairn.

On the Gardom's Edge research project in Derbyshire (Barnatt *et al.* 2002; Edmonds and McElearney 1999), the prehistoric archaeology included many complex stone and earth features. Along with their subsequent exposure to soil and chemical weathering processes, they were a real challenge to excavate and understand. Whilst excavating the cairns, enclosure and field banks, many of us working at Gardom's Edge found that conventional context sheets and scale drawings were often inadequate means of describing many of the subtleties of construction encountered. At the time, and with subsequent reflection, we realised that we needed to develop a 'grammar of stone'.

Many of the archaeological features on Gray Hill also have a stone component, and constructional histories featuring meshes of stone, earth and organic materials such as turf or timber that have since rotted away. Cairns and banks may have quite subtle differences in construction, and might consist of dumps of stone, or more carefully placed rocks, or mixtures of both. The degree of wear and weathering is also important. The recording of these attributes requires a more specialised stone structure sheet. Our approach has also been influenced by recent theoretical work on prehistoric architectural complexities (McFadyen 2000; McFadyen and Pollard 2002).

Conventional finds-recording procedures incorporate a number of theoretical and practical problems, including the rather uncritical notion of 'small finds'. This designation gives an object a reified and privileged status (explicitly or implicitly) over other objects from the same context. It may attribute meanings to objects that reflect contemporary preoccupations rather than those they might have had in the past, and is predicated on values derived from antiquarian approaches (Cumberpatch and Dunkley 1996, 7). Objects are considered to have some importance in their own right, rather than their potential for the interpretation of past human practices. Yet the 'small find' may not offer any greater insights into past

human activities or beliefs than other material from the context. A coin from a secondary pit deposit may tell us little about the nature of occupation on a particular site, but the pottery, animal bone and palaeo-environmental remains may provide much more information, and thus have more inference potential. There is also the practical problem of another layer of recording being necessary to link separate 'small finds', sample and context numbers, which increases the danger of mixed or poorly numbered bags.

Instead, we followed the approach pioneered by John Collis (Collis 2001; Loughton 2000) and developed by the now defunct South Yorkshire Archaeology Unit, for whom I used to work. Under this system, objects are bagged separately from bulk finds according to individual conservation needs, but they are assigned different *bag numbers* within the overall context number (Collis 2001, 84-86; Cumberpatch and Dunkley 1996, 7), restoring the individual context as the primary unit of recording. Bulk palaeo-environmental samples, soil samples for pollen or micromorphological analyses and Optically Stimulated Luminescence (OSL) dating, charcoal samples for species identification and ^{14}C dating can all have different bag numbers attributed to them, rather than separate sample numbers. With the context number still paramount, finds, samples and context information remain more closely linked, and communication between specialists during post-excavation is also facilitated.

Archaeological study of the Gray Hill landscape
Survey and excavation of a possible medieval building
Makepeace (1999) identified a possible medieval or post-medieval settlement complex on the south-eastern flank of Gray Hill (Makepeace 1999) (see Fig. 1). The complex consists of a semi-circular stone bank, enclosing the remains of two stone buildings. This locale was then used as a dump for both small and very large stones that were cleared from the adjacent field when it was still under arable cultivation, in some cases as late as the 1960s (R. Micklethwait pers. comm.). The present field boundary wall bank appears to overlie the north-west end of the building. As this field bank may represent a late medieval or earlier post-medieval intake, it is therefore possible that the building is medieval in date, and its form is similar to medieval longhouses.

Detailed offset survey revealed a western rectangular stone building, orientated roughly north-east to south-west, and approximately 10 metres long and 4.5 metres wide. It appears to have had an entrance facing north-west, with one side of a doorway formed by a large sandstone orthostat. A possible entrance through the enclosure bank lies just to the east of this building. Behind it are several subtle earthwork features that may represent the platforms for small wooden structures or for garden plots. Further to the north-east is a more substantial building 14.5 metres long and 5 metres wide. There is a cross-passage formed by two entrances in the middle of the structure, with an additional small entrance in the north-east end. To the north-east is a semi-circular stone feature, probably a livestock pen or a small ancillary structure. The possible cross-passage building was partially excavated in April 2003 (Trench 1).

Trench 1 was located across the north-east wall of the building. Underneath the modern stone clearance piles, turf and topsoil were several layers of stone tumble from wall collapse, but a worked stone hone or whetstone was recovered from one of these deposits. The tumble partially overlay a wall of angular sandstone and conglomerate blocks, roughly dressed but laid in courses, and surviving to a height of 0.43 metres. The wall had an internal face formed by large blocks, with a core of smaller stone fragments and earth. The external face of the wall was partially revetted into the slope, and had a dump of soil placed against it. Within the building, a compact, internal floor surface abutted the internal face of the wall, and several stakeholes and postholes were identified, though only some were excavated. A second whetstone was recovered from the surface of a postpipe in one of the postholes, and the cross-passage entrance was confirmed. Unfortunately, no dateable artefacts were recovered, but the excavated structure would seem to have been a late medieval or early post-medieval longhouse.

Excavation of the D-shaped enclosure bank
Excavation of Trench 2 revealed that the D-shaped enclosure bank was abutted by a later, roughly north-west to south-east aligned co-axial boundary (Figs. 1 and 2). The 'corner' formed by the intersection of these two structures was the focus for later stone robbing to create a gap through the two walls, and masonry from both was deliberately pushed over to form a 'ramp' leading up to the gap. A metalled stone surface was created north of the gap, presumably to facilitate livestock movement. Fragments of a late 19th or early 20th century glass beer bottle intermingled with some of the fallen rubble suggested that this activity was relatively recent in date. The north-west to south-east aligned boundary was a right-angled section of faced and coursed walling, whose corner respected an earlier entrance through the enclosure bank. This walling was of regular and evenly coursed stone up to 0.5 metres high, initially thought to be a rebuild of an earlier boundary, and might even be of medieval or post-medieval date. Some of the Bronze Age reaves excavated on Dartmoor were similar in form, however (e.g. Fleming 1988, 83, 86), and so a later date should not be assumed.

The D-shaped enclosure boundary consisted of a roughly north-east to south-west stone bank up to 1.3 metres wide with large facing blocks on the southern 'outer' face, and smaller, irregular stones 'tying' these into a fabric of tabular fragments (Chadwick *et al.* 2002; 2003). It had a lower course of very large, rectangular facing blocks on the southern, 'outer' face, and may have originally stood to a height of 1.5-2 metres. Some of the lower stones were disturbed or robbed, with several stone impressions left in the underlying natural subsoil. A mineralised sand deposit

beneath the bank was sampled for OSL dating, and for pollen and soil micromorphology analysis.

The rounded end of the D-shaped enclosure bank excavated in Trench 2 was probably a later addition formed by smaller sandstone fragments (see Fig. 2, Phases 1 and 2). Extension of the trench to the west revealed the butt end of another section of bank, forming an inturned entrance nearly 2 metres wide, with a wear hollow between the two structures. Two large postholes formed part of a timber entrance structure or wooden marker posts. The addition of smaller stones to the end of the one section of bank might represent a deliberate act of constricting or 'closing down' of the entrance after the removal of the posts. To the north of the banks, and post-dating both of them, was a stone surface forming part of a revetment or platform. On the basis of construction technique and general character, it still seems likely that the D-shaped enclosure wall bank is prehistoric, and the co-axial boundary wall may be too. Some of the possible phasing is shown in Fig. 2, and consists of:

1. A timber setting, forming part of an entrance structure.
2. The removal of one post and the burning of another, followed by a narrowing of the entrance through the enclosure banks. It is not clear if the horizontal stone surface 229 was created at this stage, as a separate Phase 3, or during Phase 4.
3. Possible construction of the stone surface?
4. The partial robbing of the enclosure banks.
5. The construction of a co-axial field boundary, forming a right angle to the D-shaped enclosure wall, but perhaps incorporating it into a field system.
6. The partial collapse of the D-shaped enclosure wall and the co-axial boundary.
7. A deliberate slighting of the junction between the two walls, creating a gap, a rough stone ramp and a metalled surface through which stock could be driven.

Another section of D-shaped enclosure bank was excavated at Trench 4, revealing some variations in construction, and large fragments of charcoal were found in a deposit at the base of the bank, hopefully suitable for species identification and ^{14}C dating.

Excavation of co-axial boundaries
Trench 6 was located to the south, across the same north-west to south-east co-axial wall boundary recorded in Trench 2. The wall was up to 0.83 metres wide and 0.46 metres in height, and consisted of small sandstone and conglomerate blocks, laid in rough courses, although in places larger subrounded stones were used. No spalls or fragments from working stone were found, indicating that the stones had not been trimmed *in situ*. The wall was built on top of a podzolised deposit that may have been original subsoil, and this was sampled for pollen analysis.

Trench 5 was excavated across a wall that appeared to be part of the same co-axial boundary in Trench 6, but which was double orthostat in form. It was located where a clearance cairn had been built on top of the boundary. The cairn was up to 2.60 metres wide and 0.50 metres high, with both 'fresh' and fractured, and more worn and weathered stones. Spalling was only present on a few, indicating that most stones were placed on the cairn rather than simply thrown onto it. On the eastern side of the boundary, the stones of the cairn were partially embedded in a deposit of dark greyish brown sandy clay loam, only present on the western side of the wall. This deposit overlapped a linear group of stones which represented clearance against the eastern face of the wall.

The double orthostat wall was 1.14 metres wide and 0.95 metres high, with two lines of large tabular and subrectangular blocks (Fig. 3), including a particularly prominent upright stone around which the later clearance cairn had been constructed. In between the two faces was a core of small sandstone fragments and soil. The facing stones on the western side were much larger than those on the east, but many were tilting outwards at a roughly 45° angle. The difference in wall facing between the western and eastern sides, the different soils, and the greater evidence for clearance on the eastern side, all suggest that different subsistence and social practices were taking place on either side of the boundary, perhaps related to pastoral and arable activities. However, these might also reflect tenurial differences. The tilting stones appeared to have been deliberately pushed over at some time in antiquity, possible representing a 'slighting' of the boundary, or tensions and arguments over it. The soil deposits beneath and on either side of the wall were sampled for pollen and micromorphological analyses, which might resolve some of the land use questions.

In 2004, Trench 7 was opened up over a double orthostat boundary running along the contours of the hill (Fig. 1), revealing further evidence for clearance on both sides of the wall, but also that the wall was constructed over an earlier, partially flattened clearance heap or cairn. This work all demonstrates how more detailed surface survey, combined with excavation, can begin to produce more complex sequences of land division, boundary construction and clearance, reflecting changes in the use and perception of Gray Hill by past communities.

Excavation of a ring cairn and Beaker burial (Adrian M. Chadwick and Joshua Pollard)

Trench 3 was located where Makepeace (op. cit.) identified a possible ring cairn, approximately 170 metres south of the D-shaped enclosure (Fig. 1). The centre of the feature was markedly concave, and it initially appeared that antiquarian digging had disturbed it, but despite some later stone robbing, perhaps for a post-medieval boundary 30 metres to the south, much of the cairn was left intact, and antiquaries may have presumed that someone else had investigated it first. Excavation demonstrated that the feature was a large ring cairn approximately 13 metres in total diameter, slightly ovoid in plan, with its southern, downslope extent still surviving to nearly 1.2 metres in

height. Some 60% of the cairn was excavated – total excavation was not felt to be appropriate for logistical and ethical considerations. As so many cairns on Gray Hill have been disturbed, it seemed inappropriate to completely excavate this example.

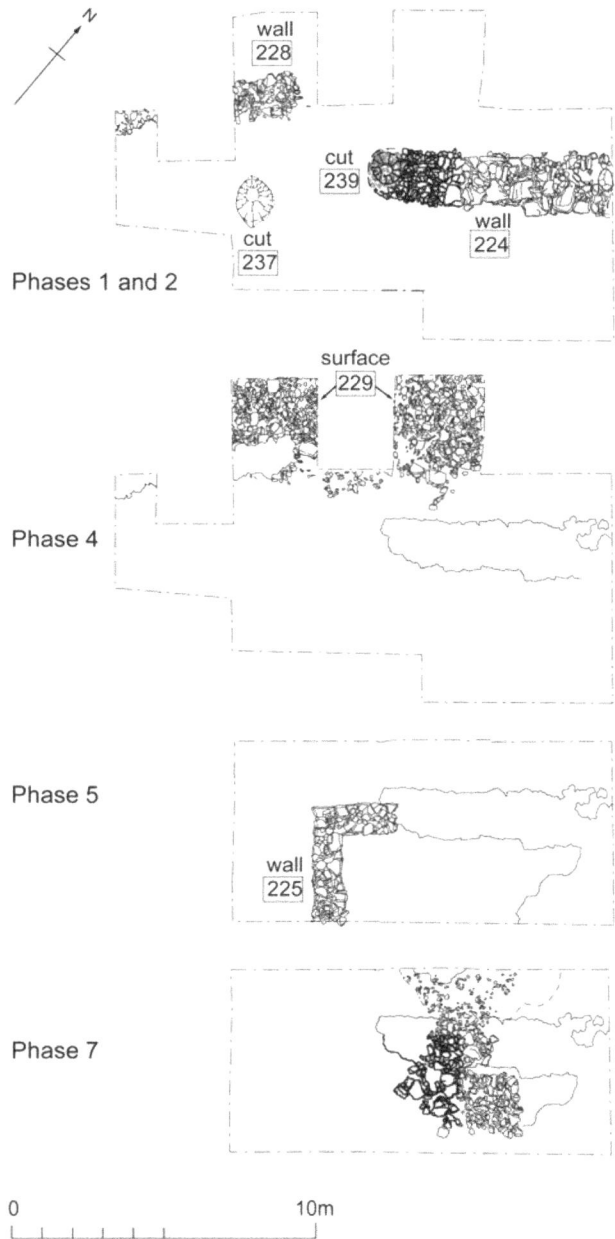

Figure 2 The proposed stratigraphic sequence at Trench 2 (P. Huckfield and A. Leaver).

The ring cairn itself consisted of a low stone structure roughly 12 metres in diameter and 2 metres wide, with regularly spaced, upright tabular sandstone slabs set at steep angles against the inner face of a broadly circular and convex stone rubble bank (Fig. 4). Between the larger orthostats were occasional smaller, though still substantial, near-upright blocks; these facing slabs were all set within a narrow, round ring slot, and many were supported on levelling and packing stones. The rubble ring bank was actually quite an intricate construction, with some evidence of radial divisions formed by further tabular blocks, and hints that individual 'cells' were filled with different stone rubble material – some freshly quarried and fractured, with red-marl or sand still adhering, whilst other pieces were weathered and worn, and derived from freestone or clearance. To the north-west, a possible gap in the upright slabs was deliberately filled in with smaller stones, reflecting the blocking of an entrance into the ring cairn. To the south-east, one large horizontal slab marked another probable original entrance. Beneath the ring bank was a heavily mineralised, manganese-stained deposit, and several small stakeholes, although it was not clear if the ring bank was preceded by an earlier timber stake ring structure. At least three circular postholes were excavated in the south-east quadrant, lying underneath stone that had been added later to the southern and south-eastern side of the cairn. In an earlier phase therefore, the southern side of the ring cairn was probably marked by upright timber posts 2-3 metres high.

In the interior of the embanked space was a roughly horizontal surface or platform formed by two or three courses of angular sandstone slabs. In the centre of the ring cairn a small mound of smaller, more fractured stones had sunk into a large, steep-sided pit lined with very large sandstone blocks. Underneath an upper fill of angular sandstone fragments was a smaller stone setting about 1 metre across, associated with charcoal and burnt stone, and probably part of a later, secondary deposit. From this came a segmented, blue-grey faience bead, the first recorded from South Wales, and one of only eight known from Wales as a whole (Lynch 2000, 112; Sheridan 2004). Analysis of the bead by Alison Sheridan of the National Museum of Scotland and Mary Davis of the National Museum of Wales could not determine its mineralogical source, but in form it is similar to examples from southern England.

At the very end of the 2003 season, two fine barbed-and-tanged flint arrowheads were found near the base of the pit. These arrowheads, both intact and 'fresh', seem to have been made of flint from a chalkland source to the east. Further excavation in 2004 found five additional barbed-and-tanged arrowheads. The two found in 2003 and two from 2004 were clearly two 'pairs', each pair made in a similar style and on almost identical flint, but perhaps by two different flintknappers. Of the three remaining arrowheads, two were more unusual forms made on flakes. The same deposit also produced some sherds of Beaker pottery from at least two different vessels, and possible sherds of a Collared Urn. Most of the pots had probably been removed in antiquity, before the secondary stone setting and faience bead were added. Although no traces of human bone were found, or even staining of the soil, a stone-free area of the deposit was probably where an inhumation burial was originally located. This is the first definite Beaker burial known from south-east Wales (c.f. Hamilton 2004, 88).

Figure 3 Double orthostat co-axial wall in Trench 5, looking north.

Figure 4 Photograph of the ring cairn, following removal of tumble and clearance cairns (A. Leaver).

The deposit containing the finds lay within a rectangular area defined by narrow slots for horizontal timbers and small postholes (Fig. 5). These appear to have formed a timber mortuary structure approximately 2 metres long and 1.5 metres wide, set within a much larger, subrectangular grave pit 3.80 metres long, 3 metres wide and 0.90 metres deep. The north-west side of the grave seemed to have been disturbed, perhaps during the insertion of the later stone setting. The backfill between the pit sides and the timber structure included a large, upright sandstone block on the south-eastern side. Here, a large horizontal sandstone slab was laid at the edge of the pit cut, with possible carvings on its upper surface, including a cup-and-ring mark. This stone was close to the south-eastern entrance through the ring bank, and may have been a platform where people could stand and look down into the open grave before it was backfilled. Following the infilling of the central grave, further stone was progressively added to the cairn, particularly on its southern side, where a 1-2 metre wide band of additional sandstone blocks was perhaps linked to clearance of adjacent ground, leaving the structure as a large platform or mound in the centre of the ring cairn (Fig. 4). On top of the circular rubble ring bank on the eastern side of the cairn, a small hearth associated with a microdenticulate flint blade was excavated.

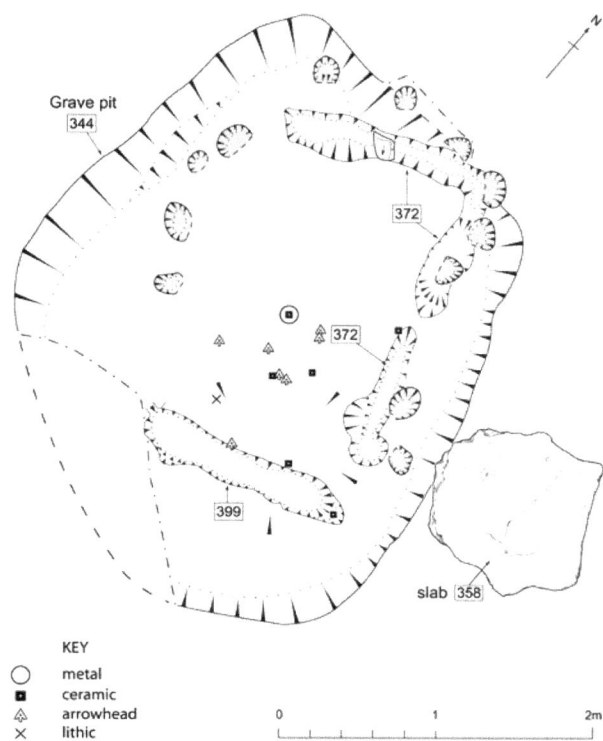

Figure 5 Plan of central pit cut 344, showing the timber mortuary structure and the horizontal slab with cup and ring decoration (A. Leaver).

The north-west to south-east co-axial, double orthostat boundary ran downslope towards the large cairn, but kinked slightly and stopped just before it, apparently respecting its position (Fig. 1). Between this boundary and the main cairn is an unexcavated 'satellite' cairn, and further earthworks suggest more satellite cairns quite regularly spaced around the ring cairn. Two were excavated in 2002 and 2003, and proved to be small, regular rounded mounds of worn sandstone fragments approximately 3 metres in diameter. These did not produce any finds. It is likely that they were derived from field clearance, but they were not simply loose, unstructured piles of stone. One had a rough kerb formed of larger blocks, whilst the other had a formal setting of upright slabs demarcating the junction between this and the larger ring cairn, which was clearly of considerable social significance when this activity was being carried

out. During removal of the topsoil on top of the cairn, a horseshoe was found. Along with the example placed in the robbed cist of the cairn further downslope, this suggests an early modern vernacular tradition of adding horseshoes to upstanding cairns on Gray Hill, perhaps to bring good luck

The Beaker pottery and the barbed-and-tanged arrowheads suggest an early Bronze Age date for an original inhumation within the central pit, with the primary deposit around 2300-1800 BC, and the possible Collared Urn sherds and the faience bead a date of between 1800-1600 BC for the disturbance and secondary deposit. Radiocarbon dating of charcoal samples should provide absolute dating for the sequence. While the structure seems to have developed around an individual burial, later phases need not have been linked to funerary activity. It is difficult to be certain how long the cairn remained in active 'use', but the complexity of later constructional detail – with extension on the southern side, and the creation of the satellite clearance cairns – implies a reasonable temporal depth, perhaps extending into the later Bronze Age or even the early Iron Age. Over this period, the structure may have been transformed from an open, bank-defined monument in what was perhaps a largely 'open' landscape, to an essentially 'closed' construction in an increasingly enclosed setting of land allotment and land division.

The landscape context of the archaeological features
There has been much recent discussion within British archaeology about phenomenology, or how in the past, human consciousness and experiences of the world were created, through the location or movements of the human body and the stimulation of the senses (e.g. Bender *et al.* n.d.; Bender *et al.* 1997; Thomas 1993; Tilley 1994; 1996; 2004; Tilley *et al.* 2000). Although these approaches offer many potentially interesting insights, aspects of them have been cogently criticised for ignoring cultural and historical specificity in the past, and for failing to consider issues such as identity, power and social structure (Brück 1998). We should be extremely careful not to establish universal ideas of human encounters with the material world, such that our own experiencing bodies automatically stand in for those of the people inhabiting the past. People in prehistory may have had very different ideas about the human body, identity and gender, sociality and the landscape. Furthermore, we must not concentrate on ritual monuments and ritual practices, at the expense of understanding how landscapes structured the routine, daily existence of different people and communities in the past. We do not want to write archaeologies where landscapes are populated only by the dead or the disembodied (Chadwick 2004, 22).

We have been working towards more nuanced accounts of the archaeology of Gray Hill that acknowledge the dynamic, mutable nature of the constructions and varied human experiences of the landscape. As elsewhere in Britain, the locations of some of the archaeological features on Gray Hill were carefully chosen in the past. The standing stone outlier and the orthostat by the possible entrance into the stone circle both line up with a distinctive 'notch' in the skyline across the Severn estuary, formed by the gorge of the River Avon. On the midwinter solstice the sun rises from behind this notch. Perhaps more significantly, when standing in the stone circle you can look out across the coastal plain, the Gwent Levels, and the Severn itself. The stone circle is built within a slight 'bowl' or natural amphitheatre in the hillside, which may have allowed practices taking place within the stone circle to be visible and audible to a larger number of people.

The D-shaped enclosure boundary was built close to the stone circle, enclosing it *within* the enclosure, which may have been socially and politically significant. Although the chronological relationship between them is not yet known, neither appears to have been robbed for stone in order to build the other, perhaps indicating some respect. No platforms or similar evidence for occupation have been detected within the area delineated by the D-shaped enclosure, and its 'function' remains unknown, although one of its roles might have been to define an area of upland pasture. Although it had entrances to the south, east and south-west, it is nevertheless different in form to upland causewayed enclosures such as Gardom's Edge in Derbyshire and Green How in Cumbria, which have been presumed to be Neolithic in date (Ainsworth and Barnatt 1988; Barnatt *et al.* 2002; Horne *et al.* 2001). A later Neolithic or Bronze Age date is still possible, but this will have to be established through ^{14}C or OSL analysis. The stone bank was much more imposing on its 'outer' face, perhaps indicating that it was at least in part a statement of tenurial control. The fact that Gray Hill is so visible from the coastal plain, and such a distinctive shape, might also have been a significant factor.

The possible wide south-western entrance into the D-shaped enclosure is close to a subtle natural depression in the ground, not visible on the coarse contour plan in Fig. 1, that can be followed downslope to the south-east, and which runs just below the group of cairns. This may have formed a natural holloway, allowing livestock to be brought up onto the hill, as the western slopes are very steep. Routine movements onto and off Gray Hill might thus have entailed people and animals passing by clearance and burial cairns, perhaps keeping them under the watchful gaze of ancestors or spirits, and also creating links between the living, the dead and the land. The close physical relationship between the D-shaped enclosure and the large westernmost cairn might also have been significant, and again may have had implications for tenurial relations.

Several cairns seem to have been sited at very specific locales. The large cairn on the highest, westernmost point on Gray Hill has extensive views out over the Severn and the Gwent Levels, and also to the Black Mountains to the north. It would have been intervisible with two large round barrows on the Wentwood ridge nearly two kilometres to the north-west. Other barrows and cairns are recorded from the area now covered by the Wentwood Forest plantation. A series of springs emerge along the ridge, and it is possible that prehistoric people may have made some links between death, rebirth and the appearance of life-giving waters. The ring cairn is false-crested, and although its landscape location (though probably not the actual cairn itself) might once have been visible from the plain around Caerwent, at the foot of the southern slope of Gray Hill it cannot be seen. It is only when you walk upslope towards it and are only some 40m away that the cairn appears in front of you once more. This phenomenon has been noted with other Bronze Age cairns and barrows across Britain, other notable Welsh examples including the Bryn Cader Faner cairn circle in North Wales. In prehistory, the timber posts on the southern side of the Gray Hill ring cairn, later replaced by additional stone, would have made the structure more pronounced when approached from downslope.

More detailed examination of the double-orthostat, co-axial field walls has revealed particularly prominent stones at irregular intervals along their lengths. This may simply reflect the presence of large, nearby earthfast boulders when they were built, but some, such as the example excavated in Trench 5, may have served as initial boundary markers at some point prior to wall construction. Alternatively, they may record the progress of wall building, or might mark the contributions of different 'gangs', families or clans. Two boundaries were aligned on the ring cairn, and the boundary running downslope towards the ring cairn respected its position. One north-south boundary on the southern flank of the hill seems to have been aligned on a small islet (Denny Island) in the Severn estuary. The roughly 50 metre wide gaps in the walls south and south-east of the stone circle and D-shaped enclosure appear to have been intentional, although we do not yet know if there were fences or hedges in these apparent gaps. The gaps may have been to facilitate the movement of livestock. However, the evidence for clearance could suggest that the natural terraces of the southern and south-eastern slopes might have been cultivated. But if this were the case, how were areas of arable and pasture effectively separated from one another? Pollen and soil micromorphology analyses may go some way to answering these questions.

Discussion (*A.M. Chadwick and Joshua Pollard*)
Many recent landscape archaeology projects in Britain have proved that much information can be gained through targeted contextual excavation undertaken at an extensive landscape scale (Adams 1999; Barnatt *et al.* 2002; Brück *et al.* 2003; Frodsham and Waddington 2004; Johnston and Roberts 2004). Our work at Gray Hill has likewise shown that there was far more constructional complexity and time depth to many of the features than is apparent on the surface, suggesting long and complex histories, rather than a few phases of widespread construction imposed upon the landscape. In addition, through the development of more reflective and reflexive on-site recording sheets

102

Figure 6 Working on Gray Hill. Photomontage: Anne Leaver.

(Chadwick 2003), we have been able to examine more closely our physical engagements with stone and earth (Fig. 6). So far, this has proved very successful in allowing excavators to voice their own understandings of these subtleties of construction. These ideas should help us to explore key issues such as land allotment, land tenure and land use that are the focus of much theoretical interest and discussion (e.g. Johnston 2001; Kitchen 2001).

At the ring cairn, activity did not end with the creation of the central mound over the burial pit, but further stone was added over time, and the creation of the

clearance cairns followed, perhaps without any hiatus. The ring cairn continued to be an important focus after more formal construction had ceased, and was woven again and again into the lives and stories of those who followed. Linear field boundaries eventually followed, two of them still referencing or respecting it. We should not see the cairn as a 'monument', constructed as a fully planned and fully finished entity, and set into a static notion of a landscape 'palimpsest' (Chadwick 2004, 4-5). Nor can its constructional development be neatly sub-divided into self-contained phases. Instead, here there were many different materialities, a sense of different connections being made, and perhaps even different groups of people making them. Attempting to fit the ring cairn into an artificial archaeological typology would be to ignore the fluidity and organic character of its coming into being (Chadwick and Pollard in prep.). Indeed, this structure, like the other cairns and boundaries on Gray Hill, was undoubtedly 'worked at' by many successive generations and/or different groups visiting the hill, beginning from the latest third or early second millennium BC.

Our project will inform the future management of Gray Hill, and it is clear that many more of its archaeological features (such as the large western cairn) should be given statutory protection, as some are unusual in form and extremely rare in a Welsh context, particularly for south-east Wales (Peterson and Pollard 2004). The co-axial field system is unlike the more irregular and nucleated later prehistoric fields and boundaries in the Black Mountains and Brecon Beacons (e.g. RCAHMW 1997). The D-shaped, scarp-edge enclosure is also different to known Iron Age, Romano-British, post-Roman and medieval or post-medieval boundaries and enclosures. The large cairns on Gray Hill are highly significant, especially now that excavation of one has produced such an important burial, and the potential links with the region across the Severn are also intriguing. Yet there is a remarkable lack of lithic material from Gray Hill, although our test-pitting has begun to discover some evidence for this. The apparent lack of pottery, even from the Romano-British or medieval periods, is also notable. These are amongst the many questions future work in this landscape will have to address.

Acknowledgements
We would like to thank Helen Lewis for inviting us to contribute, and for her editorial suggestions and tolerance of missed deadlines. We are extremely grateful to Ray and Mandy Stephens and Richard and Victoria Micklethwait for their continued support and co-operation, Graham Makepeace for his knowledge and enthusiasm, and all of the students and volunteers who took part. Adrian Chadwick, Joshua Pollard and Mike Hamilton directed the 2002-2004 excavations, with the assistance of Paul Huckfield, Rick Peterson and Helen Wickstead (Research Assistants), and Jane Masters, Hazel O'Neill, Adrian Pigeon, Dave Roberts and Chris Timmins (Site Supervisors). Daryl Williams and Jonathan Burton discovered the scarp-edge section of the D-shaped enclosure, and Dave Roberts and Samantha Williams surveyed the cairns in more detail. Anne Leaver provided vital administrative and logistical assistance, and produced the illustrations. Helen Lewis, then of the University of Oxford, undertook soil micromorphology and pollen sampling, and Phillip Toms of the University of Gloucestershire carried out sampling for Optically Stimulated Luminescence dating. Mary Davis of the National Museum of Wales and Alison Sheridan of the National Museum of Scotland conserved and studied the faience bead. The work at Gray Hill has been funded by grants from the Board of Celtic Studies, the British Academy, the Prehistoric Society and the SCARAB Research Centre.

Bibliography
Adams, M. 1991. A logic of archaeological inference. *Journal of Theoretical Archaeology* 2, 1-11.

Adams, M. 1992. Stratigraphy after Harris: some questions. In Steane, K. (ed.) *Interpretation of Stratigraphy: A Review of the Art. Proceedings of the 1st Stratigraphy Conference, Lincoln*, 13-16. Lincoln: City of Lincoln Archaeology Unit.

Adams, M. 1999. Beyond the Pale: some thoughts on the later prehistory of the Breamish Valley. In Bevan, B. (ed.) *Northern Exposure: Interpretative Devolution and the Iron Ages in Britain*, 111-22. Leicester Archaeology Monographs 4. Leicester: Leicester Archaeology.

Adams, M. and Brooke, C. 1995. Unmanaging the past: truth, data and the human being. *Norwegian Archaeological Review* 28(2), 93-104.

Ainsworth, S. and Barnatt, J. 1988. A scarp-edge enclosure at Gardom's Edge, Baslow, Derbyshire. *Derbyshire Archaeological Journal* 118, 5-23.

Bagnall-Oakeley, M.E. and Bagnall-Oakeley, W. 1889. *An Account of Some of the Rude Stone Monuments and Ancient Burial Mounds in Monmouthshire*. Newport: Monmouthshire and Caerleon Antiquarian Association.

Barber, J.W. (ed.) 1993. *Interpreting Stratigraphy. Proceedings of the 2nd Stratigraphy Conference, Edinburgh*. Edinburgh: AOC Scotland Ltd.

Barnatt, J., Bevan, B. and Edmonds, M. 2002. Gardom's Edge: a landscape through time. *Antiquity* 76, 51-6.

Bender, B., Edmonds, M., Hamilton, S. and Tilley, C. No date. The rituals of routine practice. Unpublished paper.

Bender, B., Hamilton, S. and Tilley, C. 1997. Leskernick: Stone worlds; alternative narratives; nested landscapes. *Proceedings of the Prehistoric Society* 63, 147-78.

Blinkhorn, P.W. and Cumberpatch, C.G. 1998. The interpretation of artefacts and the tyranny of the field archaeologist. *assemblage* 4. http://www.shef.ac.uk/~assem/4.

Bowden, M. (ed.) 1999. *Unravelling the Landscape. An Inquisitive Approach to Archaeology*. Gloucester: Tempus.

Brück, J. 1998. In the footsteps of the ancestors: a review of Christopher Tilley's 'A Phenomenology of Landscape: Places, Paths and Monuments'. *Archaeological Review from Cambridge* 15(1), 23-36.

Brück, J., Johnston, R. and Wickstead, H. 2003. Excavations of Bronze Age field systems on Shovel Down, Dartmoor, 2003. *Past* 45, 10-12.

Chadwick, A.M. 1998. Archaeology at the edge of chaos – further towards reflexive excavation methodologies. *assemblage* 3. http://www.shef.ac.uk/~assem/3.

Chadwick, A.M. 2003. Post-processualism, professional-isation and archaeological methodologies. Towards reflective and radical practice. *Archaeological Dialogues* 10(1), 97-117.

Chadwick, A.M. 2004. 'Geographies of sentience' – an introduction to space, place and time. In Chadwick, A.M. (ed.) *Stories from the Landscape: Archaeologies of Inhabitation*, 1-31. British Archaeological Reports International Series S1238. Oxford: BAR Publishing.

Chadwick, A.M. Forthcoming. What have the post-processualists ever done for us? Towards an integration of theory and practice, and a radical field archaeology. In Roskams, S.P. and Beck, M. (eds.) *Interpreting Stratigraphy. Contemporary Approaches to Archaeological Fieldwork: Democracy versus Hierarchy.* British Archaeological Reports International Series. Oxford: BAR Publishing.

Chadwick, A.M. 2008. Fields for discourse? Towards a more self-critical and interpretative approach to the archaeology of field systems and land allotment. In Chadwick, A.M. (ed.) *Recent Approaches to the Archaeology of Land Allotment.* British Archaeological Reports International Series. Oxford: BAR Publishing.

Chadwick, A.M. and Pollard, J. In prep. Shades of Gray – prehistoric cairns and field boundaries on Gray Hill, Llanfair Discoed, Monmouthshire, South Wales.

Chadwick, A.M., Pollard, J., Peterson, R., Hamilton, M. and Wickstead, H. 2002 [2003]. Gray Hill (Mynydd Llwyd), Llanfair Discoed (ST4360 9360). *Archaeology in Wales* 42, 101-3.

Chadwick, A.M., Pollard, J., Peterson, R., Hamilton, M. and Wickstead, H. 2003. The Gray Hill Landscape Research Project. *Past* 44, 1-3.

Collis, J.R. 2001. *Digging up the Past: an Introduction to Archaeological Excavations.* Stroud: Sutton Publishing.

Cumberpatch, C.G. and Dunkley, J. 1996. Introduction. In Cumberpatch, C.G., Dunkley, J., Latham, I.D. and Thorpe, R. (eds.) *Excavations at 16-20 Church Street,*

Bawtry, 1-9. British Archaeological Reports British Series 248. Oxford: BAR Publishing.

Edmonds, M. and McElearney, G. 1999. Inhabitation and access: landscape and the Internet at Gardom's Edge. *Internet Archaeology* 6. http://intarch.ac.uk/journal/issue6/ edmonds_index.html.

Fleming, A. 1988. *The Dartmoor Reaves.* London: Batsford.

Frodsham, P. and Waddington, C. 2004. The Breamish Valley Archaeology Project 1994-2002. In Frodsham, P. *Archaeology in Northumberland National Park*, 171-89. CBA Research Report 136. York: Council for British Archaeology.

Hamilton, M.A. 2004. The Bronze Age. In Aldhouse-Green, M. and Howell, R. (eds.) *The County History of Gwent*, 84-110. Cardiff: University of Wales Press.

Hodder, I. 1998. *The Archaeological Process. An Introduction.* Oxford: Blackwell.
Horne, P.D., MacLeod, D. and Oswald, A. 2001. A probable Neolithic causewayed enclosure in northern England. *Antiquity* 75, 17-8.

Johnston, R. 2001. 'Breaking new ground': land tenure and fieldstone clearance during the Bronze Age. In Brück, J. (ed.) *Bronze Age Landscapes. Tradition and Transformation*, 99-109. Oxford: Oxbow.

Johnston, R. and Roberts, J.G. 2004. The Ardudwy early landscapes project. http://www.bangor.ac.uk/history/site_english/research/res_projects/archaeology/ardudwy.

Kitchen, W. 2001. Tenure and territoriality in the British Bronze Age: a question of varying social and geographic scales? In Brück, J. (ed.) *Bronze Age Landscapes. Tradition and Transformation*, 110-20. Oxford: Oxbow.

Llobera, M. 1996. Exploring the topography of mind: GIS, social space and archaeology. *Antiquity* 70, 612-22.

Loughton, M. 2000. Problems and potential for recording systems on proto-urban sites in France. In Darvill, T., Afanas'ev, G. and Wilkes, E. (eds.) *Anglo-Russian Archaeology Seminar: Recording Systems for Archaeological Projects*, 19-21. School of Conservation Studies Research Report 6. Bournemouth: School of Conservation Studies Research.

Lucas, G. 2001. *Critical Approaches to Fieldwork. Contemporary and Historical Practice.* London: Routledge.

Lynch, F. 2000. The later Neolithic and earlier Bronze Age. In Lynch, F., Aldhouse-Green, S. and Davies, J.L. (eds.) *Prehistoric Wales*, 79-138. Stroud: Sutton.

Makepeace, G.A. 1999. Gray Hill (Mynydd Llwyd), Llanvair Discoed (ST 43 93). *Archaeology in Wales* 39, 71-2.

Makepeace, G.A. 2000. Gray Hill (Mynydd Llwyd), Llanvair Discoed, Monmouthshire. Archaeological Assessment. Unpublished report for Monmouthshire County Council.

McFadyen, L. 2000. *Bad press*. Unpublished paper delivered at the 22nd Theoretical Archaeology Group conference, Oxford University, December 2000.

McFadyen, L. and Pollard, J. 2002. *Entwined assemblages*. Unpublished paper delivered at the research day on Monumentality in Early Neolithic Britain, Cardiff University, January 2002.

Peterson, R. and Pollard, J. 2004. The Neolithic. In Aldhouse-Green, M. and Howell, R. (eds.) *The County History of Gwent*, 56-83. Cardiff: University of Wales Press.

Pollard, J. and Gillings, M. 1998. Romancing the stones. Towards a virtual and elemental Avebury. *Archaeological Dialogues* 5(2), 143-64.

RCAHMW 1997. *Brecknock (Brycheiniog): An Inventory of the Later Prehistoric Monuments and Unenclosed Settlements to 1000 AD*. RCAHMW/ Sutton.

Shepherd, L. (ed.) 1994. *Interpreting Stratigraphy 5. Proceedings of the 5th Stratigraphy Conference, Norwich*. Norwich: Norfolk Archaeology Unit.

Sheridan, A. 2004. A segmented faience bead from Gray Hill, Monmouthshire, South Wales. Unpublished report.

Steane, K. (ed.) 1992. *Interpretation of Stratigraphy: A Review of the Art. Proceedings of the 1st Stratigraphy Conference, Lincoln*. Lincoln: City of Lincoln Archaeology Unit.

Thomas, J. 1993. The politics of vision and the archaeologies of landscape. In Bender, B. (ed.) *Landscape. Politics and Perspectives*, 19-48. Oxford: Berg.

Tilley, C. 1994. *A Phenomenology of Landscape. Places, Paths and Monuments*. Oxford: Berg.

Tilley, C. 1996. The power of rocks: topography and monument construction on Bodmin Moor. *World Archaeology* 28(2), 161-76.

Tilley, C. 2004. *The Materiality of Stone. Explorations in Landscape Phenomenology*. Oxford: Berg.

Tilley, C., Hamilton, S., Harrison, S. and Anderson, E. 2000. Nature, culture, clitter. Distinguishing between cultural and geomorphological landscapes; the case of hilltop tors in south-west England. *Journal of Material Culture* 5(2), 197-224.

Wickstead, H. 2002. *From maps to model: exploring the bounded spaces of 2nd millennium BC Dartmoor*. Unpublished paper presented at the 24th TAG conference, Manchester University, December 2002.

Wickstead, H. 2004. *Getting over the wall: concepts of inclusion and exclusion when considering movement and tenure during the later prehistory of Dartmoor*. Unpublished paper presented at the 26th TAG conference, Glasgow University, December 2004.

The topography of outdoor assembly in Europe with reference to recent field results from Sweden

Alexandra Sanmark and Sarah Semple

Moot-sites or meeting-places, also termed assembly-sites and thing-sites, can be defined as locations selected from the natural landscape for the purposes of administrative and political group discussion. Documentary sources imply these sites were functioning in various parts of northwest Europe by the tenth century AD. A meeting-site could serve a local community, a region or a kingdom, and it is clear that different moot-sites had different statuses. Although in some parts of late Roman Iron Age and Migration Period Europe (notably in Frankia) assembly could take place within houses, palaces, settlements, churches and cathedrals (e.g. Barnwell 2003; Airlie 2003; Kosto 2003), a great range of moots or meetings were also held outdoors, focussed upon distinctive natural markers such as rocks, water-courses or hills. Outdoor assemblies seem to have been popular particularly within the British Isles, Ireland, Scandinavia and the North Atlantic, although here too palaces, churches and cathedrals, settlements, farms and special structures or buildings all featured as locations of judicial and administrative council and debate.

Work on comparative European continental assemblies focuses almost wholly on the procedures, officials and development of the Frankish *mallus* and the Germanic *Ding*, and although it is clear that the role of palaces was significant, the location of outdoor meeting-sites, which included large open areas such as fields, especially when a large assembly was necessary (Kosto 2003), remain as yet an almost totally unexplored area of study (Beck 1984; Wenskus 1984; Weitzel 1986; Goessler 1938). Comparative work with these parts of Europe, which would be a fruitful approach in determining the wider topographic trends for assembly location, is thus currently almost impossible without extensive new research. This paper is therefore orientated to the North Atlantic communities of Britain, Ireland, Iceland and Scandinavia, where recent studies have revealed new information on open-air or outdoor assembly and inauguration sites, and where, in the case of Britain and Scandinavia, new fieldwork has been conducted by the authors.

Moot-sites as places of local administration and justice survived into the twelfth, thirteenth and fourteenth centuries AD, sometimes even later, although their role and status both varied and changed over time. How this system of government evolved, how it was structured and created, and how it changed and developed over time all remain obscure, and many suspect the origins of these structures, and the sites themselves, lie in late prehistory.

New perspectives on the origins and formation of administrative geographies in central Sweden are presented here, and traditional view-points challenged. To clarify the chronological terminology used in this discussion, English assembly places are assumed to have functioned sometime within the period 450-1100 AD, broadly referred to here as the early medieval or early historic period. Swedish assembly sites, largely contemporary with the English examples, are however described using Swedish chronological terminology, as functioning in the Migration Period (400-550 AD), the Vendel Period (550-750 AD) and through to the Viking Age (790-1050 AD) and beyond.

Mootscapes: shared European themes

The natural landscape

In Ireland, Scotland, England and Scandinavia it seems both the natural landscape and ancient remains were highly significant factors necessary for an assembly site. Natural topography played its part. Fording points and river crossings, islands, hills and spurs and open land were all selected as locations for meetings (Meaney 1997) – visible natural features that provided obvious 'landmarks' for assembly (*ibid.* 204). The Icelandic site of the Althing, Thingvellir, for example, must have presented an obvious and easily locatable point of assembly (Jóhannesson 1994). Some of these 'landmarks', however, seem transient in today's environment: the selection of specific trees or shrubs, for example in England, such as Esch Hundred, Warwickshire (OE *Æsc*, ash), and Willey, Bedfordshire (OE *wilig*, willow), seem unusual landmarks for assembly places conceived of as long-term meeting locations.

Audrey Meaney's (1997, 204-6) chronological appraisal of the English evidence has identified fords and river crossings as well as crossroads as some of the earliest 'primary' meeting-locations. Accessibility being key, conjunctions of land and water routes are conceived as natural meeting points for people moving through the landscape, with an underlying implication that such places may also lie at divisions or boundaries, and present themselves as neutral territory (*ibid.*). The significance of routes and communications is also supported by Aliki Pantos' (2002; 2003) study of English meeting-places, in which road proximity is shown to be a major facet of meeting-place topography. The significance of conjunctions of roads and river crossings is re-emphasised by Stefan Brink and Mats G. Larsson, who have shown that fords, bridges and major routes frequently formed components in the topography of early assembly sites in Sweden (Brink 2004a; 2004b; Larsson

1997 1998). In England many sites are named after stones and trees or significant natural landmarks, such as a fresh-water source or pits, and these are considered by Mearey (1997, 206-11) to be a secondary development. The topographic feature in these instances is chosen to distinguish the meeting-place in its surrounding landscape and act as a landmark for the meeting (*ibid.* 206), thus implying selection, planning and organisation, in contrast to the organic development of meetings at fords and crossroads.

Renegotiating the past: re-use, continuity, longevity
Despite such a varied number of meeting-sites fixed in reference to the natural world, the re-use of surviving monumental remains of the pre-medieval era for assembly is an acknowledged theme throughout northern Europe (Pantos and Semple 2004; also see Fitzpatrick 2004a; 2004b). There is a need to make a clear distinction, however, between two different aspects of re-use. Individual monuments were re-used as places of assembly, especially mounds and sometimes megalithic remains (Fitzpatrick 2004b, 52-68); however, it is equally as frequent to find that the place of assembly lies within a heartland of ancient remains spanning a multitude of periods, most dramatically seen at Kjula ås (Södermanland, Sweden) (Fig. 1).

The use of specific ancient monuments can be found in Irish and Icelandic sources, most significantly the use of the barrow as a platform or focus for meetings, and as a tool in the process of inauguration: a special place where the supernatural world and the world of the living collided. Here a king could be accepted, gain inspiration or communicate with the ancestors (Ellis 1943, 90-6, 106-11; Doherty 1985, 52; Warner 2004, 39-41; Semple 2004, 135-6; Fitzpatrick 2004b, 41-91). Mounds are well attested in the English place-name record as the foci for moots, but how they were used remains uncertain. In Ireland, early historic written sources as late as the sixteenth century AD allude to kings sitting on mounds during inauguration ceremonies, whilst the Scandinavian sagas at a much earlier date mention kings sitting on mounds to seek inspiration as well as power (see Fitzpatrick 2004b, 99-122). In England, Meaney (1995, 36) postulates that mounds presented a platform for speakers (Reynolds 1999, 100, fig. 4), whilst Williams (2004) and Semple (2004) have both pointed to the potential relationship between the presence of the dead in the burial mound and the use of such features as places for discussion and decision-making, linking the English predilection for mounds with the Irish and Icelandic written evidence for a need to meet at places where the dead, the spirits or the ancestors can also assemble. An absence of field research means, however, that these English meeting mounds are disputed as funerary locations. Adkins and Petchey (1984) have argued for man-made, non-sepulchral structures, based on an absence of evidence for burials, prehistoric or otherwise, in excavated assembly mounds. A cautionary approach to both the Scandinavian and Irish evidence is also advisable, as Warner (2004) and FitzPatrick (2004b, 68-

80) have emphasised that some early medieval royal mounds seem to have been *de novo* constructions, and in Sweden, although many well-known assembly places lie in ancient burial grounds, few meeting-mounds have been excavated. Signhilds kulle, located in Fornsigtuna (Uppland), an Iron Age chieftains' settlement situated by Lake Mälaren, and the predecessor of the town of Sigtuna, is the only thing mound that has been subject to a large-scale excavation (Fig. 2). This mound is flat-topped, and *c.* 3 meters high. Excavations showed it was built around an unusual stone construction and did not contain a burial, perhaps thus specifically built as a thing mound. The date of construction has been estimated at 400–1100 AD (Allerstav *et al.* 1991, 38-42, 124). The partially excavated 'Thing Mound' in Gamla Uppsala also seems to be non-sepulchral (Christiansson 1958; Christiansson and Nordahl 1988-9; Persson and Olofsson 2004).

Figure 1 Kjula ås, Södermanland, Sweden.

Figure 2 The 'thing mound', Signhilds kulle, Fornsigtuna, Uppland, Sweden.

Despite this, it is certain that in Scandinavia, as in Ireland and Scotland, assembly-places on occasion comprised more extensive areas, with not one, but multiple foci Brink 2004a; 2004b; Fitzpatrick 2004b; Pantos and Semple 2004). Rather than a single re-used feature, a complex of ancient remains could form a backdrop to the assembly/inauguration site. In Ireland different monuments may have provided foci for different administrative, ritual and royal activities in the Iron Age (Newman 1997; Lynn 1992; 1994; 1996; Warner 2004, 31-2). At Kjula ås the conjunction of a major route, a river crossing, a stone-lined avenue, a stone circle of prehistoric date, an impressively large rune stone, and an extensive burial site used from the early Iron Age through to the Viking Age, formed the arena for the early medieval assembly. These palimpsests have been considered as 'sacral' or 'cultic' landscapes where the assembly was sited in reference to ancient barrows, stones and enclosures and also extensive cemeteries (Driscoll 1998; 2003; 2004; Warner 1988; 2000; 2004; Brink 2004a; 2004b; Larsson 1997; Antikvariskt-topografiskt arkiv). Within these assembly areas in Sweden and Ireland, the mound could be a designated focus for the proceedings, for the seating of the king in Ireland, and for the assembly as a whole (Warner 2004).

The acquisition of power and authority by re-use of ancient remains or indeed by the emulation or re-creation of ancient rites, rituals and objects, is a long-held and acknowledged tradition, not exclusive to the British Isles, Ireland and Sweden (e.g. James 1988, 61; Milner 2005, 687). From burials to churches and from castles to thrones, ancient monuments have been used to lend credence and power to new burgeoning authorities (Williams 1997; Semple 2003; 2009). A newly-established place of assembly may well have been sited to take advantage of one or more ancient monuments to draw on the power of the past and the ancestors (Bradley 1987; Lucy 1992; Williams 1997). In these terms the adoption of such monuments could be seen as exploitative, used to enhance the credibility of a new authority or power structure (see Fitzpatrick 2004b, 68-80). At the same time, these were ancient and powerful places with a long role as central sites. The antiquity of these places and the continuous human involvement in their creation and enhancement is attested by the remains themselves; the conjunctions of Neolithic, Bronze Age, Iron Age and early medieval remains at Tara (Meath, Ireland), and Scone (Perthshire, Scotland), for example, are no accidents but testaments to the repeated and intentional renegotiation over time of places of great power, importance and significance.

The use of ancient remains and the longevity of activity at certain key sites have contributed to a growing belief that there is a connection between pagan cultic activity and moot-sites (Meaney 1995). The conjunction of royal or political assembly sites with cult sites is a facet of meeting-places in Ireland, and has been argued more recently for Swedish meeting-places (Warner 2004; Brink 2002; 2004a; 2004b; Fitzpatrick 2004a; 2004b). The possible association of ancient remains, early medieval burial and meeting-sites in England has been reviewed by Meaney (1995), Williams (2004), Semple (2004) and Fitzpatrick (2004a; 2004b), and this suggests that these types of places might have provided ideal assembly locations for early medieval communities. The archaeological evidence offers little support as yet for a link between burial and assembly, or indeed cult and assembly in England.

Better understanding of the longevity of meeting-places has crucial implications for identifying the origins of assembly as a political and administrative structure in European terms. British historians argue for the emergence of the assembly only within the early historic period, perhaps within the period of major restructuring and power-sharing in the seventh century AD, and for the full functioning of meeting-sites within the tenth or eleventh centuries AD (Loyn 1974; Wormald 1999; Reynolds 1999). Some European centres stand in complete contrast to this English evidence; indeed the archaeological biography of sites such as Tara or Anundshögen (Västmanland, Sweden), greatly exceeds their documented period of life as places of assembly, pointing to an antecedent, late prehistoric origin for the emergence of some ritual/royal centres, if not the administrative and judicial structures and arrangements documented later in time. Such early origins for assembly as a place of decision-making, dispute settlement and justice are supported by the descriptions of Tacitus (1877, Ch 11, 87-110) of the assemblies of the Suebi and other German tribes of the Roman Iron Age.

It may be the case that there has been a tendency to focus predominantly on the long-lived well-known sites. These potentially generate a model of a multi-focal, long-lived cultic assembly place which may have evolved, or been adopted or created in special circumstances, but this does not necessarily represent a common model at a regional and local level. Indeed it may be the case in Sweden, as Warner (2004) and Fitzpatrick (2004a; 2004b) have demonstrated in Ireland, that although several great major archaic centres of inauguration, kingship and assembly existed from the late Iron Age, many early medieval assembly places may be both later in conception, and very different in their topography and status from the conventional model (Fitzpatrick 2004a; 2004b).

Early medieval/historic period meeting-sites may have been created and set out according to a topographic plan related more to access, visibility, and personal and royal prestige than to a pre-existing archaic framework of ceremonial ancient meeting sites. Indeed mapping of late Iron Age and early medieval sites in Sweden is showing that the majority are located very close to major river routes. The conceptual association of cult, kingship and assembly may thus not be relevant for understanding site formation beyond the Migration Period, surviving only at some rare and special sites with ancient origins, which, for exactly this reason, developed as places associated not just with assembly but also with inauguration rites and kingship.

Enhancement

Assembly-places are not generally considered good candidates for archaeological intervention. After all, they were used only periodically and any kind of inhabitation would have been as temporary and transient as short-lived camps. There is evidence, however, for enhancement of meeting-places in the early medieval era. At Tynewald Hill (Isle of Man), several phases of remodelling or alteration of the site have been identified, presumably to aid the performances and events that took place in the area around the mound (Darvill 2004, 218-224). As late as the fifteenth century AD the place was maintained by the annual construction of a fence enclosure (Clucas 1925). In Iceland, booths are found at many thing sites, and are mentioned in the sagas describing meeting-places. Although the number and layout of these booths varied between different sites, at some places booths may have been added to the thing sites and altered over time, a process clearly evident at Thingvellir, where the course of the river Öxará, which now runs close to the Lögberg, was changed during the Icelandic Commonwealth period (930–1262 AD). The reason for this must have been to make sure that the participants of the thing meetings had constant access to fresh water (Friðriksson *et al.* 2002, FS 183-02141; Friðriksson 2004, FS 233-02142; Vésteinsson *et al.* 2004; Jóhannesson 1994, 41; Ólafsson 1987). Far from cultic, this archaeology implies a general care and maintenance of sites, with additions and alterations to aid access, performance and ease of use. At the Frostathing in Norway, below the assumed location of the Viking Age and medieval meeting-site, the remains of a large jetty or harbour have been found (Ødegård 2005). This enormous construction, which dates between 1005 and 1160 AD (*ibid.* 5), was most likely used by the participants in the meetings of the thing, and again shows how sites could be re-landscaped to provide better accessibility and the better functioning of the meeting-site. This type of auxilliary structure has largely been overlooked, through its ephemeral and perhaps mundane nature. Such evidence of caretaking, however, might represent the type of activity undertaken by communities or families responsible for meeting-sites, and has important implications for how we should see the functioning and care of the assembly.

The creation or setting-up of thing sites is attested by runic inscriptions in Sweden, such as those found at 'Arkel's thing site', at Bällsta (Uppland) (Fig. 3). At this site, there are two rune stones, which together bear the inscription: "Ulfkell and Arnkell and Gýi, made here a thing site. There shall be no mightier memorial than this, which Ulf's sons made in his memory... They raised the stones and made the staff, also the mighty one, as marks of honour" (Jansson and Wessén 1943, U 225 and 226). Next to the two rune stones there is a square stone-setting, which has been interpreted as the arena for the thing proceedings, and the site consists of two terraces, which most likely were created for the purposes of the thing meetings. At Aspa Löt in Södermanland, there is a rune stone bearing the inscription: "...this stone stands after Öpir at the thing site" (Brate and Wessén 1924-36,

Sö 137). This stone may have been placed there when the thing was created, but could also be a monument added to an existing thing site by Öpir's family in order to claim supremacy over the site or to commemorate their responsibility or good citizenship in maintaining the location. English place-names also indicate associated structures, including OE *stapol*, standing post, OE *scæmels*, benches, and OE *hus*, house, and these names might imply the augmentation and development of sites by early medieval communities or individuals, presumably for the greater good of the community and to enhance personal status. This evidence for the life of the assembly site shows these places were not static but changing environments. Perhaps even more significant is that it provides an archaeology for assembly sites that attests more frequently to regular, ritualised maintenance of sites by communities or individuals, rather than the regular use of these places for religious or cultic activities such as funerals or votive deposits. This also points to the usefulness of archaeological exploration: these sites do have a tangible history awaiting discovery.

The mounds themselves were often new constructions and thus preserve a history of meeting-sites. Either created initially as part of a meeting-site or even added to a site as a kind of public work for the benefit of the meeting, the mound may have become a necessary component to be built or added to a place of assembly in the early medieval period: an archaic reference to the ancient past needed to legitimate the assembly and create the right atmosphere and theatre for proceedings. The meeting-mound is a shared characteristic of administrative geographies in Britain and Scandinavia. Compared to fords, trees and stones, the meeting-mound is a resource: it is a built structure with an archaeological profile and thus an important and still under-exploited surviving aspect of these early political systems.

Figure 3 'Arkel's thing site', Bällsta, Uppland, Sweden.

Combined research and investigations in the last five years have offered more insight into the assembly as a political and social mechanism. Common themes have emerged including the importance of landscape as a tool in the creation of power, and of places of power and governance, the direct and indirect use of ancient remains, the extensive biographies of some sites, and as a consequence the firm belief that assembly was intimately linked with ancestors, cult and kingship. Anomalies have also emerged, though they have generally been overlooked. They include the striking absence of a direct relationship between burials and assembly at all but a small handful of significant and well-known sites, a common absence of a direct correspondence between prehistoric and early medieval material remains, and an archaeology that, where accessible, points more to administrative and civil rather than cultic motivations (see Adkins and Petchey 1984; Pantos 2002; and summary by Fitzpatrick 2004b, 75).

Recent field results from Sweden

A comparative programme of archaeological investigation was implemented by the authors in 2004, centred on Swedish and English assembly sites. The motivations behind this project were these apparently shared themes: use of ancient monuments at assembly sites, use of mounds/barrows, and possible associations with cultic and funerary activity and royal associations. By undertaking comparative fieldwork, it was hoped that research in each country would benefit from a less insular approach, one that took account of shared European traits and examined evidence within the common framework of both Swedish and English societies during the Iron Age to Migration Period or medieval period, which, although differing in religious orientation, shared the developing political and social geographies of emerging complex organisation and kingdom formation. Comparative research has also provided an opportunity to use theories and approaches prevalent in Scandinavian scholarship, but less-accepted within English early medieval studies. The use of long-term trajectories for social and ritual practice encompassing the prehistoric to early historic eras has only recently become more acceptable within Anglo-Saxon studies (see, for example, Semple 2007; Yeates this volume). This subject area has tended to be defined by the historically-documented discontinuities between Romans and incoming Germanic settlers (overviewed by Lucy 1998 and Hills 2003). In this new framework, assembly could be examined in terms of its longevity as a social practice, its possible duality with cultic or ritual concerns, and its potential as a tool for emerging kingship in early proto-historic and historic societies.

Two seasons of excavations were carried out at Aspa Löt, Sweden (Fig. 4) (Sanmark 2004; Sanmark and Semple forthcoming). These investigations have raised significant questions regarding the reality of cultic/funerary activity at assembly sites in Sweden. Aspa was the thing site of Rönö hundred from 1302 until 1458 AD (Ahlberg 1946, 120). The site is complex, marked by a range of monumental features, including four rune stones, one of which was erected "after Öpir at the thing site", dating to the late tenth/early eleventh century AD (Brate and

Wessén 1924-36, Sö 137; Larsson 1997, 67), and implying assemblies or meetings were held at Aspa at least between this time and the mid-fifteenth century AD. This rune stone is not alone; another stands opposite it (Brate and Wessén 1924-36, Sö 138), and two further standing stones are located c. 150 meters to the north, at the modern bridge crossing the stream (Storån) with another two rune stones. The inscription on one of these reads: "Slode and Ragnfrid made this bridge and erected this stone after Igulbjörn, their son" (ibid. Sö 141). According to the seventeenth-century AD Rannsakningarna, representing the first efforts at recording Swedish ancient sites and monuments, there was once a third rune stone by the bridge as well (ibid. Sö 136). These rune stones are presumed to be more or less in their original position. About 300 meters south of the bridge is a flat-topped mound, c. 4 meters high and 30 meters in diameter, marked with another standing stone. The rune stones on the different sides of the bridge represent two families, each of which had substantial landholdings on their respective sides of the water. It therefore seems likely that the Storån constituted an estate boundary at this time (Larsson 1997, 66-69).

Figure 4 Aspa Löt, Södermanland, Sweden.

The Rannsakningarna names the mound at Aspa the Tingzhögh, 'thing mound', and one of the writers stated that he had seen an "ancient letter" issued at the "thing at Aspa mound" (Ståhle and Schell 1938, 39). In the same source is a drawing of eight burial mounds located at "Aspa Löther". The name Aspolöt, attested in the Middle Ages, can be translated as 'the pasture belonging to Aspa village' (Söderwall 1884-1918; Per Vikstrand, pers. comm.). Today, Löten is located c. 300–400 meters north of the mound, but this component of the place-name may have referred to a considerably larger area in the late Iron Age to Middle Ages. Thus the exact location of the thing site is uncertain (Brink 2002; 2004a; 2004b; Larsson 1997, 65-9; Sundqvist 2001, 635), however fieldwork in 2004 strongly suggests that the conjunction of the mound, bridge, fording-place and rune stones do provide evidence of the original focus of activity.

A geophysical survey of the area around the mound revealed a range of anomalies (Persson 2004). Nine trenches were opened, radiating from the mound. On the eastern side a road was revealed which may have ancient origins, although nothing was found that could provide a date for its construction or period of use. The excavations showed the road had moved over time, suggesting longevity of use, and early maps indicate a road existed in this position as late as the 1930s. Roads in mid-Sweden altered little between the Middle Ages and the late 1920s. From medieval documents, it seems clear that the royal road named the *Eriksgata* ran past the thing site at Aspa (Mannerfelt 1930, 138-9; 1936, 67), and it is likely that the excavated road represents this route. Other than this, no further activity was evident in the vicinity of the mound. In 2005 an extensive geophysical survey was undertaken to the west of the mound, and west of a natural knoll that mirrors the 'Thing mound' in size and shape. Trial trenching was carried out in this area, but no archaeological features were revealed. Extensive fieldwalking was also carried out across the site and the surrounding fields. Only a small number of prehistoric and medieval pottery fragments were retrieved.

These results refute a purported connection between assembly and burial at Aspa Löt. It has been assumed that the eight burial mounds depicted in the *Rannsakningarna* are located next to the 'Thing mound' (Brink 2004a; 2004b; Larsson 1997, 63-4). Indeed this is the view presented in the Swedish Sites and Monuments Record (Antikvariskt-topografiskt arkiv). The fieldwork in 2004/5 has shown that there are no associated satellite burials. Significantly, in the *Rannsakningarna* the 'Thing mound' and the eight burial mounds are in fact contained in two separate drawings and their geographical connection has never been clear (Schnell and Ståhle 1938, 39).

The absence of finds connected to the thing site could be explained by the possibility that the Löten area was once more extensive than it is today. The earliest reference to a settlement or a farm by the name of Aspa (*aaspo*) dates from 1455 AD. *Aaspo* seems to be based on an earlier name of the Storån, 'Aspen stream'. This has been seen as an indication that the farm was originally located next to the stream (Larsson 1997, 63; Strandberg 2001-2), and can be verified by an eighteenth-century map which locates a farm just south of the stream (Rivell 1763). Since this farm was named after a natural feature, it has been seen as the oldest settlement located along the stream, from which other farms, such as one called 'Ryssinge', were parcelled out (Larsson 1997, 63; Strandberg 2001-2). But this need not necessarily be the case. Indeed Ryssinge might well be an older settlement than Aspa, since the suffix *-inge* suggests the name relates to an older Iron Age/Migration Period settlement (Ståhle 1949). The modern farm of Ryssinge is, moreover, located on the north side of the stream, on the opposite side from the Aspa farm. On this side of the stream there are four large terraces, which presumably were foundations for a number of structures forming part of an Iron Age farm (Antikvariskt-topografiskt

arkiv:Ludgo 177:1-4). Close to these terraces there are two smaller burial grounds of the same period (*ibid.*). The seventeenth-century AD reference to burials at Aspa Löther may refer to burials situated within a larger area around the 'Thing mound', perhaps at the Iron Age cemetery located *c.* 600 meters northwest of the mound, close to the south bank of the stream (Antikvariskt-topografiskt arkiv:68:1), which comprises ten circular stone settings covered by small turf mounds, as well as two mounds without any kerb stones. This would fit in well with the drawing of eight small mounds with kerb stones found in the *Rannsakningarna* (*ibid.*; Schell and Ståhle 1938, 39). The supposed burial ground being thus located elsewhere, and a complete dearth of archaeological findings from an extensive area around the 'Thing mound', might call into question the site of the assembly place, but the proximity of the mound to the ancient route and the collection of rune stones, including one that refers to the moot, are compelling evidence that the administrative focus was at the bridging point of the Storån.

The royal route mentioned previously appears to have bypassed the mound immediately to the east. The *Eriksgata* was the ceremonial journey that a newly elected king travelled in order to be accepted by the population in the various districts of his kingdom. The earliest reference to this route is found in the Older Law of Västergötland, the oldest Swedish provincial law (Holmbäck and Wessén 1946, 109). Versions of this regulation appear in the Law of Uppland (Holmbäck and Wessén 1933, 430), the Law of Södermanland (Holmbäck and Wessén 1940, 42), and the Later Law of Västergötland (Holmbäck and Wessén 1946, 292). The earliest complete extant manuscript of the Older Law of Västergötland dates from 1280 AD. Today it is, however, generally accepted that this law contains elements from earlier times (Holmbäck and Wessén 1946; Sundqvist 2001; c.f. Sjöholm 1988). Several scholars have argued that the custom of travelling the *Eriksgata* originated in late prehistoric times and many pieces of evidence support this (for a comprehensive overview see Sundqvist 2001). According to the various medieval documents, a king had to be elected at a place called Mora thing or Mora stone, which was located outside Uppsala. After this, the new king should travel the *Eriksgata*, which linked some of the local things in the kingdom. At these things, the population accepted or rejected the king; once accepted, the lawman should 'deem' him king, meaning that the king had to swear an oath to guard the peace and law. The provincial laws also state that bishops should be elected in this manner and, as this is contradictory to canon law, this seems to be a tradition of pre-Christian origin (Holmbäck and Wessén 1946, 109; 1933, 430; Vestergaard 1990, 121; Sundqvist 2001) .

Continental parallels serve to re-enforce the suggestion that this royal/ritual journey has its roots at least in the Migration Period. Written sources state that Merovingian rulers travelled through their realms on ceremonial journeys, and the Carolingian courtier Einhard recounted that Childeric III travelled through his kingdom in a special chariot, visiting "the palace and also the public assembly of his people". None of these sources give any indication of the routes taken by these kings, and no attempts have thus far been made to reconstruct the royal journeys (Sundqvist 2001, 634; Hoffman 1990, 138; Schmidt 2001; Hultgård 2001, 439-40; Dutton 1998, c. 1).

Archaeological evidence from the area around Aspa implies powerful magnates were present in the region during the Iron Age. The sizeable burial mound, Uppsa kulle, possibly dating from the Migration Period, lies some 5 kilometres to the south, and a large number of later Iron Age burials are known from the surrounding area. It is possible that minor kings had been passing Aspa on ceremonial journeys from prehistoric times onwards, although it important to note that the custom of travelling the *Eriksgata,* if it existed in prehistoric times, would not have taken the same form as that seen in the provincial laws. This ceremony as described in the medieval laws is usually accepted as "a sign of the progress toward a state in Sweden, i.e. it should be dated to the twelfth century at the earliest" (Sundqvist 2001, 635).

At Aspa, the presence of the early road, flanked by rune stones and standing stones where it bridged the Storån (a navigable water course connected to the Baltic Sea in the Viking Age), and the position of the mound in immediate proximity, all suggest that the assembly area was entered where the royal road crossed the watercourse, and although activity might have concentrated around the mound, the assembly area might have been significantly larger. The route and its crossing of the Storån seem to be significant, with the mound adding to the sense of monumentality and fixing the location in visual terms. Even today, despite the extensive vegetation, the mound is clearly visible from the old river approach.

The mound at Aspa seems to have no associated funerary archaeology and trial trenching close to the barrow provided no finds or associated features. This seems to be a 'clean' site, without any long-term cultic activities. Aspa and Fornsigtuna are not alone in being non-sepulchral. At Bällsta in Uppland, runic inscriptions indicate the thing was constructed by three sons to the memory of their father Ulf (Jansson and Wessén 1943, U 225 and 226), and the two terraces constituting the thing site appear to have been constructed by Ulf's sons at the same time as they erected the stones and pillars referred to in the inscriptions. This implies the intentional construction of a thing site by aristocratic individuals in memory of their father. Significantly, there are no documented Iron Age graves on or around the site, and the absence of these or of other ancient features at the thing site was confirmed by geophysical survey (Sanmark and Semple forthcoming). Thus the sons made no use of ancient monuments and did not bury their father at the site, although they did dedicate the site to his memory. Ulf's grave is thought to lie by his family home in Skålhamra, several kilometres away from the thing site, based on a rune stone dedicated to the memory of the

same Ulf, who "lived in *Skolhamarr*". The inscription ends: "May God and God's mother help his spirit and soul; grant him light and paradise". This stone is decorated with an elaborate cross (*ibid.* U 160). A cross, although of simpler design, is also found on one of the stones at the Bällsta thing site (*ibid.* U 225). The Skålhamra family were thus clearly Christian at this time and may not have experienced the need for a thing site with connections to the ancestral past.

This example has particular significance for understanding the genesis of assembly at Aspa and the creation of the thing site. Although dedicated to Öpir, his family seems to have resided several kilometres south of the thing site in Aspa (Larsson 1997, 68), a far more likely location for his burial. This is indicated by another rune stone dedicated to Öpir's memory (Snædal Brink and Strid 1982). This stone is also decorated with a cross, suggesting that Öpir's descendants, at least, had adopted the Christian religion. There is no reason why the thing site at Aspa was not also constructed, like Bällsta, *de novo* as a complex of new monuments. The Aspa site may not, however, have been created at the same time as the erection of the rune stone commemorating Öpir. Torun Zachrisson (1998) has argued that runic inscriptions containing the word 'stands' refer to monuments on the familial estate that were already in existence, while rune stones erected at a newly created monument tend to explicitly state this, as do the stones at Bällsta. The absence of burials and other prehistoric monuments suggests that the creation of the thing site at Aspa does not go very far back in time. A plausible suggestion is that the site was constructed by Öpir, and that it is for this reason that the thing site was mentioned on the rune stone commemorating his death (Larsson 1997, 68).

Thus the impetus for siting the assembly could be the juncture of the royal/ceremonial route with another communication route, the Storån, offering a useful place of gathering within the territory. The establishment of a collection of monuments memorialised the meeting-site, whilst the dedication, in this case to Öpir, remembered the individual and marked the assembly as a place of meeting under the authority of his kin. The assembly site here seems more representative of a significant location within a larger maintained administrative system, located at the conjuncture of the royal itinerary with other communications and perhaps local divisions relating to landownership. It may represent something personally or familially created and maintained. This argument is strengthened by the indications that the Storån seems to represent a Viking Age estate boundary.

In the tenth and eleventh centuries AD a system of hundredal organisation – an organisation of landscape into defined units (hundreds[1]) to better facilitate the

---

administrative organisation of growing territories – seems to have come into existence in Sweden, as a consequence of strengthening of royal power in conjunction with the establishment of Christianity. These developments also led to the construction of a large number of roads and bridges during the eleventh century AD, as demonstrated by the many rune stones from this period mentioning bridge building. Falling water levels meant that the number of navigable rivers was reduced and land routes gained increasing importance (Ambrosiani 1987, 14-15).

The description of the royal itinerary in the Law of Uppland highlights the significance of river crossings. The law reads:

> 'Now he [the king] shall ride the *Eriksgata*. They [the men of Uppland] shall follow him and give him hostages and swear him oaths...From Uppsala they shall follow him to Strängnäs. There the men of Södermanland shall receive him and with safe conduct and hostages follow him to Svintuna. There the men of Östergötland shall meet him with their hostages and follow him through their land to the middle of the forest Holaved. There the people of Småland shall meet him and follow him to Junabäck [Juna Stream]. There the people of Västergötland shall meet him with safe conduct and hostages and follow him to Ramundeboda. There the people of Närke shall meet him and follow him through their land to Uppbåga bridge. There the people of Västmanland shall meet him and with safe conduct and hostages and follow him to Östen's bridge. There the people of Uppland shall meet him and follow him to Uppsala' (Holmbäck and Wessén 1933).

The implication of this law is that the king should be met by representatives of the local population when he entered each new province. He would then be escorted to the local assembly site where he should be accepted or rejected as the new king, after which ceremony he should be taken to the boundary of the next province where another handover would take place. All seven handover points mentioned in the law can be shown to be located on river or lake crossing points, whilst in three instances the place-names themselves emphasise this geographic association: Junabäck (Juna Stream), Uppbåga bridge and Östen's bridge.

The very late description of the *Eriksgata* in the Law of Uppland is significant, because although we are dealing with different time periods and other administrative divisions, this law seems to describe exactly the process implied by the physical remains at Aspa, a significant crossing point where the royal route traversed a major watercourse. The crossing points described in the law obviously relate to later divisions. This law may, however, fossilise crossings as significant points in the royal itinerary, specifically related to meetings with the king.

Discussion and conclusions

By means of broad inquiry and preliminary field results it is suggested here that currently-accepted European models for the emergence of assembly and the establishment of meeting-sites are far from accurate for Sweden and Britain. No assembly site is identical, and the variety of shapes and forms across northwest Europe is vast and varied, but these can be broadly divided into rare assembly sites with long biographies and those that appear newly-constructed in the early medieval period.

Recent fieldwork in Sweden implies that some assembly sites, such as Aspa and Bällsta, are not long-lived cultic and ceremonial places but newly-created non-cultic, administrative locations. Monumentality is still central, but may be more a process of marking the site, maintaining its function, and demonstrating public or private ownership, rather than augmenting or reinforcing any sacred or religious associations. Most significantly, these sites draw upon the past through a new invented monumentality, perhaps referencing ancient ritual centres, by means of newly-constructed mounds, terraces, standing stones and rune stones. This suggests communities were often actively engaged in 'creating the past' by means of newly-constructed monuments (mounds, stone rows, etc.): monuments chosen perhaps as emblems of the ancient past offering authenticity and legitimation to the assembly. Such a process could allow for the re-use of some ancient remains, which would explain the second category of assemblies, such as Anundshögen and Kjula ås.

Anundshögen is a large mound, presumably a thing mound, located in a burial ground dating from at least the sixth century AD (Bratt 1999). The setting of this site is strikingly similar to that of Aspa. To the east of the mound is a stream which appears to have been navigable during the Iron Age. There was also a ford where the *Eriksgata* crossed the water route. The *Eriksgata*, lined by 14 standing stones, then continued across the site. In front of the large mound is a rune stone, which has been dated to the first half of the eleventh century AD. The inscription reads "Folkviðr raised all of these stones in memory of his son Heðinn, Ônundr's brother", which suggests that the rune stone and the road monument were erected at the same point in time (Jansson 1964, Vs 13; Bratt 1999, 4-5; Brink 2004b, 309-10). The construction date for the large mound is unknown, despite a partial excavation in 1998. The investigation did ascertain, however, that the mound was built on top of settlement-like remains, dating from 200–400 AD, which provides a *terminus post quem*. The external features of the mound have led the excavator to propose that it was constructed in the tenth century AD (Bratt 1999). Altogether the evidence suggests that the thing site was integrated into the new administrative system of the tenth and eleventh centuries AD, and enhanced at this time, when the stone-lined road, and possibly also the large mound, were added

---

the 12th century AD *härad* became more and more common and was eventually adopted across Sweden (Hafström 1961; 1962).

to this long-lived site. Further investigation of the mound would establish whether it was sepulchral or a purpose-built thing mound.

Kjula ås (see Fig. 1) was also located on an old burial ground, this one going back to the Roman Iron Age (Antikvariskt-topografiskt arkiv, Kjula 11:1), and here too a road lined with standing stones passes through the site. Along this road is a large mound (15–20 meters in diameter), which, according to the *Rannsakningarna*, was called *Tingh-höge, i.e.* the 'Thing mound' (Ståhle 1969, 127-9; Larsson 1997, 18-27; Brink 2004b, 310-11). At the foot of this mound is a rune stone dated to *c.* 1025–50 AD (Brate and Wessén 1924-36). This site is thus rather similar to Anundshögen, in terms of location and its eleventh-century enhancement. These similarities show that these sites were chosen as moots within the new administrative system in response to the underlying need for accessibility and route-proximity. Kjula ås was not located directly on the *Eriksgata,* but was connected to this circuit by one of the roads and the water route in close proximity (Mannerfelt 1930, fig. 6). The place-name associated with the site, Kungshållet (Vikstrand 2001, 343-4), 'the king's stopping place', further strengthens the significance of the location.

There is, however, one sense in which Anundshögen and Kjula ås are different. Anundshögen was used as a thing site until at least the seventeenth century AD, while the Kjula ås site was moved *c.* 8 kilometres to Fagrahed some time before 1380 AD. The most likely reason is a settlement shift within the hundred (Emmelin 1944; Larsson 1997, 24-5; Vikstrand 2001, 343).

The location of these assembly sites thus implies that movement through the landscape by land and/or water was a primary motivation, and crossing points such as at Aspa, where a royal and perhaps ancient circuit crossed a significant, navigable watercourse, may have provided ideal ideological and politically important locations for new assembly sites in the late Viking Age or early Middle Ages. This further supports the idea that some sites could be entirely created as new monuments by individuals or groups staking their claims, in an emergent regulated system of division and land ownership in the tenth and eleventh centuries AD. Motivations may have included the need to create or maintain personal and familial links with the aristocracy, as well as providing a forum for administration and debate.

Rather than ancient cultic centres, sites such as Aspa emerge far more comfortably as newly-built, suitably furnished locations developed within a planned system of division and administration that perhaps came about in response to expanding royal authority in the tenth to twelfth centuries AD. Such a system might have encompassed, continued to use, or re-use the great archaic assembly sites, such as Kjula ås and Anundshögen, reconfiguring these within a new and/or modified system that required new assembly sites.

There also remains the exciting proposition that individual groups or families might contend for such privileges; disputes over 'ownership' are indicated by the eleventh-century AD rune stones at Aspa. This may explain the fabrication of monumentality: an assembly needed its trappings. Whether groups were making reference to the past, or adopting certain necessary 'furniture', or even creating the past to strengthen claims to the moot, mounds, stones, rune stones and platforms were all useful additions. The archaeology of assembly is more likely to comprise evidence of re-modelling, maintenance and housekeeping than of cultic and funerary practices.

The existence of some ancient and long-lived judicial, royal and sacred locations such as Gamla Uppsala cannot be disputed, however, and may now be demonstrable in England too (Sanmark and Semple 2008). It is interesting to note, in regard to the idea of surviving archaic moots, that Gamla Uppsala was never integrated into the larger administrative hundred system, but remained an *althing* for the *Svear*, essentially a meeting place serving an old tribal unit of territory. Moreover, by 1350 AD the site had fallen out of use and its functions were removed to Mora thing (Sundqvist 2001, 623-5).

Archaic and pre-eminent sites should perhaps be considered a less common phenomenon, rare survivals of a first-tier framework of central places generated in late prehistory, at a point when prehistoric communities began to form strong tribal identities, kingship emerged and elites found that aspects of social control and organisation were necessary to emerging authority. These centres, however, survived only as components either within a gradually emerging system of land organisation, division and ownership, or were encompassed intentionally, perhaps even re-used, within a newly-planned administrative system, the origins of which may lie in the eighth to tenth centuries AD. Throughout, however, from the Roman Iron Age to the tenth and eleventh centuries AD, the use of the past, whether appropriated, adopted or remodelled, was a key attribute of creating such power centres and places of government, and when there was no 'past' to exploit communities may have drawn inspiration from the landscape around them to add *gravitas* and legitimacy to the moot.

Acknowledgements
The fieldwork in Sweden has been enabled by generous grants from Berit Wallenbergs Stiftelse, Helge Ax:son Johnsons stiftelse and *Societas Archaeologica Upsaliensis'* research fund. We would also like to express our gratitude to the County Administration in Nyköping for their advice and assistance. Finally, Dr. Per Vikstrand at The Institute for Dialectology, Onomastics and Folklore Research in Uppsala has generously shared his expertise in place-names. Our thanks go as well to two anonymous peer-reviewers and to audiences at the EAA 2006 and UEA 2006 for their comments and suggestions.

Bibliography

Adkins, R.A. and Petchey, M.R. 1984. Secklow hundred mound and other meeting-place mounds in England. *Archaeological Journal* 141, 243–51.

Ahlberg, O. 1946. Tingsplatser i Södermanland och Närke före tillkomsten av 1734 års lagar, *Rig* 29, 96-119.

Airlie, S. 2003. Talking heads: assemblies in early medieval Germany. In Barnwell, P.S. and Mostert, M. (eds.) *Political Assemblies in the Earlier Middle Ages*, 29-46. Turnhout: Brepols.

Allerstav, A., Damell, D., Gustafsson, J.H., Hammar, T., Hedman, A., Königsson, L.-K., Sandén, B., Sjösvärd, L, Stenström, G. and Strid, J.P. 1991. *Fornsigtuna. En kungsgårds historia*. Upplands-Bro: Stift Upplands-Bro Fornforskning.

Ambrosiani, B. 1987. Vattendelar-eller Attundalandsvägen. In *Runor och runinskrifter. Föredrag vid Riksantikvarieämbetets och Vitterhetsakademiens symposium, 8–11 September, 1985*, 9-16. Stockholm: Almcvist and Wiksell International.

Barnwell, P.S. 2003. Kings, nobles, and assemblies in barbarian kingdoms. In Barnwell, P.S. and Mostert, M. (eds.) *Political Assemblies in the Earlier Middle Ages*, 11-28. Turnhout: Brepols.

Beck. H. 1984. Ding. In Jankuhn, H., Ranke, K., Beck, H. and Wenskus, R. (eds.) *Reallexikon der Germanischen Altertumskunde von Johannes Hoops, Zweite, völlig neu bearbeitete und stark erweiterte Auflage unter Mitwirkung zahlreicher Fachgelehrter*, Vol. 5, 433-65. Berlin and New York: de Gruyter.

Bradley, R. 1987. Time regained: the creation of continuity. *Journal of the British Archaeological Association* 140, 1-17.

Brate. E. and Wessén, E. 1924-36. *Södermanlands Runinskrifter* Stockholm: Almqvist Wiksell internaional.

Bratt, P. 1999. *Anundshög. Del 1. Delundersökning för datering: arkeologisk delundersökning av Anundshög, raä 431, Långby, Badelunda Socken, Västerås Stad, Västmanland*. Stockholm: Stockholms Läns Museum.

Brink, S. 2002. Law and legal customs in Viking Age Scandinavia. In Ausenda, G. and Jesch, J. (eds.) *The Scandinavians from the Vendel Period to the Tenth Century*, 87-112. Woodbridge: Boydell.

Brink, S. 2004a. Legal assembly sites in early Scandinavia. In Pantos, A. & Semple, S. (eds.) *Assembly Places and Practices in Medieval Europe*, 205-16. Dublin: Four Courts.

Brink, S. 2004b. Mytologiska rum and eskatologiska föreställningar i det vikingatida Norden. In Andrén, A., Jennbert, K. and Raudvere, C. (eds.) *Ordning mot kaos: studier av nordisk förkristen kosmologi*, 291-316. Lund: Nordic Academic Press.

Christiansson, H. 1958. Gamla Uppsala ur fortifikationssynpunkt. *Tor* 4, 170-82.

Christiansson, H. and Nordahl, E. 1988-9. Tingshögen and Kungsgårdsplatåerna in Gamla Uppsala. A preliminary report of trial excavations. *Tor* 22, 245.

Clucas, G.F. 1925. Tynwald in ancient days. *Proceedings of the Isle of Man Natural History and Antiquarian Society* 2, 160-2.

Darvill, T. 2004. Tynwald Hill and the 'things' of power. In Pantos, A. and Semple, S. (eds.) *Assembly Places and Practices in Medieval Europe*, 217-32. Dublin: Four Courts.

Doherty, C. 1985. The monastic town in early medieval Ireland. In Clarke, H.B. and Simms, A. (eds.) *The Comparative History of Urban Origins in Non-Roman Europe*, 45-76. British Archaeological Reports International Series 225. Oxford: British Archaeological Reports.

Driscoll, S.T. 1998. Picts and prehistory: cultural resource management in early medieval Scotland. *World Archaeology* 30(1), 142-58.

Driscoll, S.T. 2003. Govan: an early Medieval royal centre on the Clyde. In Welander, R., Breeze, D. and Clancy, T.O. (eds.) *The Stone of Destiny: Artefact and Icon*, 77-84. Edinburgh: Society of Antiquaries of Scotland.

Driscoll, S.T. 2004. The archaeological context of assemby in early medieval Scotland – Scone and its comparanda. In Pantos, A. and Semple, S. (eds.) *Assembly Places and Practices in Medieval Europe*, 73-94. Dublin: Four Courts.

Dutton, P.E. 1998. *Charlemagne's Courtier. The Complete Einhard*. Peterborough: Broadview Press.

Ellis, H.R. 1943. *The Road to Hel, A Study of the Conception of the Dead in Old Norse Literature*. Cambridge: Cambridge University Press.

Emmelin, A. 1944. Om tingsställen i Uppland och Västmanland före tillkomsten av 1734 års lag. *Rig* 27, 89-112.

FitzPatrick, E. 2004a. Royal inauguration mounds in medieval Ireland: antique landscape and tradition. In Pantos, A. and Semple, S. (eds.) *Assembly Places and Practices in Medieval Europe*, 44-72. Dublin: Four Courts.

FitzPatrick, E. 2004b. *Royal Inauguration in Gaelic Ireland c. 1100-1600: A Cultural Landscape Study*. Studies in Celtic History 22. Woodbridge: Boydell Press.

Friðriksson, A., Guðmundsson, G. and Roberts, H.M. (eds.). 2002. *Þinghald til forna. Framvinduskýrsla.* Reykjavík: Fornleifastofnun Íslands.

Friðriksson, A. 2004. *Þinghald að fornu – Fornleifarannsóknir 2003.* Reykjavík: Fornleifastofnun Íslands.

Goessler, P. 1938. Grabhügel und Dingplatz. In Bihl, H. (ed.) *Festgabe für Karl Bohnenberger, Tübingen, zum 75 geburtstag, 26 August, 1938, dargebracht von Freunden, Kollegen und Schülern,* 15-39. Tübingen: Verlag von J.C.B. Mohr (Paul Siebeck).

Hafström, G. 1961. Herred. In Granlund, J. (ed.) *Kulturhistoriskt lexikon för nordisk medeltid: från vikingatid till reformationstid,* 6, col. 491-2. Malmö: Allhem.

Hafström, G. 1962. Hundare. In Granlund, J. (ed.) *Kulturhistoriskt lexikon för nordisk medeltid: från vikingatid till reformationstid,* 7, col. 74-8. Malmö: Allhem.

Hills, C. 2003. *The Origins of the English.* London: Duckworth.

Hoffman, E. 1990. Coronations in medieval Scandinavia, In Bak, J.M. (ed.) *Coronations. Medieval and Early Modern Monarchic Ritual,* 125-51. Berkeley: University of California Press.

Holmbäck, A. and Wessén, E. (eds.) 1933. *Svenska landskapslagar. Tolkade och förklarade för nutidens svenskar, första serien: Östgötalagen och Upplandslagen.* Stockholm: Geber.

Holmbäck, A. and Wessén, E. (eds.) 1940. *Svenska landskapslagar. Tolkade och förklarade för nutidens svenskar, tredje serien: Södermannalagen och Hälsingelagen.* Stockholm: Geber.

Holmbäck, A. and Wessén, E. (eds.) 1946. *Svenska landskapslagar. Tolkade och förklarade för nutidens svenskar, femte serien: Äldre Västgötalagen, Yngre Västgötalagen, Smålandslagens kyrkobalk och Bjärkörätten.* Stockholm: Geber.

Hultgård, A. 2001. Kultische Umfahrt. In Jankuhn, H., Ranke, K., Beck, H. and Wenskus, R. (eds.) *Reallexikon der Germanischen Altertumskunde von Johannes Hoops, zweite, völlig neu bearbeitete und stark erweiterte Auflage unter Mitwirkung zahlreicher Fachgelehrter,* Vol. 17, 437-42. Berlin and New York: de Gruyter.

James, E. 1988. *The Franks.* Oxford: Blackwell.

Jansson, S. B. F. 1964. *Västmanlands runinskrifter.* Stockholm: Almqvist S Wiksell international.

Jansson, S.B.F. and Wessén, E. 1943. *Upplands Runinskrifter. Andra delen, första häftet.* Stockholm: Almqvist Wiksell international.

Jóhannesson, J.A. 1994. *History of the Old Icelandic Commonwealth.* Winnepeg: University of Manitoba Press.

Kosto, A. 2003. Reasons for assembly in Catalonia and Aragón 900-1200. In Barnwell, P.S. and Mostert, M. (eds.) *Political Assemblies in the Earlier Middle Ages,* 133-149. Turnhout: Brepols.

Larsson, M.G. 1997. *Från stormannagård till bondby: En studie av mellansvensk bebyggelseutveckling från äldre järnålder till medeltid.* Acta Archaeologica Lundensia nr 26. Lund: Lunds Universitet.

Larsson, M.G. 1998. Runic inscriptions as a source for the history of settlement. In Düwel, K. and Nowak, S. (eds.) *Runeninschriften als Quellen interdisziplinärer Forschung, Abhandlungen des vierten internationalen Symposiums über Runen und Runeninschriften in Göttingen vom 4.-9. August 1995,* 639-46. Ergänzungsbände zum Reallexikon der Germanischen Altertumskunde 15. Berlin: de Gruyter.

Loyn, H.R. 1974. The hundred in the tenth and early eleventh centuries. In Hearder, H. and Loyn, H.R. (eds.) *British Government and Administration,* 1-15. Cardiff: University of Wales Press.

Lucy, S. 1992. The significance of mortuary ritual in the political manipulation of landscape. *Archaeological Review from Cambridge* 11(1), 93-105.

Lucy, S. 1998. *The Early Anglo-Saxon Cemeteries of East Yorkshire: An Analysis and Reinterpretation.* Oxford: BAR Publishing.

Lynn, C. 1992. The Iron Age mound in Navan Fort: a physical realisation of Celtic religious beliefs? *Emania* 10, 33–57.

Lynn, C. 1994. Hostels, heroes and tales: further thoughts on the Navan mound. *Emania* 12, 5–20

Lynn, C. 1996. That mound again: the Navan excavations revisited. *Emania* 15, 5–10.

Mannerfelt, M. 1930. Där svenska riksvägar mötas. *Svenska turistföreningens årsskrift,* 34–144.

Mannerfelt, M. 1936. *Svenska vägar och stigar.* Studentföreningen Verdandis Småskrifter N^r 379. Stockholm: Bonnier.

Meaney, A.L. 1995. Pagan English sanctuaries, place-names and hundred meeting-places. *Anglo-Saxon Studies in Archaeology and History* 8, 29–42.

Meaney, A.L. 1997. Hundred meeting places in the Cambridge region. In Rumble, A.R. and Mills, A.D. (eds.) *Names, Places and People: An Onomastic Miscellany in Memory of John McNeal Dodgson,* 195-240. Stamford: Paul Watkins.

117

Milne, G.R. 2005. Complex societies of North America. In Scarre, C. (ed.) *The Human Past*, 687-91. London: Thames and Hudson.

Newman, C. 1997. *Tara: An Archaeological Survey.* Discovery Programme Monograph 2. Dublin: Royal Irish Academy/Discovery Programme.

Ødegård, Ø. 2005. Rapport fra arkeologisk utgraving av kaianlegg fra vikingtid på Fånes gnr/bnr. 19/1, Frosta i Nord-Trøndelag, 09.11 – 25.11.2004. Trondheim: Unpublished manuscript.

Ólafsson, G. 1987. Þingnes by Elliðavatn: the first local assembly in Iceland?. In Knirk, J. (ed.) *Proceedings of the Tenth Viking Congress, Larkollen, Norway, 1985*, 343-349. Universitetets Oldsakssamlings Skrifter. Ny Rekke 9. Oslo: Universitetets Oldsaksamling.

Pantos, A. 2002. *Assembly-places in the Anglo-Saxon Period: Aspects of Form and Location.* Unpublished Dphil thesis, Oxford University.

Pantos, A. 2003. On the edge of things: the boundary location of Anglo-Saxon assembly-sites. *Anglo-Saxon Studies in Archaeology and History* 12, 38-49.

Pantos, A. and Semple, S. 2004. Introduction. In Pantos, A. and Semple, S. (eds.) *Assembly Places and Practices in Medieval Europe*, 11-23. Dublin: Four Courts.

Persson, K. 2004. *Rapport geofysisk prospektering Tingsplatsen i Aspa, Ludgo sn (Raä 62) i Södermanland.* Stockholm: Unpublished manuscript.

Persson, K. and Olofsson, B. 2004. Inside a mound: applied geophysics in archaeological prospecting at the Kings' Mounds Gamla Uppsala, Sweden. *Journal of Archaeological Science* 31, 551-62.

Reynolds, A. 1999. *Later Anglo-Saxon England: Life and Landscape.* Tempus: Stroud and Charleston.

Rivell, M.J. 1763. *Wägwisare igenom Södermanlands höfdingedöme.* Nyköping: Kongl. Tryckeriet.

Sanmark, A. 2004. *Tingsplatsen som arkeologiskt problem. Etapp 1: Aspa. Med bidrag av Eva Bergström och Kjell Persson.* SAU Rapport 2004:25. Uppsala: SAU.

Sanmark, A. and Semple, S. Forthcoming. *Tingsplatsen som arkeologiskt problem. Etapp 2: Aspa och Arkels tingstad.* SAU Rapport. Uppsala: SAU.

Sanmark, A. and Semple, S. 2008. Places of assembly: recent results from Sweden and England. *Fornvännen* 103, 4:2008, 245-59.

Schell, I. and Ståhle, C.I. (eds.). 1938. *Rannsakningar om antikviteter i Södermanland 1667-1686. Sörmländska handlingar.* Nyköping: Södermanlands hembygdsförbund.

Schmidt, R.. 2001. Königsumritt. In Jankuhn, H., Ranke, K., Beck, H. and Wenskus, R. (eds.) *Reallexikon der Germanischen Altertumskunde von Johannes Hoops, zweite, völlig neu bearbeitete und stark erweiterte Auflage unter Mitwirkung zahlreicher Fachgelehrter*, Vol. 17, 139-41. Berlin and New York: de Gruyter.

Semple, S. 2003. Burials and political boundaries in the Avebury region, north Wiltshire. *Anglo-Saxon studies in Archaeology and History* 12, 72-91.

Semple, S. 2004. Locations of assembly in early Anglo-Saxon England. In Pantos, A. and Semple, S. (eds.) *Assembly Places and Practices in Medieval Europe*, 135-54. Dublin: Four Courts.

Semple, S.J. 2007. Defining the OE Hearg. *Early Medieval Europe* 15(4), 364-85.

Semple, S. 2009. Recycling the past: ancient monuments and changing meanings in early medieval Britain. In *Antiquaries and Archaists: The Past in the Past, the Past in the Present.* London: Spire Books Ltd.

Sjöholm, E. 1988. *Sveriges medeltidslagar. Europeisk rättstradition i politisk omvandling.* Stockholm: Institutet för rättshistorisk forsking.

Snædal Brink, T. and Strid, J.P. 1982. Runfynd 1981. *Fornvännen* 77, 233–51.

Söderwall, K.F. 1884-1918. *Ordbok öfver svenska medeltids-språket.* Lund: Berling.

Ståhle, C.I. 1949. *Studier över de svenska ortnamnen på –inge: på grundval av undersökningar i Stockholms län.* Uppsala: Lundequistska bokh.

Ståhle, C.I. (ed.) 1969. *Rannsakningar efter Antikviteter. Band 2. Södermanland, Närke, Värmland, Västergötland, Östergötland, Gotland.* Stockholm.

Strandberg, S. 2001-2. Ortnamn berättar i Lid och Runtuna. *Krönikan. Runtuna-Lids Hembygdsförening*, IX, 41-3. Nyköping: Runtuna-Lids hembygdsförening.

Sundqvist, O. 2001. Features of pre-Christian inauguration rituals in the medieval Swedish laws. In Stausberg, M. (ed.) *Kontinuitäten und Brüche in der Religionsgeschichte. Festschrift für Anders Hultgård zu seinem 65. Geburtstag am 23.12. 2001*, 620-650. Berlin and New York: de Gruyter.

Tacitus. 1877. *Germania.* Translated as *The Agricola and Germania* by Church, A.J. and Brodribb, W.J. London: Macmillan.

Vésteinsson, O. Einarsson, A. and Sigurgeirsson, M.Á. 2004. A new assembly site in Skuldaþingsey, NE Iceland. In Guðmundsson, G. (ed.) *Current Issues in Nordic Archaeology. Proceedings of the 21st Conference of Nordic Archaeologists, 6–9 September, 2001, Akureyri,*

Iceland, 171–79. Reykjavík: Society of Icelandic Archaeologists.

Vestergaard, E. 1990. A note on Viking Age inaugurations. In Bak, J.M. (ed.) *Coronations. Medieval and Early Modern Monarchic Ritual*, 119-24. Berkeley: University of California Press.

Vikstrand, P. 2001. *Gudarnas Platser: förkristna sakrala ortnamn i mälarlandsckapen*. Uppsala: Kungl. Gustav Adolfs akademien för svensk folkkultur.

Warner, R. 1988. The archaeology of early historic Irish kingship. In Driscoll, S. and Nieke, M. (eds.) *Power and Politics in Early Medieval Britain and Ireland*, 47-68. Edinburgh: Edinburgh University Press.

Warner, R. 2000. Keeping out the otherworld: the internal ditch at Navan and other Iron Age 'hengiform' enclosures. *Emania* 18, 39-44.

Warner, R. 2004. Notes on the inception and early development of the royal mound in Ireland. In Pantos, A. and Semple, S. (eds.) *Assembly Places and Practices in Medieval Europe*, 27-43. Dublin: Four Courts.

Weitzel, J. 1986. Ding (Thing). *Lexikon des Mittelalters*, Vol. 3, col. 1058-1063. München and Zürich: Artemis.

Wenksus, R. 1984. Ding. In Jankuhn, H., Ranke, K., Beck, H. and Wenskus, R. (eds.) *Reallexikon der Germanischen Altertumskunde von Johannes Hoops, Zweite, völlig neu bearbeitete und stark erweiterte Auflage unter Mitwirkung zahlreicher Fachgelehrter*, Vol. 5, 443-65. Berlin and New York: de Gruyter.

Williams, H.M.R. 1997. Ancient landscapes and the dead: the reuse of prehistoric monuments as early Anglo-Saxon burial sites. *Medieval Archaeology* 41, 1-32.

Williams, H.M.R. 2004. Assembling the dead. In Pantos, A. and Semple, S. (eds.) *Assembly Places and Practices in Medieval Europe,* 109–34. Dublin: Four Courts.

Wormald, P. 1999. *The Making of English Law: King Alfred to the Twelfth Century*. Oxford: Blackwell.

Zachrisson, T. 1998. *Gård, gräns, gravfält: sammanhang kring ädelmetalldepåer och runstenar från vikingatid och tidig medeltid i Uppland och Gästrikland*. Stockholm Studies in Archaeology 15. Stockholm: Stockholms Universitet.

* 9 7 8 1 4 0 7 3 0 5 7 9 0 *